For Graham Willis,
in tribute to past and
future academic collaboration,
abraços, Joe Blackmore
Feb. 24, 2023

THE INNER SEA

The Inner Sea

MARITIME LITERARY CULTURE
IN EARLY MODERN PORTUGAL

Josiah Blackmore

The University of Chicago Press   CHICAGO AND LONDON

The University of Chicago Press, Chicago 60637
The University of Chicago Press, Ltd., London
© 2022 by The University of Chicago
All rights reserved. No part of this book may be used or reproduced in any manner whatsoever without written permission, except in the case of brief quotations in critical articles and reviews. For more information, contact the University of Chicago Press, 1427 East 60th Street, Chicago, IL 60637.
Published 2022
Printed in the United States of America

31 30 29 28 27 26 25 24 23 22   1 2 3 4 5

ISBN-13: 978-0-226-82046-0 (cloth)
ISBN-13: 978-0-226-82047-7 (e-book)
DOI: https://doi.org/10.7208/chicago/9780226820477.001.0001

The University of Chicago Press gratefully acknowledges the generous support of the Robert C. Smith Jr. Fund for Portuguese Studies at Harvard University toward the publication of this book.

Page ii: Alfredo Roque-Gameiro, aftercastle of a fifteenth-century Portuguese caravel. From *História da Colonização Portuguesa do Brasil* (Porto: Litografia Nacional, 1921). Photograph: © DeA Picture Library / Art Resource, New York.

Library of Congress Cataloging-in-Publication Data

Names: Blackmore, Josiah, 1959– author.
Title: The inner sea : maritime literary culture in early modern Portugal / Josiah Blackmore.
Description: Chicago : University of Chicago Press, 2022. | Includes bibliographical references and index.
Identifiers: LCCN 2021062111 | ISBN 9780226820460 (cloth) | ISBN 9780226820477 (ebook)
Subjects: LCSH: Camões, Luís de, 1524?–1580—Criticism and interpretation. | Sea in literature. | Seafaring life in literature. | Portuguese literature—Classical period, 1500–1700—History and criticism.
Classification: LCC PQ9196.Z9 B47 2022 | DDC 869.09/32162—dc23/eng/20220103
LC record available at https://lccn.loc.gov/2021062111

♾ This paper meets the requirements of ANSI/NISO Z39.48-1992 (Permanence of Paper).

Deep in the mind there is an ocean
I would fall within it . . .

JACK SPICER,
  "A Portrait of the Artist as a Young Landscape"

CONTENTS

LIST OF FIGURES *ix*
LIST OF ABBREVIATIONS *xi*
NOTE ON TEXTS AND TRANSLATIONS *xiii*

Introduction:
Immense and Possible Oceans *1*

1. Saltwater Poetics *19*

2. Epic Seas *47*

3. Lyric Seas *91*

4. The Sunken Voice *146*

ACKNOWLEDGMENTS *171*
NOTES *175*
WORKS CITED *203*
INDEX *217*

FIGURES

1. St. Brendan celebrates Mass (1621) *23*
2. African landscape (1576) *61*
3. Illuminations of ships (1543) *62*
4. Miniatures of ships (ca. 1563) *69*
5. Vasco da Gama (ca. 1563) *70*
6. Isle of Love (1772) *88*
7. Sea nymphs (1772) *128*
8. Nereids (1502) *129*

ABBREVIATIONS

HDCI	Fernão Lopes de Castanheda, *História do descobrimento e conquista da Índia pelos Portugueses*
LFN	Fernando Oliveira, *Liuro da fabrica das naos*
NSB	*Navegação de S. Brandão* (*Navigatio Sancti Brendani*)
PLP	Robert Durling, trans. and ed., *Petrarch's Lyric Poems: The* Rime sparse *and Other Lyrics*
RAS	Manuel de Mesquita Perestrelo, *Roteiro da África do sul e sueste desde o Cabo da Boa Esperança até ao das Correntes*
RSV	Manuel de Mesquita Perestrelo, *Relação sumária da viagem que fez Fernão d'Álvares Cabral, desde que partiu deste Reino por capitão-mor da Armada que foi no ano de 1553 às partes da Índia até que se perdeu no cabo de Boa Esperança no ano de 1554*
TMP	Rebecca D. Catz, ed. and trans., *The Travels of Mendes Pinto*

Full bibliographic citations appear in the Works Cited section of this book.

NOTE ON TEXTS AND TRANSLATIONS

Citations of the medieval Galician-Portuguese *cantigas* are from *Cantigas medievais galego-portuguesas: Corpus integral profano*, 2 vols., ed. Graça Videira Lopes (Lisbon: Biblioteca Nacional de Portugal; Instituto de Estudos Medievais; Centro de Estudos de Sociologia e Estética Musical, 2016).

Citations of *Os Lusíadas* (keyed to canto, stanza, and verse numbers) are from Luís de Camões, *Os Lusíadas*, ed. Emanuel Paulo Ramos (Porto: Porto Editora, n.d.).

Citations of Camões's lyric poetry are from *Rimas*, ed. Álvaro J. da Costa Pimpão (Coimbra: Atlântida, 1973).

All translations into English are mine, unless otherwise indicated.

❋ Introduction ❋

Immense and Possible Oceans

In the middle of the thirteenth century, Paio Gomes Charinho, a Galician nobleman, admiral, and accomplished poet, makes the following declaration in one of his poems:

> Eno mar cabe quant' i quer caber;
> e mantém muitos; e outros i há
> que x'ar quebranta e que faz morrer
> enxerdados
>
> (The sea has room for everything that wishes to be in it; and it sustains many, but there are also others whom it destroys and makes them die disinherited)

In this political satire, Paio Gomes is equating the mercurial personality of the king with the sea.[1] But apart from the metaphor that fuses the unstable character of the monarch with the nature of the sea, the poet's observation expresses a truth that underlies many of the arguments of this book: in its ability to contain "everything that wishes to be in it," the sea is both a place and an idea, a capaciousness, a principle of expansiveness, possibility, literary imagination, and even the arbiter of life and death. Three centuries later, the sixteenth-century Portuguese poet Diogo Bernardes (1530–ca. 1595) makes a similar claim in two of his poetic letters or *cartas*. In these letters, written on the occasion of a friend's departure to India, Bernardes writes:

> Que por mais qu'antre nós deixes aberto
> Do curvo lenho largo mar no meyo
> Sempre da minha Musa estarás perto.
> Contigo o pensamento, sem receyo,
> Passará novos mares, novos climas (*Carta* 25)
>
> Rompia a proa o liquido elemento,
> Eu com sospiros d'alma o ar rompia,
> Com lagrimas mostrando o sentimento.
> Cos olhos saudosos te seguia
> Em quanto divisei as brancas vellas,
> E depois disso com a fantesia. (*Carta* 26)[2]

(For however much you leave the wide sea open between us by the curved wood, you will always be near to my Muse. Alongside you, boldly, my thoughts will travel new seas, new climes // The prow cleaved the liquid element, I cleaved the air with sighs from my soul, my sorrow showing with tears. With longing eyes I followed you for as long as I could discern the white sails, and after that I followed with my imagination.)

In both letters, Bernardes imaginatively accompanies his friend on the sea voyage to new aquatic and climatic realms, metonyms for the new worlds revealed by Iberian seafaring in the early modern period. Specifically, it is Bernardes's *pensamento* or thought that undertakes the journey here—in the passage from *Carta* 26 the flight of the imagination unfolds as it envisions the smooth sea voyage overseen by nymphs and Neptune. Together, both of Bernardes's letters propose that the exercise of poetic creativity is a form of sea voyaging, that there is a dynamic affinity between poiesis and nautical movement.

The Inner Sea is a book about the maritime imagination in early modern Portugal and Iberia, especially in the work of Luís Vaz de Camões (ca. 1524–80), author of the epic poem *Os Lusíadas* (The Lusiads, 1572) and of a corpus of lyric poetry published posthumously as *Rhymes* in two editions (1595 and 1598).[3] Camões is arguably the maritime poet par excellence of the early modern period, not only in Iberia but in western Europe generally, and his oeuvre is the epicenter of the maritime literary consciousness of the sixteenth century. *Os Lusíadas* tells the tale of Vasco da Gama's sea voyage from Portugal to India (and back) in 1497–99, the first maritime journey between

Europe and the subcontinent which established the *carreira da Índia* (India voyage), "the great transoceanic route that linked Lisbon to the Portuguese establishment in Goa on the western Indian coast and to a series of maritime commercial loops that tied various places in Asia to Goa and the carreira."[4] Camões's poem is often touted as a culminating expression of Portugal's imperial ideologies and expansionist designs, but it also consolidates Portugal's identity as a seafaring nation.[5] "The whole idea of the [Portuguese] nation," Bernhard Klein writes, "is filtered from the start through the image of a seafaring venture—the nation becomes a ship's crew, the state a vessel, national destiny a sea voyage."[6] In another study, Klein notes that "few other sixteenth-century instances of epic poetry are so heavily invested in the culture of seafaring."[7] Likewise, in Maria Vitalina Leal de Matos's assessment, "if *Os Lusíadas* is an epic, it is because it is an epic of the sea."[8] And for Hélio J. S. Alves, no other text in Western literature symbolically embodies the ocean to the degree we find in *Os Lusíadas*.[9] Many of Camões's lyric poems also reveal a multifaceted engagement with the empirical and metaphoric realms of the sea and nautical culture. This perhaps comes as no surprise given that Camões himself traveled extensively by sea to Africa, Asia, and the Middle East over a period of almost twenty years. The maritime sojourns of the sailor-poet are undoubtedly partially responsible for the vitality and eyewitness immediacy of his epic and lyric compositions. If *Os Lusíadas* conjoins nation, destiny, and seafaring, Camões's maritime lyric poetry turns on more problematic contemplations of fate, existential disquiet, and global itinerancy that often stand in opposition to seafaring as a coherent and bold exercise of "worldmaking" (to borrow Ayesha Ramachandran's term) infixed in the epic poem. Yet seafaring in both Camões's epic and lyric poetry underlies aspects of identity—collective and historical in the former, and individual, amorous, and existential in the latter.

As a wide-reaching treatment of seafaring, *Os Lusíadas* embraces *navegação* as historical achievement and literary structure. The Portuguese political dominion over the world's oceans is the "governo do mar." The singular *mar* in *governo do mar* is an expression of a global totality. With Gama's voyage, and in the many Portuguese seafaring ventures that preceded it, a world previously divided by the seas becomes one interconnected by those same seas. This is the epic moment at the heart of the poem. It was a shift that occurred incrementally over many years. If medieval views of seas were characterized by understanding them as barriers and frontiers, unfathomable spaces of danger, the opening up of Atlantic space began to wrench the world's oceans free from a sense of separateness and apartness. Joyce E. Chaplin asserts that "the Spanish and Portuguese were like cousins who squabbled over a meager patrimony. That bleak treasure was their access to the Atlantic, a very unpromising part of the Ocean Sea, but an entryway, at least, to the outer world."[10] But these "squabbles" had a far-reaching effect, which was an ever-widening connectivity of the world's oceans, one of the transformations of world oceanic geography that Camões's poem touts.[11]

The world-embracing seafaring of the Portuguese would not have been possible without the collective, technical knowledge of Portuguese mariners.[12] Margaret Cohen, in the case of nineteenth-century sea adventure fiction, calls this nautical knowledge "craft," the "routinization of the work of the sea" that is a form of "practical reason," while Steve Mentz, in casting his focus further back in time, uses *metis* as a Homeric Greek term associated with seamanship.[13] It is this routinely practiced navigational skill of Portuguese sailors that allows Camões to designate the world ocean as a Portuguese domain. And the sea, in its apparent boundlessness and magnitude, permits the acquisition of knowledge on an unprecedented scale. The movements of ships have made the oceanic world mensurate. Yet Gama's status as the *capitão-mor* of the *São Gabriel* did not at all vouch for his skill as a navigator, and Camões subtly overlooks this. Francisco Contente Domingues notes that (royal) appointments of sea captains on the *carreira da Índia* were made primarily on the basis of social class, not on skill as a navigator, and that there is no evidence that Gama was able to pilot a ship.[14] In the world of *Os Lusíadas*, Camões compresses Gama's all-encompassing scopic agency into a presumed technical expertise. Camões never mentions Gama's chief pilot, Pero de Alenquer—there are only brief references to an unnamed *mestre*. The implication is that, unlike Aeneas, Gama needs no Palinurus (the *gubernator*), so Gama consequently emerges as the *primus inter pares* of the tradition of seafaring "barões assinalados" (outstanding men) who set sail from Lusitanian shores, the exemplar of a seafaring collective that steers Portugal into a global, maritime order. The Portuguese mariners safely complete their voyage to India following the perilous storm in canto VI without the need to sacrifice a member of the crew to placate Neptune, the reason for Palinurus's death at the end of book 5 of the *Aeneid* when the pilot falls overboard. If such a sacrifice is requisite for ensuring the success of the sea voyage in the Mantuan's epic,[15] no such supernatural bargain is necessary in Camões, since the nautical skills of Gama's crew allow for the fleet's making port in India and therefore mitigate the vicissitudes of Fortune.

Prior to Camões's oceanic worldview in the sixteenth century, Portuguese thinkers and writers had established a connection between knowledge and seafaring. In the mid-fifteenth century, Gomes Eanes de Zurara (ca. 1410–74) loosely aligned knowledge and navigation in the *Crónica dos feitos notáveis que se passaram na conquista de Guiné por mandado do infante D. Henrique* (Chronicle of the Famous Feats That Occurred in the Conquest of Guinea by Order of Prince Henry, hereafter *Crónica de Guiné*), the chronicle that first recorded the Portuguese expeditions along the west coast of Africa that rapidly developed into the traffic in slaves with the capture of Black Africans who lived south of Cape Bojador and who were transported to Portugal for the slave markets. In an early chapter, Zurara details five reasons why Henry ordered the expeditions to the lands of "Guiné" (West Africa): (1) to explore the lands south of Bojador and the Canaries, which were until then only the matter of legend; (2) to discover if there were populations of Christians with whom the Portuguese could enter into trading alliances; (3) to ascertain the degree and geographical reach of "Moorish" (i.e., African) military strength; (4) to discover if there were any Christian princes in the lands; and (5) to convert non-Christians to the Christian faith. In sum, Henry's putative motives were all related to knowledge gathering, implicitly reflecting Aristotle's opening claim in the *Metaphysics* that "all men by nature desire to know."[16] The navigational frame of the history Zurara recounts is significant: Prince Henry's knowledge-gathering project is realized through a series of nautical excursions that by and large determine the structure of chapters. Zurara gestures toward a correlation between forms of new knowledge and seafaring, of the epistemological importance of ships as vessels of historical reality and historiographic truth, what we might think of as a seafaring epistemology.

Another example of the nautico-epistemological mindset prior to Camões is the diary of Gama's India voyage, Álvaro Velho's *Roteiro da primeira viagem de Vasco da Gama* (The Journal of the First Voyage of Vasco da Gama). Velho's eyewitness account is one example of the nautical genre of the *roteiro* (a "rutter" or ship's diary), and in this author's hand the *roteiro* is a combination of eyewitness travel account, historical chronicle, and nautical diary. Gama's voyage is parsed into daily entries, with accompanying technical information regarding wind, weather, and nautical movements. What Velho's account shares with Zurara's chronicle is not only an interest in documenting newly uncovered geographical regions and peoples but the unfolding of history and historical eyewitnessing as a nautical voyage. Nautical travel itself lays implicit claims to empirical truth, credibility, and reliability, and therefore, by association, these ideas ratify whatever seemingly unbelievable phenomena that might be reported within this frame. In the maritime, imperialist mentality, few people wield as much uncontested authority as the mariner-eyewitness.

The inchoate seafaring epistemology of the fifteenth century reaches its plenitude in the sixteenth. João de Castro (1500–48), the fourth viceroy of India, was also an accomplished cosmographer and a nautical scientist. He penned *roteiros* describing the technical specifics of sea voyages between Portugal and points in the Middle East and India (which also happen to be compendia of the state of nautical science to Castro's time), as well as the *Tratado da Sphæra* (Treatise on the Globe, written 1545–48). The *Tratado*, in dialogue form, explores astronomical and geographical knowledge and the authority of Portuguese thinkers on these sciences. One of the interlocutors ("D") inquires how it is possible to dismiss and disprove the knowledge of the ancients, and interlocutor "M" replies:

> A muyta experiencia dos modernos, E principalmente a muito nauegação de Portugal. Por que despois que os Portugueses pella parte Oriental, E os outros Espanhois por seu exemplo pera o Occidente nauegarão toda a redondeza do mundo, E descubrirão tātas, E tão varias terras nunca desdo principio do mundo descubertas.[17]

(The vast experience of the Moderns, and mainly the extensive seafaring of Portugal. For the Portuguese went to eastern realms, and afterwards the Spaniards [following the Portuguese example], to western parts; all together they navigated the entire circumference of the world, and discovered so many and so varied places as had never been encountered since the beginning of the world.)

Castro, like Zurara and Velho before him, equates seafaring with knowledge. In Castro's treatise, and in *Os Lusíadas*, boats and ships perform an epistemological function in that they are the means to new forms of knowledge and to knowledge of the world in general.

THE MARITIME SUBJECT

The pervasiveness of maritime voyaging as a quotidian experience in early modern Iberia is one of the realities underlying the texts I study here. The coexistence of lived experience and the historical, scientific, and imaginative configurations of seafaring in texts is a distinguishing characteristic of early modern Portugal. The ubiquitous presence of the sea traveler in practice and in literature written under the aegis of empire marks one of the shifts away from the medieval world. In writing of the very early Iberian voyages as "extensions of the medieval universe, undertaken in response to the needs of a feudal economy in crisis," Shankar Raman argues that "the discovery of lands unknown to the ancients transformed their significance. The colonial voyages of discovery came to embody a new relationship to the world and ultimately to offer a different kind of stability."[18] While Raman's claims are arguments about the metaphor of the voyage in the Camonian relationship between ancient and Christian conceptions of the cosmos and of subjectivity in philosophical thought, the "new relationship to the world" points to a new positionality of the traveler and writer in a worldspace increasingly and persistently, over time and in multiple forms, defined by maritime travel and an expanded, oceanic consciousness. A new subjectivity is the result: a maritime subject, created by a reconfigured relationship to the world forged by a practice of sustained seafaring.[19] Collectively, it is a subject that occupies different categories of maritime experience: mariner, traveler, pilot, captain, ship passenger, cartographer, and cosmographer. Experiences of difference and otherness that early modern voyaging produced are, for Roland Greene, the basis of an "anaculturalism" or the seeking out of forms of difference by writers who "want to maintain their privileged, culturally particular standpoints."[20] While experiences of otherness are indispensable to an international outlook in the sixteenth century in Greene's argument, I would add that, especially in the case of Iberian writers, such an outlook was frequently mobilized and realized by nautical means.

The maritime subject, then, was as much a historical reality as it was a literary construct and outlook on the world. One of the many seafaring realities that *Os Lusíadas* records is the emerging, ocean-wide presence of the "gente marítima de Luso" (maritime people of Lusus; I.62.i). There is a historical dimension to Portugal's identification with the sea. While the "gente marítima de Luso" definitively emerges with Gama's voyage as a world-reaching demographic, the years of seafaring prior to this moment invest Portuguese mariners with a transhistorical importance. The early modern sea is the stage of Portuguese history, a measured, plotted, known, and managed element of nature. If the sea voyage is a "kind of modern epistemology of uncertainty"[21] because knowledge is always preliminary or partial, the project of traveling and qualifying the sea, and the science of navigation itself, are the basis of knowledge of the world and of Portuguese cultural authority in non-Western or unknown realms. Lyrically, as I show in chapter 3, the maritime subject in Camões is the self that creates and expresses itself in the real and metaphoric realms of the sea. There is a tight intertwining of sea and self in many of Camões's lyric poems, and of sea and national self in *Os Lusíadas*. The merger of subjectivity and the sea and seafaring is a characteristic dimension of Camonian poetic ipseity. The maritime subject, even lyrically, emerges in the culture of oceanic empire, and is therefore itself often tacitly ideological insofar as it reflects on or situates itself within imperial expansion. The seafaring epistemology of early modern Portuguese expansion creates maritime subjects through the interpenetration of human bodies, ships, and oceanic spaces.

THE SHIP

The ship or nautical vessel is the defining material object of seafaring. It is pragmatic and technical, a human achievement over nature and over nonseafaring peoples, and symbolic and metaphoric, of Portuguese culture and history itself.

The ship is an artifice, a product of theory, knowledge, and skilled material application that mediates the relationship to the aquatic environment. One of the more notable examples of ship theory and nautical science is the treatise by Fernando (Fernão) Oliveira (1507–85), the *Livro da fábrica das naus* (Book of Shipbuilding, written 1570–80). Oliveira led an adventurous seafaring life. He entered a

Dominican convent at an early age and made voyages from Spain to Italy before returning to Portugal and being recruited to serve as pilot of a French galley. Over the years he was a prisoner of both the French and the Turks. Oliveira traveled to England in the mid-1500s and returned to Portugal in 1547 where he ran afoul of the Inquisition because of his support of King Henry VIII.[22] In addition to his work on naval architecture, Oliveira authored the first-ever grammar of the Portuguese language (*Gramática da linguagem portuguesa*, Grammar of the Portuguese Language, 1536) and a book on naval war strategy, the *Arte da guerra do mar* (Art of War at Sea, 1555).

The *Livro da fábrica das naus* is encyclopedic in its treatment of naval architecture. Oliveira's book describes the specifics of naval construction in addition to numerous other details such as the kinds of woods best suited for certain types of vessels, the ideal times for harvesting wood, the different kinds of ships for different kinds of voyages, and descriptions of ancient and "Moorish" ships. The ship is a product of many traditions of learning, so shipwrights and those involved in the craft of shipbuilding command a knowledge of both the scientific and natural worlds. Navigation is necessary for the survival of Portugal itself, Oliveira notes, since the gathering of food and the governance of overseas territories by the Crown depend on it. In the spirit of Camões's boast of Portuguese seafaring as outstripping that of the ancients, Oliveira also extols Portuguese ships as superseding those of the Greeks and Latins whose vessels were only capable of navigating Mediterranean waters: "Os nossos agora são capazes tambem do oceano todo per todo o mũdo, ou mayor parte delle" (Ours now are capable [of sailing] the entire ocean in the whole world, or the better part of it).[23] Oliveira claims that, in its scope, his book is the first of its kind, although he places it in the tradition of the French humanist Lazaro Bayfio (Lazare de Baïf), whose *De re vestiaria, vascularia, & nauali* (On Clothing, Vessels, and Ships; 1553) contains detailed descriptions of many types of ships.

For Oliveira, shipbuilding is a form of human industry over nature, so the ship should imitate nature. With citations of Pliny and Aristotle, for instance, Oliveira identifies a kind of fish (*nautilo*, "mollusc") that uses a shell as a vessel. Oliveira emphasizes the equation between ships and the natural world by observing that fish are kinds of ships, and that both fish and birds possess bodily structures that are ideal models for ships (LFN 110–11, 122). The parallel in effect naturalizes the ship and, by extension, any uses to which the ship might be put, such as imperial voyaging. The mimetic relationship between ships and nature is not limited to fauna, however—the human body also figures in the discussion. The overall measurements of the parts of the ship should, Oliveira says, obey a standard of proportion like the body that the architectural theorist Vitruvius terms the *rata pars* or "certain part" (LFN 86). Oliveira likens the sturdiness and strength of the components of a high-seas India ship to the members of the body necessary for supporting weight. In this vision, planks are like skin or leather that covers bones and sinews (LFN 116–17). With the reference to Vitruvius, the atomization of a ship's components as anatomical parallels to the human body conscripts ships into the aesthetics of proportion of the Roman author so that a ship might be considered an example of *l'uomo vitruviano* (Vitruvian man) at sea.

Oliveira's discussion of ships as a result of many traditions of scientific learning and craft points to the nimble semantics of the ship I consider in the pages to follow. For example, epic ships are the means of encountering new peoples, geographies, languages, religions, and natural phenomena, or the new worlds revealed by early modern seafaring. On the ship, knowledge and experiences of new realities are recorded and assessed as an ongoing activity concomitant with the directed movement of the vessel. The ship itself is a contained space of specialized knowledge, the *metis* or science of seamanship. The confines of this knowledge space also harbor a set of hierarchical and political relations. In the *Arte da guerra do mar*, Oliveira notes the authority of the *capitão-mor* in a fleet, who is like the head of the body to which all members respond.[24] The *capitão-mor* exercises supreme authority over the onboard society of seafaring warriors who must obey him "em tudo como ao princepe" (in everything as they would a prince).[25] Oliveira presents the membership of a fleet as a sort of seaborne *polis*, a structure of governance that represents the transferal of land-bound orders of law, state, and citizenry to the waters of the sea.

A ship does not realize its essence, of course, until it moves over water. Chronological and historical time travel with and in the vessel, as does the idea of concerted purpose, which might be thought of nautically as "orientation" or "compass." Time on a ship "is both linear and cyclical: Time is linear in the sense that voyages have beginnings and endings . . . in the unfolding of chronological time; yet time is also cyclical, just as the rhythm of waves is cyclical, because the pattern of a ship's daily routine ... highlights endless recurrence."[26] The temporal dimensions of vessels vary in epic and lyric ships. While Vasco da Gama's flagship, the *São Gabriel*, bears a consciousness of the historical past and future, time on lyric vessels turns inward, since sea voyages can be occasions for reflection on emotional pasts, states of being, and existential quandaries. The forward movement of epic conquest and the anxious melancholy of lyric nostalgia is an idea that recurs in this book. In the chapters to follow, individual and collective relationships to ships emerge and underlie a general truth: ships wield subject-forming power. Ships define a subject's relation to itself and to the world, and in their enclosed, seaborne space, nautical vessels promote a heightened consciousness of the conditions of the self that underlie literary expression. Subject boats appear regularly in *The Inner Sea*.

The arguments I present encompass a number of texts that contribute to an understanding of seafaring as a hermeneutic of early modern culture in Portugal (and Iberia generally), including poetry, historiography, hagiography, nautical documents, and scientific treatises. I use "literary" broadly to refer to texts across genres and intellectual disciplines. The sea, ships, and nautical travel in this diverse archive exfoliate into a variety of empirical, metaphoric, and symbolic dimensions, creating alliances between ostensibly discrete genres of thought and literature. The oceans that were traversed in the late fifteenth and sixteenth centuries correspond to oceans within the literary self, vast reaches and depths of emotion, consciousness, memory, and identity. Interior or "lyric" space, for instance, is oceanic in its fluid connectivity between emotion, intellect, the senses, and experiences of the world. One of the guiding tenets of *The Inner Sea* is that the sea and seafaring are not merely themes in literary creativity—these themes date to the dawn of Western culture—but, in the Portuguese sixteenth century, become a *forma mentis*, a principle of culture and literary creativity that creates individual and collective subjects according to oceanic and nautical modes of perception and thought.

Although Portugal remained primarily an agrarian country, from the fifteenth to the seventeenth century Portuguese and Iberian ships sailed unsleepingly to Africa, Asia, and the Americas. Even a brief perusal of the inventories of India-bound vessels in books such as the *Livro de Lisuarte de Abreu*, the *Relação das náos e armadas da India*, and Carlos Alexandre de Morais's *Cronologia geral da Índia portu-*

guesa, 1498–1962 reveals that hundreds of Portuguese ships made the voyage across the Indian Ocean following Gama's pathfinding expedition. Inevitably, references and allusions to the sea and seafaring pervade literary culture in early modern Portugal and Iberia. The texts chosen for this study are representative of this culture, but are by no means exhaustive, and other scholars might well make different selections. My assertion that Camões is early modern Europe's preeminent maritime poet underlies the presence of Camões's writings as the centerpiece of many of the book's arguments. However, I do not want to suggest that Camões is a synecdoche of Portuguese literature itself, but rather that the literary treatment of and imaginative engagement with seafaring and the maritime realm reach an accomplished level in the poet's oeuvre that is singular in the literary landscape of early modern Iberia.

THE CAMONIAN DEEP

The sea in *Os Lusíadas* washes to all corners of the globe. It is not confined or contained. It reaches nations, peoples, languages, and geographies, and is the medium and guarantor of Portuguese political claims and exercises of power in realms far beyond western European shores. Camões recognizes the plurality and distant reach of the globe's oceanic realms with the locution "mares nunca dantes navegados" (seas never sailed before) and speaks of the Portuguese dominion over the *mar*—a singular noun that marshals into one entity the many marine components of the world. It's possible to think of Camões's unified *mar* as an early modern example of what some scholars now refer to as the "world ocean," an oceanic space of connectivity that, "with its interwoven patterns of currents and prevailing winds, drove the populations of the separated continents back together."[27] To be even more precise, Camões regularly designates his epic, world ocean as *profundo*, a polysemous word that is consonant with some of the overarching concepts throughout the poem and brings the oceanic depths to the semantic surface, as it were, of Camões's maritime world.

Profundo in its most immediate senses means "deep," "toward (or at) the bottom," "vast," and "spacious." It derives from Latin *profundus* (*pro* [in the direction of] + *fundus* [bottom, base]).[28] The common adjectival use in an expression like *mar profundo* corresponds to the substantive *profundo*, which can refer to the maritime deep itself. In a few instances, Camões uses the noun to mean an infernal underworld. Of all the uses of the adjective *profundo*, which include political allegiance and goodwill (III.25.v), a depth of emotion (IV.43.v), an enlightened, searching capacity for reason (IV.102.v), far-reaching and consequential prophecy (VI.36.iv), and an eternal, divine knowledge (X.80.iii), it is the expression *mar profundo* that most reflects the multivalent nature of the Camonian sea world. In the word's first appearance in the poem, Gama has just arrived in Melinde (Malindi), and the king of Melinde visits the Portuguese flagship. There, prior to the African potentate's request to hear the history of Gama's country and of the origin of the voyage, Gama thanks his new ally for his singular and welcoming reception: "Tu só, de todos quantos queima Apolo, / Nos recebes em paz, do mar profundo" (You alone, of all whom Apollo scorches, receive us in peace, from the wide sea; II.105.i-ii); Gama and his companions originate in the sea, and the *capitão-mor* brings the sea with him to the port of Melinde. The adjective's inaugural use denotes a wide expanse of sea over which the fleet has traveled—an indicator of geographical distance—as well as a locus of cross-cultural encounter. As Gama's historical peroration progresses, the *mar profundo* appears in canto III when the *capitão-mor* addresses "noble Lisbon" as the princess of world cities "a quem obedece o Mar profundo" (whom the wide sea obeys; III.57.v). This *mar profundo* identifies all the seas of the globe, the domain of Lisbon's worldwide political and cultural reach. It is also an ever-expanding sea that extends out to the world from the west, the "Ocidental praia Lusitana" (western Lusitanian shore; I.1.ii), hence the significance of the first use of *mar profundo* as the place of meeting between East and West in Africa. Seafaring (*navegação*) conscripts the eastward-expanding ocean into the imperial domain of Manuel I. Moreover, the term *navegação* bears a political meaning beyond the first sense of nautical voyaging. Following Gama's return from India, Manuel I adopted the grandiose and geographically vast regal title of "Rei de Portugal e dos Algarves, d'Aquem e d'Além-Mar em Africa, Senhor da Guiné e da Conquista, Navegação e Comércio da Etiópia, Arábia, Pérsia e Índia" (King of Portugal and of the Algarves, and of Near and Far Seas in Africa, Lord of Guinea and of the Conquest, Navigation, and Commerce of Ethiopia, Arabia, Persia, and India). *Navegação* designates the entire, interconnected imperial enterprise of seafaring as exercised by the monarch and the geographic domain circumscribed by such enterprise. The *mar profundo* is both an attested domain of imperial interests and a sea *in potentia*, the stage for and raw stuff of future, as-yet unrealized political pursuits. Gama invokes the *mar profundo* to describe the singularity of his voyage and of his world-witnessing at the end of canto V as he brings his historical narrative to a close. He asks the king of Melinde:

> Julgas agora, Rei, se houve no mundo
> Gentes que tais caminhos cometessem?
> Crês tu que tanto Eneias e o facundo
> Ulisses pelo mundo se estendessem?
> Osou algum a ver do mar profundo,
> Por mais versos que dele se escrevessem,
> Do que eu vi, a poder de esforço e de arte,
> E do que inda hei-de ver, a oitava parte? (V.86)

(Judge now, King, if there have been such people in the world who have undertaken such paths? Do you believe that Aeneas and the eloquent Ulysses had reached such corners of the world? Has anyone dared to see what I have seen of the vast sea, in however many verses that might have been penned, or seen even an eighth of what I have yet to see?)

Gama claims an exceptional place in history and in the literary tradition of seafaring history. This exceptionalism stems from the epic passion of *ousadia*. The *mar profundo* is at once an expanse of history, a space of origin and of exemplarity, of historical protagonism and historical memory. Coming as it does on the heels of the Adamastor episode, the use of *mar profundo* in this passage inevitably resonates with Gama's description of Adamastor's voice some stanzas earlier: "Cum tom de voz nos fala, horrendo e grosso, / Que pareceu sair do mar profundo" (With a horrible and booming tone of voice he speaks to us, a tone that seemed to rise up from the deep sea; V.40.v-vi). There is a tacit correlation through the use of *mar profundo* between the oceanic depths as the origin of Adamastor's troublingly prophetic voice and Gama's imperial, seafaring agency. But if Adamastor is possessed of the gift of prophecy—itself a form of historical speaking—he also represents a knowledge and conceptualization of worldspace that Gama's trip symbolically renders obsolete. In this respect, Gama's claim to the *mar profundo* picks up where Adamastor leaves off.

The poem's final conjugation of *profundo* and the sea occurs in canto IX, as Venus prepares her isle of amorous delights for the Portuguese seafarers. In the vision she paints, she remarks to Cupid:

E pera isso queria que, feridas
As filhas de Nereu no ponto fundo,
De amor dos Lusitanos encendidas,
Que vem de descobrir o novo mundo,
Todas nũa ilha juntas e subidas,
Ilha que nas entranhas do profundo
Oceano terei aparelhada. (IX.40.i-vii)

(And to this end I would ask that the daughters of Nereus in the very depths where they reside be inflamed with love for the Lusitanians who are coming from discovering a new world, and that they all assemble in fine form on an island in the heart of the ocean that I will have prepared.)

With the locution "profundo oceano" Camões construes an oceanic vastness that is the locus of desire and maritime-imperial enterprise. Venus situates her island in the very heart of that expansive ocean; the isle is pelagic in location and in essence, and as such is a final corroboration of the maritime realm as both space and structure of the past, present, and future. Placed in the *entranhas* or epicenter of the vast, historically agentive, and temporally ubiquitous ocean, the waters that surround the Isle of Venus are the very *eidos* of the Camonian sea.

Through the texts I study here, the arguments of *The Inner Sea* present notable moments of the intellectual and literary histories of the human-ocean encounter. My hope is that these chapters add to discussions taking place in the maritime humanities as well as elucidate some of the historical precedents to more contemporary topics of interest to scholars working in blue cultural studies. My work shares methodological approaches and an interest in literary texts (flexibly defined) with the work of critics like Steve Mentz, Dan Brayton, Heather Blum, and Margaret Cohen. While I do not claim to practice ecocriticism, it is not implausible to read some of these arguments as providing a dimension, historically attested in Iberian cultures, to the kind of "fluidity and fluid thinking" requisite for interdisciplinary mixing that Sidney I. Dobrin explores, or as deepening our understanding of the role of (literary) texts "in their contribution to our engagements with ocean."[29] Many of the texts and concepts I study provide a Portuguese and Iberian historical rootedness to ecocritical tenets that understand the ocean as a distinct form of thought—I'm thinking, for instance, of Melody Jue's *Wild Blue Media: Thinking through Seawater*, in which Jue posits the ocean as a distinct environment (as opposed to land) for perception and thought.[30]

Chapter 1, "Saltwater Poetics," focuses on two key moments in the Middle Ages when the genealogy of the Portuguese maritime imaginary most patently begins. The first moment is the early tenth-century hagiographic narrative *Navigatio Sancti Brendani* (Voyage of St. Brendan), and the second is the medieval Iberian poetry of the thirteenth to the fourteenth century known as the Galician-Portuguese *cantigas*. The tale of St. Brendan is one of the earlier stories of (imagined) westward expansion, composed and circulated in the land-bound confines of monasticism. This story is important as much for its status as a first moment in envisioning westerly nautical voyaging as it is for the survival of this legendary journey in the decades of expansion when it broke free from the learned circles of monasteries and entered into the imaginations of cartographers. The second moment is the Galician-Portuguese lyric "school," a culture of poetry widely practiced and diffused throughout the kingdoms of the medieval Iberian Peninsula. In a relatively small but important subset of these performed poems or *cantigas*, poets imagine water, sea, nautical travel, and emotional relationships in relation to the maritime and aquatic worlds in ways that anticipate the lyric expressivity of Camões and other poets of the sixteenth century. In select Galician-Portuguese *cantigas* we find women poetic protagonists engaging with the sea as part of their emotional and experiential worlds, an expressivity that brings love and carnal yearning into a seaward projection of a putative female lyric consciousness in the minds of the male poets who authored these compositions.

Chapters 2 and 3 focus on the work of Luís de Camões. Chapter 2, "Epic Seas," reads *Os Lusíadas* as the most preeminent and extensive expression of the Iberian maritime imaginary of the early modern period. This epic poem situates a world-reaching Portuguese practice of seafaring at its core with Vasco da Gama's first-ever maritime voyage between Portugal and India in 1497–99, a round-trip voyage known as the *carreira da Índia* (India voyage) that would become a mercantile mainstay of Portugese imperial trading interests. The poem's overall narrative and the many dimensions of its imagined and historical worlds rely on the oceanic, the aquatic, and the nautical as organizing principles and integral components of Camões's epic, poetic logic. This seafaring infrastructure reflects, in part, the political dimensions of Camões's epic that chart the eventual Portuguese dominion over the sea or the *governo do mar*. While other imperial epics in the Renaissance center on the conquest of and rule over land, *Os Lusíadas* explores the rule over the sea and thus differs from epic tradition, especially in its Virgilian form. Yet while Camões's poem follows other political dimensions of Virgilian epic, such as the founding events of history that culminate in world empire, the ties of epic to a specific national history, and the capacity of political power to fashion human history into narrative,[31] Camões unmoors the epic narrative from its landlocked trajectory and situates it on the sea. If, as David Quint argues, Virgil "wants to depict the character that would build the future greatness of Rome, . . . a city built by farmers into a world power,"[32] Camões depicts how Lisbon was built into a world power by seafarers.

Chapter 3, "Lyric Seas," addresses maritime lyric subjectivity and the manners in which seafaring and oceanic experience bear on love, exile, and a dispersed state of being in the world. With initial reflections on the nautical Petrarch (a predecessor of the lyric, seafaring Camões), I consider expressions and constructions in Camões's lyric poetry that establish the maritime subject as an existentially fraught lyric consciousness at odds with the triumphalist tone and claims of the epic. Key components of this lyric consciousness are the shipwreck swimmer, experiences of displacement and exile, and a poetic self dispersed and fragmented throughout the spaces of the world as a result of incessant oceanic travel.

Chapter 4, "The Sunken Voice," analyzes forms of depth and sinking and their relationship to narrative and poetic voice in Manuel de Mesquita Perestrelo's narrative of the wreck of the *São Bento* (*Relação sumária que fez Fernão d'Álvares Cabral*) and in canto VI of *Os Lusíadas*. The argument demonstrates how speaking from the depths is part of the metaphoric and discursive dimensions of the maritime subject. I argue that depth, sinking, and the abyss are concepts that inform the apprehensions and terrors underpinning nautical travel and shape narrative and poetic moments of voice. To sink into the depths is also to create discrete moments of speaking and sound; poetic voice in the maritime world of imperialism can originate in the oceanic abyss.

1

Saltwater Poetics

To initiate the study of the maritime imaginary we must reach back to the Middle Ages and to two distinct spheres of literary history. Both of these spheres—hagiography and medieval, orally transmitted poetry—configure the maritime and the aquatic as part of their literary expressivities. While the learned, ecclesiastical circles of hagiographic writing and the public domain of performed poetry are discrete discursive cultures, they nonetheless construe human engagements with the ocean that are notable in their own right and that will resonate in the intellectual and literary domains of early modern seafaring. This study begins with the salt water of medieval seas.

The hagiographic narrative in question is the Latin *Navigatio Sancti Brendani*, or *Voyage of St. Brendan*, and the poetry is a subset of the body of poems known as the Galician-Portuguese *cantigas* or "songs," a poetic tradition cultivated in Iberia from the late twelfth to early fourteenth century. The anonymous, tenth-century St. Brendan narrative exists in two Portuguese versions, one in Porto, and the other in Santa Cruz de Coimbra.[1] The *Voyage of St. Brendan* was a widely diffused story in medieval Europe as evidenced in numerous manuscript testimonies and versions. The narrative tells of the sea journey of the sixth-century Irish Benedictine abbot Brendan (died ca. 575) with his company of monks through a group of islands west of Ireland in a quest for the Promised Land or the *Terra repromissionis sanctorum*. These islands, which would be known as the St. Brendan Isles, became legendary. On their voyage, the monastic brethren encounter isles full of sheep, birds, and grapes; *mirabilia* such as sea monsters; the whale

Iascónio, on whose back, thinking it an island, the monks celebrate Mass; a crystal column in the middle of the sea; and the savage island on which labor the blacksmiths of hell. Though nautically framed, the journey is spiritual in nature and is structured by the temporality of the liturgical calendar.[2] As an imagined, spiritual *peregrinatio*, the Portuguese testimonies do not specify navigational or geographical details, apart from the observation that the monks travel west, a fact that will ensure the survival of the legend of St. Brendan's isles in later centuries. A central conceit in the *Voyage* is the sea as a specific place of human itinerancy and not merely as a symbol or allegory. For even if a symbolic reading of the ocean is possible as "the instability and contingency of all human existence," as one critic puts it,[3] there is a pronounced consciousness of being at sea, of pursuing an oceanic itinerary from locale to locale. Moreover, the aquatic element is home to marvels, a geographical habitus of mirabilia akin to the East that will continue to be envisioned as the space of the wondrous in later centuries. The Irish saint reached the Promised Land only because he committed to the ocean first, "quia deus uoluit uobis ostendere sua diuersa secreta in oceano magno" (because God wanted to show [him] His many secrets in the wide sea; NSB 114). But Brendan's sea, a conduit to spiritual grace and salvation, also participates in divine punishment and retribution. So it is that Brendan and his company encounter Judas Iscariot in eternal, maritime torment, placed on a rock in the open sea and forever battered by the waves, which are thick and congealed, as if this viscous state of water expresses a divine repulsion at the betrayal of the sinner. The moralization of the sea and the overlapping of ocean water and the divine anticipates the sea in early modern expansionist texts that present Christian seafaring as a confederate of divine will.

In this tale, the symbolism and functionality of the ship itself reiterate the dual valence of the sea as both allegorical and a specific, lived placement in which the divine and the marvelous coexist. In both Portuguese versions, the initial references to Brendan's boat are to its construction by the monks and the outfitting of the vessel with the necessary provisions. Brendan's vessel (*nauicula*) is therefore first a product of communal, nautical knowledge, and the brotherhood of monks is a sort of shipwright's guild. This brief reference to the building of the vessel is a glimpse of what will become, in later centuries, the idea of maritime "craft" or the deliberate execution of seafaring labor as "elaborate professional practices, which [mariners] shared, compared, and refined. These practices included specific skills, and they included a characteristic set of demeanors."[4] The *Voyage of St. Brendan* makes no further mention of skilled seamanship on the part of the monks apart from general references to the ship's movements from one locale to the next.[5] Once built, Brendan's small craft acquires metaphoric dimensions related to its impending spiritual voyage as Brendan invites his brethren to board by intoning: "In nomine patris et filii et spiritus sancti intrate in nauim" (In the name of the Father, Son, and Holy Spirit, board the ship; NSB 84). With this one rhetorical move, the saint converts the *nauicula* into a seafaring community with its own organization and laws—in this instance, a community of believers, a church.[6] We find one pronounced instance of this forty days into the journey when Brendan's company encounters a deserted island where one of the clerics, on finding a valuable silver necklace, takes it. Brendan reprimands the monk for the theft, thus foregrounding the maritime community as governed by strict ethical standards. God's will presides over the spiritual and ethical dimensions of the shipboard community as evident in nautical steerage: "Sulcabant uento ueloci cursu, quia deus dux est eorum" (They sailed swiftly with the wind, since God was their guide; NSB 150). The motif of the ship moving briskly forward under favorable winds as a demonstration of the divine approval of a seafaring voyage is one of the images Camões repeatedly invokes in *Os Lusíadas*.

Generally, the ship as the product of the exercise of technical knowledge, built for a specific purpose, implies a maritime journey with a deliberate purpose and even telos. A ship's multivalence in terms of its different forms of law-bound communities, its symbolic significance as the iterative reconstitution of orders of law, knowledge, and agency in successive "de-territorializations" (to use Kado's term),[7] the mobility and transportability of such orders, and the ship's status as a visible sign of divine will in its unobstructed, free movements is an early registration of ideas that will inform, to varying degrees, many of the texts written during the years of maritime expansion. The location of the Isles of St. Brendan, never mentioned in the hagiographic narrative itself, fueled speculation for centuries afterward. Gomes Eanes de Zurara, for example, refers in passing to St. Brendan in an early chapter of the *Crónica de Guiné*. In comments on the principal motives behind Henry's African expeditions, Zurara notes that no historical memory nor documents exist that treat of the features of the lands lying south of Cape Bojador: "Nem per scriptura nẽ per memorya de nhuũs homeẽs nunca foe sabudo determinadamẽte a callidade da terra que hya aallem do dicto cabo. Bẽ he que alguũs deziam que passara per ally sam brandam" (Neither in writing nor in the memory of any person was the nature of the lands that lay beyond said cape ever clearly known. Some said that St. Brendan had passed that way).[8] The chronicler makes this observation at the beginning of a passage in which he frames Henry's African interests as a project of knowledge gathering. Thus, initially, the prince's maritime enterprise was propelled by a desire for geographical knowledge, so the mention of Brendan's putative traversal of African waters is emblematic of a state of knowledge in flux in which historical speculation and legend are to be replaced by the empiricism of Henry's fleets. Brendan is a marker of the blurry contours of geographic and cartographic certainties, one sign of the insistent presence of legend and rumor that defined medieval knowledge of Africa and Atlantic oceanic space that the fifteenth-century fleets confirmed or disproved. As Christopher L. Pastore points out, St. Brendan's Isles were part of a group of early medieval imaginary lands that migrated on maps as geographic knowledge of the sea increased: "The islands of St. Brendan . . . moved from somewhere west of Ireland toward the Mediterranean. . . . St. Brendan's island continued to migrate westward so that by the sixteenth century it appeared somewhere off the coast of Newfoundland."[9]

The idea that the Irish saint had navigated the waters in the regions off the west coast of Iberia and Africa persisted for decades in the late medieval and early modern cartographic imagination. In the fifteenth century, for example, Brendan's Isles appear on maps that place them near the Azores, Canaries, and Madeira.[10] The well-known moment from the *Voyage of St. Brendan* when the company celebrates Mass on the back of a whale appears as an illustration on a 1513 map of the Caribbean.[11] Figure 1 presents a particularly imaginative seventeenth-century example of Brendan's whale island navigating the waters beyond the limits of knowledge.

Such cartographic examples testify to the conviction that the Irish saint had made an actual oceanic voyage in the Atlantic. Iberian travelers and mapmakers desired to conscript Brendan's sojourn into the sphere of Portuguese and Spanish voyages to Africa and to the New World. In the centuries after its original appearance, the Brendan

FIGURE 1. St. Brendan and his monastic brethren celebrate Mass on the whale's back. From Honorius Philoponus's (i.e., Caspar Plautius) *Nova typis transacta navigatio. Novi Orbis Indiæ Occidentalis* (Linz, 1621). Photograph: Houghton Library, Harvard University.

legend became mostly a matter of geographic-cartographic interest, although it is difficult to ignore the spiritual telos of the saint's oceanic voyage as anticipating, at least to some degree, the Christian imperialist rationale of many Iberian seafaring expeditions.

WOMEN'S VOICE AND SONGS OF THE SEA

The legacy of the hagiographic legend is but one instance of medieval configurations of maritime travel as important precursors to seafaring in early modernity, especially in regard to oceanic geography. Yet in comparing Brendan's voyage to the medieval Galician-Portuguese *cantigas*, a distinction becomes evident: the emotional experiences triggered by the sea and water voiced in the *cantigas* are a depth-finding counterpart to the persistent horizontality of Brendan's voyaging. The maritime saint offers a seafaring exteriorization of states of faith that contrasts to the inward and psychological dimensions of the medieval lyrics.

The Galician-Portuguese lyric tradition is so called because the language of composition was Galician-Portuguese, a poetic lingua franca employed by numerous poets and performers across the several kingdoms of medieval Iberia. This poetry boasts a number of genres, the major ones being the *cantigas de amigo* ("songs of a friend" or "lover's songs," poems in the voice of women), the *cantigas de amor* ("love songs," poems in the voice of men), the *cantigas de escarnho e mal-dizer* (joke and insult poetry), and the religious *Cantigas de Santa Maria* of Alfonso X, el Sabio, of Castile (1221–84).[12] The sea, seafaring, and water populate a small but notable subset of the woman-voiced *cantigas de amigo* with their imbrication of emotion, desire, and the real and metaphoric aspects of water and sea travel. The *cantigas de amigo* corpus numbers some five hundred compositions, and the women who poetically speak in these poems live in the countryside outside of the courtly circles that are the backdrop of the poems in the voice of men. All *cantigas de amigo* are attributed to male poets in the extant manuscripts and thus ventriloquize women's speech. They collectively turn on the representation of women's emotions. Some of the *cantigas* evoke a pronounced female corporality, either in descriptions of the physical beauty of women or in those songs in which women dance or swim. The *cantigas de amigo* are a remarkable body of poetry in the literary culture of medieval Europe; in the words of one scholar, they are "great originalities of ... Peninsular poetry."[13]

The small group of *cantigas de amigo* in which the sea, ships, and sea voyages figure are known as *marinhas* or *barcarolas*. Such compositions take as their premise the absence of a male lover or *amigo* because of his overseas travel, usually a presumed consequence of military service.[14] The women sing of their amorous yearning in the absence of their friends, their erotic desires, the uncertainty of their lover's safety, or joy at the prospect of his impending return. Other *cantigas* explore the solace to be found among female friends. This small corpus of women's songs forcefully brings aqueous and nautical motifs to bear on medieval Iberian lyric expression. The watery spaces of the poems shuttle between fresh water and salt water, so they initiate a tradition of sea poetry that will lead to the maritime poetics of seafaring in the early modern era. The poets studied here, therefore, express an affinity between water, love, longing, nostalgia, anguish, and happiness in the fluid, ever-renewing, and expansive nature of such sentiments.[15] Sometimes, these emotions are situated at specific locales along the Galician and Portuguese coastlines. We find, for instance, the Bay of Vigo in Galicia in the poems of Martim Codax, and Lisbon and the Tagus River in those by João Zorro. Such specific places tighten the bond between emotion and outer, aquatic worlds. These places become repositories of sentiment that are as characteristic of Portugal and Galicia as the seashores and waterways themselves.

The *barcarolas* or boat poems are all land-bound in that the poets never imaginatively place us on board a ship but rather incorporate seagoing vessels into the perspective of a protagonist on shore. The movement of boats or ships as a trigger to or a reflection of emotional states underlies some *cantigas* because it is the nautical voyage that removes the *amigo* from the presence of the *amiga* (young woman or girlfriend) and consequently occasions suffering. But such voyages also bring the lover home and create an anticipation of his return. In a poem by Juião Bolseiro, the *amiga* sings, "Nas barcas novas foi-s'o meu amigo daqui, / e vej'eu viir barcas e tenho que vem i, / mia madre, o meu amigo" (On the new boats my friend departed from here, and I see boats coming and believe my friend, dear mother, is on board). Nuno Fernandes Torneol emphasizes the affective power of seeing ships for the shore-bound *amiga*, who then discovers that her lover did not return:

> Vi eu, mia madr', andar
> as barcas eno mar,
>   e moiro-me d'amor.
>   . . . .
> As barcas [e]no mar
> e foi-las [a]guardar,
>   e moiro-me d'amor.
>   . . . .
> E foi-las aguardar
> e non' o pud' achar,
>   e moiro-me d'amor.

(I saw, my mother, the ships moving across the sea, and I'm dying of love. // . . . // The ships on the sea, I went to search for them, and I'm dying of love. // . . . // I went to search for them, and could not find him, and I'm dying of love.)

In observing to her mother that the sight of ships causes her to die of love, the *amiga* creates an association between the vessels and her absent lover. The seaborne ships become a sign of the emotional experience of amorous suffering, an emotion known as *coita* throughout the corpus of all of the *cantigas*.

The experience of viewing a ship from a riverbank also brings happiness in a poem by João Zorro:

> Per ribeira do rio
> vi remar o navio
> > e sabor hei da ribeira.
> ....
> Vi remar o navio,
> i vai o meu amigo
> > e sabor hei da ribeira.
> ....
> I vai o meu amigo,
> quer-me levar consigo
> > e sabor hei da ribeira.

> (Along the riverbank I saw the ship rowing, and the riverbank gives me pleasure. // . . . // I saw the ship rowing, and my friend is leaving, and the riverbank gives me pleasure. // . . . // And my friend is leaving, he wants to take me with him, and the riverbank gives me pleasure.)

Zorro elaborates his poem on a correlation between sight, movement, and sentiment. The *amiga*'s sighting of the oar-propelled vessel creates a pleasure (*sabor*) of the shore. This is a somewhat unexpected reaction, since an imminent departure of the lover would more likely occasion sadness. Zorro undoubtedly engages here in a subtle, allusional erotics. *Sabor* suggests the pleasure of a carnal tryst prior to the *amigo*'s departure, especially when we read these lines in the context of other songs by Zorro that make reference to the "pleasure" of the shore.[16] If sexual union is one dimension of pleasure here, another is the pleasure to be derived from the potential embarcation of the *amiga* along with her friend, which would obviate the *coita* or amorous torment. Zorro establishes an emotional intensity to his poem by juxtaposing the preterite action of the sighting of the ship to a continuing presentness of pleasure ("sabor hei da ribeira") in the refrain. This shift from past to present is accompanied by a pronounced nautical movement ("I vai o meu amigo"). What I would consider to be the kinesthetic aspect of Zorro's text is this conjoining of nautical movement and the experience of pleasure. Vesseled movement as an analogue to emotion finds expression in another *cantiga* by Zorro:

> Jus'a lo mar e o rio
>   eu namorada irei
> u el-rei arma navio,
>   amores, convosco m'irei.
>   . . . .
> U el-rei arma navio
>   eu namorada irei,
> pera levar a virgo,
>   amores, convosco m'irei.

(To the sea and to the river I will go, in love, to where the king prepares his ship; love, I will go with you. // . . . // To where the king prepares his ship I will go, in love, to the ship that will carry the young girl; love, I will go with you.)

There are two related movements here: the young woman's trip to the river and the seashore, and the departure of the ship, a kind of extension of the *amiga*'s journey to the water. The sea voyage affectively begins on land; the repeated "irei" creates a sense of expectation on shore of a voyage that will be emotional as well as spatial. This conflation of emotion and maritime space appears in the one surviving poem by Nuno Porco, which in part reads:

> Irei a lo mar vee'lo meu amigo;
> preguntá-lo-ei se querrá viver migo,
>   e vou-m'eu namorada.
>   . . . .
> Preguntá-lo-ei por que nom vive migo,
> e direi-lh'a coita [e]m que por el vivo,
>   e vou-m'eu namorada.

(I will go to the sea to see my friend; I will ask him if he wants to live with me, and I go in love. // . . . // I will ask him why he doesn't live with me, and I will tell him of the torment, on account of him, that I suffer, and I go in love.)

The journey to the sea is potentially one toward emotional fulfillment. The refrain "vou-m'eu namorada" in the maritime world of this and other *cantigas* presents love as a mode of travel, as in the superimposition of the space of desire and the space of oceanic voyaging in a poem by Lopo:

> Polo meu mal filhou-[s'ora] el-rei
> de mar a mar, assi Deus mi perdom,
> ca levou sigo o meu coraçom
> e quanto bem hoj[e] eu no mund'hei;
> > se o el-rei sigo nom levasse,
> > mui bem creo que migo ficasse.
> . . . .
> O meu amigo, pois com el-rei é,
> a mia coita é qual pode seer:
> semelha-mi a mi já par de morrer;
> esto vos dig'ora, per bõa fé:
> > se o el-rei sigo nom levasse,
> > mui bem creo que migo ficasse.

(To my great suffering, the king has now conquered from sea to sea, so help me God, and he took with him my heart and all good that I have in the world; if the king had not taken him, I well believe he would have stayed with me. // . . . // Since my friend is with the king, my suffering is as great as can be: it seems to me equal to death; and this I tell you, by God: if the king had not taken him, I well believe he would have stayed with me.)

The *cantiga* makes reference to the Reconquest vision of joining the Atlantic and Mediterranean worlds with Fernando III's conquest of Seville in 1248.[17] The geographic expanse of the seas is coterminous with an expansive, emotional seaspace of the *amiga*'s *coita*. Her anguish reaches beyond the confines of land like the conquistatorial dominion that reaches "de mar a mar."

The ship poems that feature the absence or imminent departure of the *amigo* create a gendered localization of emotion in that women experience heightened emotions on the shore or in coastal waters. An *amiga*'s thoughts and desires can project seaward without the young woman herself going to sea. There is thus a separation of body and emotion, where emotional constancy is expressed as an imagined voyage. Consider Paio Gomes Charinho's treatment of this conceit:[18]

> As frores do meu amigo
> briosas vam no navio,
> > e vam-s[e] as frores
> > daqui bem com meus amores,
> > idas som as frores,
> > daqui bem com [meus amores].
> > . . . .
> Briosas vam no navio
> pera chegar ao ferido,
> > e vam-s[e] as frores
> > daqui bem com meus amores,
> > idas som as frores,
> > daqui bem com [meus amores].
> > . . . .
> Pera chegar ao ferido
> servir mi, corpo velido,
> > e vam-s[e] as frores
> > daqui bem com meus amores,
> > idas som as frores,
> > daqui bem com [meus amores].

(My friend's flowers are leaving valiantly on the ship, and the flowers leave from here and with them my love; gone are the flowers from here with my love. // ... // They are leaving valiantly on the ship to arrive at battle; and the flowers leave from here and with them my love; gone are the flowers from here with my love. // ... // To arrive at battle to serve me, this beautiful body; and the flowers leave from here and with them my love; gone are the flowers from here with my love.)

What, precisely, the flowers are is a matter of conjecture. Some scholars think they are the flowers of a heraldic shield or standard (such as that of the admiral-poet himself), or that they are symbolic of the *amiga*'s love, which accompanies her departing lover.[19] It is the poetic function of the *frores*, however, that is of interest: they are the means by which the *amiga* accompanies her friend imaginatively on the ship and to the Crusader battlefield. If love is a form of travel, it serves in this *cantiga* to emphasize the physical separation of the lovers. In Stephen Reckert and Helder Macedo's reading, the flowers at first symbolize the euphoria of love while the *amigo* is still present, and, because of his eventual departure, they become melancholic.[20] Yet the distance separating the *amigo* from his *amiga* dramatizes the imaginative placement of the young woman on board the ship, so that the flowers may, even as the ship is lost from sight, connote a togetherness. In the final third of the poem, the poet introduces a moment of corporality when the *amiga* refers to herself as a body, a "corpo velido." This corporality further foregrounds the physical separation of the lovers: the woman's body remains behind, on land, while her emotional self journeys over water with the *amigo*. In this imagined projection of love at sail on the seas, Paio Gomes's *cantiga* is a notable precedent to the early modern, oceanically itinerant lyric subject, in which poetic selfhood voyages through aquatic worldspaces and states of mind and emotion.

With the *amiga* who watches her lover's ship disappear over the horizon in mind, consider a poem by Rui Fernandes de Santiago. This one is a *cantiga de amor*, and is unusual as one of the only sea-themed songs in the Galician-Portuguese love poetry voiced by men.

Quand'eu vejo las ondas
e las muit'altas ribas,
logo mi vêm ondas
al cor, pola velida:
    maldito seja'l mare
    que mi faz tanto male!

Nunca ve[j]o las ondas
nen'as altas debrocas
que mi nom venham ondas
al cor, pola fremosa:
    maldito seja'l mare
    que mi faz tanto male!

Se eu vejo las ondas
e vejo las costeiras,
logo mi vêm ondas

>   al cor, pola bem feita:
>   maldito seja'l mare
>   que mi faz tanto male!

(When I see the waves and the very steep cliffs, suddenly waves pound in my heart for the beautiful one: cursed be the sea, which does me such great harm! // I never see the waves nor the very tall rocks without waves pounding in my heart for the lovely one: cursed be the sea, which does me such great harm! // If I see the waves, and see the shores, then suddenly waves pound in my heart for the fair one: cursed be the sea, which does me such great harm!)

What is typically the female prerogative of contemplation of the sea and seascapes in the *cantigas de amigo* here belongs to the male speaker, and, like the woman-voiced poetry, the song expresses a link between maritime and emotional realms where the force of love overwhelms the speaker like the waves of the sea.[21] In her edition of the *Cancioneiro da Ajuda*, Carolina Michaëlis de Vasconcelos classifies the text as a *barcarola*, although it is not clear if her use of the term simply means a sea-themed poem (a *marinha*, the most likely hypothesis, given her comments on the text) or if it implies the presence of a ship.[22] My reading of the *cantiga* advocates for the latter. The use of *quando* implies a habitual contemplation of the waves and seacoasts, yet the location of the speaker as he gazes at the maritime environment is unclear. If we recognize that the *cantigas de amigo* present maritime or nautical scenarios as the objects of shore-bound contemplation that is part of the woman-centered, poetic perspective, then Rui Fernandes de Santiago's poem raises the possibility that the man speaks from on board a ship, or draws on a personal history of sea travel in rendering his poetic confession. This vessel-bound view of the sea and shorelines would also suggest the *amiga*'s absence on such voyages. The on-deck perspective corroborates nautical travel primarily as a masculine venture; women watch from shore in the *marinhas* or *barcarolas*, while this one maritime *cantiga de amor* consolidates a gendered practice of sea voyaging.

The personal relationship to environment in these women's sea poems is apparent in references to elements of nature such as flowers, wind, and water. The well-known sequence of seven *cantigas de amigo* by Martim Codax illustrates this linkage between nature and emotional states.[23] All of Codax's *cantigas* are set in Galicia in the Bay of Vigo. The sea (*ondas*) is the only element of nature that claims Codax's poetic attention: invocations of the waves open and close the sequence (*cantigas* 1 and 7), and reside at the center of *cantigas* 3 and 5. These waves require consideration as the central motif governing the *amiga*'s emotional states across all seven lyrics.

In the first *cantiga*, the woman addresses the waves of Vigo, asking for news of her lover:

> Ondas do mar de Vigo,
> se vistes meu amigo?
>   e ai Deus, se verrá cedo?
>
> Ondas do mar levado,
> se vistes meu amado?
>   e ai Deus, se verrá cedo?
>
> Se vistes meu amigo,
> o por que eu sospiro?
>   e ai Deus, se verrá cedo?
>
> (Waves of the sea of Vigo, by chance have you seen my friend? and, oh God, if he will come soon? // Waves of the roiling sea, by chance have you seen my beloved? and, oh God, if he will come soon? // By chance have you seen my friend, the one for whom I sigh? and, oh God, if he will come soon?)

The apostrophe to the sea establishes the maritime nature of the *amigo*'s absence and incorporates the waves symbolically into the affective trajectory of Codax's poetic sequence. In the second poem the *amiga* informs her mother that she has news that her lover is to return safely, so she will journey to Vigo. The third *cantiga* finds the woman inviting her sister (or possibly friend) to accompany her:

> Mia irmana fremosa, treides comigo
> a la igreja de Vigo u é o mar salido
>   e miraremos las ondas.
>   . . . .
> A la igreja de Vigo u é o mar levado

> e verrá i, mia madre, o meu amado
> e miraremos las ondas.

(My lovely sister, come with me to the church at Vigo where the sea is high, and we will watch the waves. // ... // To the church at Vigo where the sea is high and where there, dear mother, my love will come and we will watch the waves.)

The turbulent sea of Vigo, as Pilar Lorenzo Gradín argues, evokes amorous passion, and, for Anne-Marie Quint, connotes masculine potency.[24] The waves of Vigo in Codax's seven poems, as well as those in the *marinhas* and *barcarolas*, create a sense of sexual restlessness and urgency, the unsleeping yearning that makes the absence of the *amigo* so agonizing and the prospect of his return so exhilarating. We find the same imperative of desire collectively across a great number of the *cantigas de amigo*. The shift in function of the *ondas* from the first song as the addressee of the woman's inquiry to the symbol of emotion in the third is also a sensorial shift: the sea becomes the object of visual contemplation ("miraremos las ondas"), viewed communally by two women in the first two stanzas, after which the *amigo* becomes part of the first-person plural of the refrain in the remaining stanzas. Initially, the viewing of the waves is a gesture of hopeful expectation of the lover's arrival and subsequently becomes a form of amorous, celebratory (re-)union with the presence of the young man.

In Codax's fourth *cantiga*, the affective state of the *amiga* takes a negative turn:

> Ai Deus, se sab'ora meu amigo
> com'eu senheira estou em Vigo!
>   E vou namorada ...
>   ....
> Com'eu senheira estou em Vigo
> e nulhas gardas nom hei comigo!
>   E vou namorada ...
>   ....
> E nulhas gardas nom hei comigo,
> ergas meus olhos que choram migo!
>   E vou namorada ...

(Oh God, I wonder if my friend now knows how lonely I am in Vigo! And I am in love ... // ... // How lonely I am in Vigo, and there are no chaperones with me! And I am in love ... // ... // And there are no chaperones with me, besides my eyes, which are crying with me! And I am in love.)

The happy, communal viewing of the sea in the previous song here gives way to a despondent loneliness. There is a tide of mutable emotions flowing through Codax's lyric sequence up to this point that begins with the *amiga*'s worries about her lover's whereabouts, then shifts to joy as the woman has news that her lover will return, so she happily invites her sister (or friend) to accompany her to Vigo and to the seaside reunion. The fourth *cantiga* pulses with a sense of urgency and frustration, since the *amiga* is alone with no one to impede the amorous meeting. In this *cantiga*, presumably because the *amigo* has failed to appear, she laments her state. A sense of joy returns in poem 5:

> Quantas sabedes amar amigo,
> treides comig'a lo mar de Vigo
>   e banhar-nos-emos nas ondas.
>   ....
> Treides comig' a lo mar de Vigo
> e veeremo'lo meu amigo
>   e banhar-nos-emos nas ondas.

(All of you women who know what it means to love a friend, come with me to the sea of Vigo, and we will swim in the waves. // ... // Come with me to the sea of Vigo, and we will see my friend, and we will swim in the waves.)

In this decidedly happier song there is a return to camaraderie (first introduced in *cantiga* 3 with the invitation to the sister), except that here the scope of female society has been expanded to include all those who know the experience of love. Rather than simply contemplating the waves (poem 3), the woman proposes swimming in them, a bodily immersion that marries nautical absence to sexuality: the women will swim in the water that buoys the ships that carry their *amigos*, so contact with the water is a metonymic contact with the bodies of the young men. Scholars have noted the possible allusion of the verb *banhar* (to bathe, to swim) to ritualistic, erotic bathing in folkloric tradition,[25] so it is possible to understand the celebratory, culminating immersion in the waves as ecstatic and orgasmic. The *ondas* have become sexual substitutes for the body of the *amigo*, and as such, are capable of producing erotic fulfillment, a climatic moment of satisfaction made possible by the (haptic) chain of correspondence between young men, ships, and the sea. In *cantiga* 3, Codax employs the future tense to convey felicitous speculation and expectation: "miraremos las ondas" foresees the arrival of the amigo ("veerá i . . . o meu amado"), while the swimming in the waves likewise precedes the lover's presence ("veeremo'lo meu amigo"). These future conjugations stand in contrast to the present state of unhappy solitude in poem 4 ("com'eu senheira estou em Vigo"). Codax's *amiga*'s invitation to women experienced in love is similar to one in a *cantiga* by Airas Nunes, whose first stanza reads:

> Bailemos nós já todas três, ai amigas,
> sô aquestas avelaneiras frolidas,
> e quem for velida, como nós, velidas,
>   se amigo amar,
> sô aquestas avelaneiras frolidas
>   verrá bailar.

> (Let us dance now all three of us, oh friends, under these flowering hazel-trees, and whoever is beautiful, like us, beautiful friends, if she is in love, under these flowering hazel-trees she will come to dance.)

Pozo Garza notes the erotic connotation of the hazel-tree (*avelaneira*),[26] and this connotation ascribed to an element of nature shares an eroticism with Codax's sea. In both poems, the group of women fortify their affective, sympathetic bonds by a communal, bodily activity that is compensatory for the absence of the *amigo* and is a form of erotic encounter with the absent lover. This compensation is also liberating in that women sustain themselves through camaraderie in the absence of men. In Codax's and Nunes's poems, women swim and dance as a form of erotic activity; these *cantigas* present emotions and sexual moments as communally shared, and this is one of the features of several *cantigas de amigo*. While men suffer alone in the *cantigas de amor*, collective experiences of emotion not only find expression in the woman-voiced poetry but are also mobilized by women. So if women suffer because of the absence of a man and therefore are passively dependent on male presence, their marshaling of communal, emotional moments emancipates them from male interaction and grants them a certain emotional protagonism.

If Codax's marine immersion is celebratory, as it is in *cantiga* 5, it, like sea travel, can also be perilous. The sole surviving *cantiga* by the Galician *jogral* Mendinho depicts just such a danger:

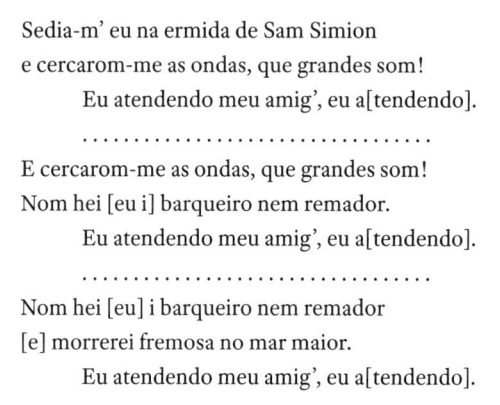

> Sedia-m' eu na ermida de Sam Simion
> e cercarom-me as ondas, que grandes som!
> > Eu atendendo meu amig', eu a[tendendo].
> > ....
> E cercarom-me as ondas, que grandes som!
> Nom hei [eu i] barqueiro nem remador.
> > Eu atendendo meu amig', eu a[tendendo].
> > ....
> Nom hei [eu] i barqueiro nem remador
> [e] morrerei fremosa no mar maior.
> > Eu atendendo meu amig', eu a[tendendo].

(I was at the sanctuary of San Simion, and the waves surrounded me, they are huge! I am waiting for my friend, waiting. // . . . // And the waves surrounded me, they are huge! I have neither boatman nor oarsman. I am waiting for my friend, waiting. // . . . // I have neither boatman nor oarsman, I, beautiful girl, will die in the turbulent sea. I am waiting for my friend, waiting.)

Mendinho sets his poem in the Bay of Vigo and, specifically, on the small island on which the church of San Simón is located. The intensity of the emotional drama of the poem derives from the young woman's impending death from *coita*;[27] rhetorically, Mendinho establishes this with the repeated use of *cercar* (to surround, to enclose) in the first four stanzas. The sea threatens to overwhelm the young woman—as Reckert and Macedo note, there is an overlapping of emotion and the maritime geography of San Simón, in that the waves of the sea are also the waves of passion that will wash over the *amiga* if her lover arrives.[28] But the emotional character of the waves is bivalent in that they are both the tide of passion and the tide of death—the *amiga* will die or drown of longing in the absence of the *amigo*.[29] This bivalence turns on the nautical analogy between the lovestruck woman as a ship without a helmsman (if the *amigo* were present, he would steer her through desire) and without whom she will wreck. Of the *barcarolas*, Mendinho's is perhaps the most dramatic in terms of the metaphoric equation between love, nautical vessels, bodies, and maritime peril, and as such is an important predecessor to early modern poetic constructions of poetic subjectivity and the realms and metaphors of nautical life. The poem exemplifies exceptionally well, in its dual valence of the sea, the polarized emotional world of the *cantigas de amigo* that moves between *sabor* (pleasure) and *coita* (suffering). The *amiga*, surrounded by water, is submersed in love while at the same time threatened vitally by the tide of passion.

Codax's seven-*cantiga* sequence comes to a close with a poem in which the *amiga* once more addresses the waves of the sea:

> Ai ondas que eu vim veer,
> se me saberedes dizer
>   por que tarda meu amigo sem mim?
>
> Ai ondas que eu vim mirar,
> se me saberedes contar
>   por que tarda meu amigo sem mim?
>
> (Oh waves that I came to see, might you able to tell me why my friend delays without me? // Oh waves that I came to watch, are you able to tell me why my friend delays without me?)

Codax ends his sequence as he began it, with an apostrophe to the sea in which the young woman expresses her preoccupation with her lover's absence. The regular presence of the ocean in every other poem of this mini-cycle unites the varying emotions of the *amiga* into a single, emotional journey, and is one more argument in favor of understanding Codax's *cantigas* as linked. Seawater is the premise for the poetic speaker to manifest a range of emotional states across the seven lyrics, from the initial worrying and fretting over the *amigo*'s absence and his possible return to the reassuring news of his arrival in Vigo and the happy invitation to the *irmana* to make a journey there. The poems explore loneliness and the ensuing celebratory expression of erotic desire amid a company of sympathetic women with the exhortation that they bathe in the sea; and finally, the sequence records jubilant, love-inspired dancing in Vigo in *cantiga* 6 and returns to a fretful interrogation of the sea regarding the delay of the lover's return. The sea not only structures the emotional voyage but also underwrites varied sensorial experiences. In the opening *cantiga*, the reference to the turbulent sea suggests that the young woman is overwhelmed aurally by the roar of the waves, while the third poem shifts to the visual ("miraremos las ondas"). The fifth poem, as we saw, emphasizes a tactile engagement with the ocean, intensified by an implicit yet evident eroticism, while the sixth lyric expresses physical sensation through a terpsichorean kineticism. The seventh lyric returns to sight as a multifaceted sense that will characterize the *amiga*'s interaction with her as-yet-to-return lover: *veer* here encompasses not only the action of seeing the *amigo* but also the emotional and erotic dimensions of the encounter. Such a range of sensorial experiences is in keeping with the *cantigas de amigo* as representing the emotions and bodies of the many young women who populate this corpus of poetry.

It is the emphasis on the sensorial that I wish to consider in a *cantiga de amigo* by King Dinis of Portugal (1261–1325), the renowned *rei trovador* (troubadour king). It is a poem about a young woman washing clothes in a mountain stream.

> Levantou-s' a velida,
>   levantou-s' alva,
> e vai lavar camisas
>   eno alto,
>   vai-las lavar alva.
>   . . . .
> [E] vai lavar camisas;
>   levantou-s' alva,
> o vento lhas desvia
>   eno alto,
>   vai-las lavar alva.
>   . . . .
>   E vai lavar delgadas;
>   . . . .
>
> O vento lhas desvia;
>   levantou-s' alva,

meteu-s' [a] alva em ira
　　eno alto,
　　vai-las lavar alva.

O vento lhas levava;
　　levantou-s' alva,
meteu-s' [a] alva em sanha
　　eno alto,
　　vai-las lavar alva.

(She woke up lovely, bright and early, and goes to wash shirts at the stream. She'll wash them bright and clean // ... // She goes to wash shirts, bright and early; they're strewn by the wind at the stream. She'll wash them bright and clean. ... // She washes chemises; ... // They're strewn by the wind bright and early; she becomes livid at the stream. She'll wash them bright and clean. // They're strewn by the breeze bright and early; she begins seething at the stream. She'll wash them bright and clean.)[30]

There are sexual overtones to Dinis's poem, according to the arguments of some scholars, on account of the washing of intimate apparel (*camisas, delgadas*) that is the young woman's matinal task and the tacit presence of the *amigo*, symbolized by the wind.[31] For Pilar Lorenzo Gradín, wind is the male principle of fertility, while Reckert and Macedo read the wind as phallic and the *velida*'s ire as the result of a violent initiation into sexuality.[32] However, since the wind is what carries off the washed clothing, and does not penetrate the young woman's body, it is unclear how the wind may be considered phallic.[33] Nonetheless, there is a latent eroticism in the *cantiga* that hinges on the synonymous emotions at the center of the poem, which are *ira* and *sanha*. Such a sentiment is opposed to the one found in a *cantiga* by Pero Meogo to which Dinis's composition is likely a response.[34] In part, Meogo's poem reads:

[Levou-s' aa alva], levou-s' a velida,
vai lavar cabelos na fontana fria;
　　leda dos amores, dos amores leda.
　　　　............................
Vai lavar cabelos na fontana fria,
passou seu amigo, que lhi bem queria;

>   leda dos amores, dos amores leda.
>   . . . .
> Passa seu amigo, que lhi bem queria,
> o cervo do monte a áugua volvia;
>   leda dos amores, dos amores leda.

(The beautiful girl arose, the fair girl arose: she goes to wash her hair in the cold fountain; happily in love, in love happily. // . . . // She goes to wash her hair in the cold fountain: her friend came by, who loves her greatly; happily in love, in love happily. // . . . // Her friend comes by, who loves her greatly, the stag from the hill agitates the water; happily in love, in love happily.)

Meogo's *cantiga* establishes an erotic connotation of water with the stag that stirs it, the same water in which the *velida* washes her hair. The water sexually links the *velida* and the *cervo*.[35] The young woman's happy disposition is due to the presence of the *amigo* with whom she carnally frolics. The plural and therefore multifaceted *amores* suggests a proliferation of bodily pleasures between *amiga* and *amigo*. Dinis's poem, by contrast, paints a picture in which the absence of the *amigo* triggers the experience of anger (*ira*, *sanha*). I want to suggest that the reason for the *amiga*'s ire is not the wind as an unsatisfactory substitute for the body of the absent lover, as Ferreira argues, but that a constellation of elements reminds the girl of why her *amigo* is not there: it is because he has left her to go overseas. Dinis's "Levantou-s' a velida" is an *alba* or dawn song, a genre of medieval poetry premised on the parting of lovers at daybreak. There is a nautical allusionality in the triad of wind, water, and cloth. The wind that carries off the clean clothing reminds the woman of the wind that fills the sails of the ship on which her lover departs, and her response to this unwanted departure and resulting (erotic) solitude is *ira*. In the practice of Galician-Portuguese lyric, in which an individual poet might invoke components of a collectively constituted repertoire of vocabulary, ideas, themes, or conceits as part of the semantic possibilities of any one *cantiga*, the absence of the *amigo* because of sea travel, as we have seen in other poems, is plausible.[36] Seafaring permits a reading in which water awakens or intensifies the young woman's desire for her absent friend. Interestingly, Reckert and Macedo find onomatopoeia in the many occurrences of *l* and *v* in Dinis's song because of the mimicking of the sound of the wind.[37] The aural evocation of the wind places the *amiga*, as well as the audience of the *cantiga* when it was performed, on board a ship as the wind suddenly fills the sails. The mountain breeze reminds the woman of the sea voyage of her *amigo* and the impossibility of a further expression of physical desire, if we grant that the washing of the intimate *camisas* follows a night of lovemaking.

Dinis's and Meogo's *cantigas*, like Codax's swimming poem or Estevão Coelho's "Se hoj' o meu amigo / soubess', iria migo: / eu al rio me vou banhar, / [e] al mar" (If today my friend knew it, he would come with me: I will swim in the river and in the sea), conjoin touch and water as compensatory for erotic congress with the lover. This sex-by-aquatic-proxy may in part be a device by which poets allow a female poetic persona the initiative in amorous adventures. The tactility associated with water in this love poetry poetically connects with some medieval formulations of the theory of touch. It was Aristotle in the *De anima* who proposed the lasting paradigm of the five senses, and of these senses touch is the most fundamental but the most difficult to locate in the body.[38] Aristotle ambivalently proposes that the organ of touch is at once the flesh and something deeper within the body.[39] In *Sense and Sensibilia*, a section of the *Parva naturalia*, the philosopher claims that "the sensory organ of both touch and taste is closely related to the heart."[40] Katie L. Walter notes that Albertus Magnus follows the Aristotelian understanding of touch when he differentiates flesh from skin in "those things perceived by touch as received first by 'the heart, then the flesh, and then the skin.'"[41] Touch, then, might conceivably be understood as cordial, not cutaneous, and this resonates strongly with the *cantigas* as a poetry of the *cor* or *coraçon* (heart). The heart as an organ of physiological sensation makes a number of the *cantigas de amigo* and the *cantigas de amor* potentially about tactile experience or touch-driven understandings of love and yearning. The *coitas no coraçon* (afflictions in the heart), so frequently invoked by the Galician-Portuguese poets, in addition to being the physiological manifestations of love in terms of cardiac palpitations, may also be understood as a longing for tactile encounters with a present or absent lover.

These *cantigas de amigo* all share an intense engagement between humans and the aquatic and maritime environments. With the presence of water and the sea, the *cantigas* present an embodiedness of young women who speak in a poetic fiction created by male poets. While the ventriloquizing of women's voices, and the depiction of women's emotions and desires as hinged to men, inevitably raise nontrivial questions for the critic, the collective, poetic portrait of women immersed in and experiencing a sensorial world—both the world of the body and the world of nature—is remarkable in medieval lyric and lends a vivacity to these poems that would no doubt have been intensified in performance. Barletta contends that nature in the Galician-Portuguese lyric is not so much an object of perception for poets and performers, but that *cantigas* set in the natural environment "work to make manifest or entail for their audience the process by which subjectivity itself emerges through a profound commerce with nature" and that the poetic engagement with nature is not a question of theme but is "primarily a matter of sensibility, a *spectacle* aimed at producing the continuous, echoing noise from which the subject emerges."[42] Barletta's focus on subjectivity is apposite. The immersion into the "noise" of the maritime world as a premise or condition of subjectivity reappears dramatically in Camões and other writers, so the correlation between aquatic or marine nature and the emergence of subjectivities is part of Portuguese literary tradition. The *donzelas* of the *cantigas de amigo* acquire an embodied presence through contact with water, and these feminine subjects are part of the creations of Galician-Portuguese poets. Role-playing partially informed the poiesis of Galician-Portuguese lyric, including those poets who spoke in women's voices and depicted what we would now consider to be stereotypical profiles of women's emotions and sexuality. This does not, of course, relieve the poets of the responsibility inherent in the constructedness of women or the absence of authentic women's speech (although some of the *cantigas de amigo* may have been based on popular women's songs), but rather acknowledges the gendered back-and-forth of so much of this lyric corpus. For if the *Arte de trovar*—at least in the extant fragments—identifies a sequence of gendered speech as constituting the generic contours differentiating the *cantigas de amigo* from the *cantigas de amor*, it is silent on authorship. For the author of the *Arte de trovar*, at least, the link between gender and voice is a matter of poetics and is not linked to the individual poet.

TWO SIXTEENTH-CENTURY *AMIGAS*

The poetic interplay of sea, water, love, desire, and women's emotions in the *cantigas de amigo* are important literary conceits in the trajectory of maritime literary culture in Iberia. This coalition of lyric elements gains new treatment in the sixteenth century in two poems by Camões. Both poems are *moto/volta* compositions, and are part of a handful of Camões's poems that boast a lighthearted spirit.

The first is Camões's gloss, in Castilian, on the *moto* "Irme quiero, madre / á aquella galera, / con el marinero / á ser marinera" (I want to go, mother, to that galley with the sailor, to become a sailoress).[43] In its four *redondilha menor* stanzas, Camões depicts a young woman subjected to Love's uncompromising imperative and who has no choice but to accompany the sailor (*marinero*) to become a *marinera*. The first stanza reads:

> Madre, si me fuere,
> dó quiera que vó,
> no lo quiero yo,
> que el Amor lo quiere.
> Aquél niño fiero
> hace que me muera,
> por un marinero
> á ser marinera.

(Mother, if I were to go wherever I am to go, I myself do not wish to; rather it is Love who commands it. That fierce child makes me die for a sailor so I must become a sailoress.)

The next two stanzas repeat the woman's unwilling subjection to the tyrannical force of love, and end with the refrains "que, si es marinero, / seré marinera" (for if he is a sailor, I will become a sailoress) and "yo me quiero / por un marinero / hacer marinera" (on account of a sailor, I want to become a sailoress). Camões's poetic characters are a young woman and her mother, a common duo in the *cantigas de amigo*. The pairing of *marinero/marinera* unites the woman and mariner in an amorous bond and infuses the nautical world with love. Love, as it were, goes to sea. But Camões's *amiga*, unlike her medieval predecessors, lives in a world saturated by seafaring and oceanic venturers. A nautical life is as natural and accessible a *modus amandi* as any other. In the final stanza, the woman speaks to the sea waves:

> Decid, ondas, ¿cuando
> vistes vos doncella,
> siendo tierna y bella,
> andar navegando?
> [Pues] más no se espera
> daquel niño fiero,
> vea yo quién quiero,
> sea marinera.

(Tell me, waves, when have you seen a maiden, delicate and beautiful, going to sea? For nothing else may be expected of that ferocious child; may I see whom I love, and may I be a sailoress.)

The address to the sea reveals the singularity of this *amiga*'s experience: we find little evidence of women mariners, since seafaring was by and large a male profession. The quasi-ironic tone of the apostrophe corroborates the intensity of the ferocious child's transformative will, since the *doncella* accedes to the only possible way of loving the sailor, which is to become one herself. The maiden's willing capitulation to love in a nautical manner—despite the gesture of resistance in the first stanza—allows women an agency in Camões's nautically inscribed realm of amorous existence.

A similar agency underwrites a two-stanza *vilancete*, which is Camões's gloss on the *moto* "Quem disser que a barca pende, / dir-lhe-ei mana, que mente" (Whoever says that this boat lists, I'll tell him, sister, that he's lying):

> Se vos quereis embarcar
> e para isso estais no cais,
> entrai logo; que tardais?
> Olhai que está preiamar!
> E se outrem, por vos fretar,
> vos disser que esta que pende,
> dir-lhe-ei, mana, que mente.

Esta barca é de carreira,
tem seus aparelhos novos;
não há como ela outra em Povos,
boa de leme e veleira.
Mas, se por ser a primeira,
vos disser alguém que pende,
dir-lhe-ei, mana, que mente.

(If you want to embark, and that is why you're on the dock, come aboard right away, why wait? Look, it's high tide! And if someone, to get you on his boat, says that this boat lists, I'll tell him, sister, that he's lying. // This is a high-seas vessel and has all new rigging; there's none like it in all of Povos, swift and with a good helm. But, if because it's your first, someone says that this boat lists, I'll tell him, sister, that he's lying.)

Here, nautical allusions and women's sexual desire meet in a bold play of amphibolic vocabulary or *equivocatio*. Couched as a woman choosing a ship on which to embark, the scenario presents a man hawking his ship-for-hire that is fit, seaworthy, and never lists. The vessel's solid construction, new rigging, and seaworthiness ludically stand for sexual and phallic stamina, where the imputed listing vessel is an allusion to flaccidity or impotence. Macedo finds here the "unconventional acceptance of the legitimacy of a woman's sexual desire and of her freedom to exercise this desire through uninhibited choice,"[44] a freedom of choice that also motivates "Madre, si me fuere" but in a much more diffident vein. One of Camões's lighthearted ambiguities in "Se vos quereis embarcar" is the question of who is speaking: it could be the owner of the boat, but it could also be a female companion of the feminine "you" who desires to travel by sea. This companion knows, by sexual experience, that "this" boat never lists. The possible gender of the speaker as female follows from the use of *mana* (literally, "sister," but also informally "friend"), a common form of colloquial address between women in the *cantigas de amigo* and in the sixteenth-century theatrical farces of Gil Vicente. A woman speaker both expresses the freedom of sexual choice and, at the same time, renders men as silent, passive objects of female erotic scrutiny. In this case Camões, in the space of one poem, participates in and revives the ventriloquizing of women's voices characteristic of the *cantigas de amigo*. If the speaker is a man, *mana* lends the dockside exchange a certain flirtatious quality, since it is his vessel that supposedly lists. In the double entendre of *embarcar* (to board) or *navegar* (to sail) as references to sex, Camões is not alone. Manuel da Costa Fontes, for example, establishes sailing as a metaphor for sex in Francisco Delicado's *La Lozana andaluza* (1528).[45] And sexual freedom and choice as a woman's initiative in Portugal is the humorous premise of Gil Vicente's *Auto da Índia* (1509), in which a woman takes advantage of her husband's overseas absence by taking on multiple suitors. In Camões's poetic frolic, a ship's architecture and rigging and male anatomy are co-referential. By sailing on the vessel, the woman engages in carnal union with a man; his body is a *barca* to be steered and enjoyed. In this nautically framed erotics, women are sexual pilots.

✳ 2 ✳

Epic Seas

The sea and water course through *Os Lusíadas*. From the second line of the first stanza to the poem's close, currents of water flow through an expanding worldspace and the many arrangements of its inhabitation. Vasco da Gama's voyage from Portugal to India (Calicut, now Kozhikode) and back in 1497–99, the backbone of Camões's poem, makes the sea a historical inevitability in the narrative of Portugal's past and future. Yet Gama's sea journey is only one aspect of the poem's maritime realm, since water and seafaring reside at the center of the Camonian epic imagination; they are organizing principles of poetic creativity that structure many of the historical, mythological, and prophetic dimensions of the narrative. For Camões and his early modern contemporaries, nothing defines Portuguese culture and history more than the sea.

The seas, oceans, rivers, ships, and boats that crowd *Os Lusíadas* shape its various narratives, its representations of the world, its ideological underpinnings, and the contours of its imagined and real spaces. Camões invests the ocean and seafaring with a wide-ranging polysemy, the raw matter of historical realities and the lenses through which the Portuguese perceive and read the worlds that unfold before the bows of Gama's ships. Gama's fleet, sailing at the orders of King Manuel I (1495–1521), achieves a desired "governo do mar" (control of the sea; I.28.iii-iv), so that all of Portugal's expansionist ambitions coalesce in the sovereignty over the world's oceans.[1] The nautical image that cogently encapsulates expansionist desires in the form of oceanic sovereignty is the piloted ship. The command of a high-seas vessel is the realization of imperial designs, for the controlled movement of a *nau* is a manifestation of both human and divine will. At the outset of canto I, Camões boasts that the Portuguese feats he is about to narrate eclipse those of Ulysses and Aeneas—specifically, their sea voyages—and thus places maritime voyaging at the heart of Western epic tradition.[2] For Camões, to navigate is to participate in a centuries-old practice of adventurous daring, a practice that, throughout the ten cantos of his poem, establishes a new historical order, but one fraught with danger and uncertainty. The poet's numerous references to the "mar irado" (angry or ireful sea) invest the humid element with the passion of anger that the Portuguese seafarers must confront in their efforts to reach "as much of India as Doris bathes" ([d]a Índia tudo quanto Dóris banha; I.31.iv).[3] *Irado* also suggests an expansive sea that is undomesticated because, in the fiction of the poem, it has not yet been navigated prior to Gama's voyage.[4] Alongside the Portuguese mariners, the sea itself exercises an agency in charting the geographic contours of the terraqueous globe that define the reach of expansion, an agency that is evident in Camões's use of *banhar* (to bathe) in the quotation above. "To bathe" here is to delineate the space of India in an inscriptionary gesture, as most landscapes exist in *Os Lusíadas* only insofar as they are created by, or juxtaposed to, bodies of water. This inscriptionary gesture, as Simone Pinet explains, can be traced to Strabo, who held that the sea "shapes and defines the land."[5] *Banhar* wields a cartographic power like ships. In their many voyages, the *naus*, *caravelas*, and *galeões* act as a collective stylus, charting and inscribing Portuguese presence in the aquatic element from Africa to Asia and the New World.

WATER AND VOICE

From the first lines of the poem, water and voice define the creation and trajectory of the many narratives embedded in *Os Lusíadas*:

> As armas e os barões assinalados
> Que, da Ocidental praia Lusitana,
> Por mares nunca dantes navegados
> Passaram ainda além da Taprobana (I.1.i-iv)
>
> (Arms, and the outstanding men, who from the western Lusitanian shore, through seas never before navigated, passed even beyond Taprobana)

These lines echo the *incipit* of the *Aeneid*:

> Arma virumque cano, Troiae qui primus ab oris
> Italiam fato profugus Lavinaque venit
> litora
>
> (Arms and the man I sing, who first from the coasts of Troy, exiled by fate, came to Italy and Lavine shores)[6]

In this initial exercise of *imitatio* Camões modifies his Virgilian model in two ways. The first is to recast the protagonist of the poem as a collectivity, substituting the plural *barões* for Virgil's singular *vir*. The second is the use of *praia* (beach or shore) as a parallel to *litora* (shores). *Praia* as a synecdoche for Portugal casts the country as a coastal nation, definitionally oriented toward the sea. Virgil's verb *venit* (came) relates the journey of Aeneas to "Italy and Lavine shores" as a journey of arrival, while Camões's reference to the "Lusitanian shore" as the launching point for voyages over time declares his poem to be one of departures. Voyages out for Camões claim precedence over voyages of return (*nostos*); these expeditions are, in part, epistemological in nature, since they challenge old traditions of knowledge and reveal new forms of knowing. The "barões assinalados" acknowledge a long-standing historical practice of seafaring, an iteration through time that is central to Camões's vision of Portuguese identity. Coastal, maritime Portugal, the endpoint of European soil and the head of Europe—"[o]nde a terra se acaba e o mar começa" (where the land ends and the sea begins; III.20.iii)—reaches expansively beyond its European borders, a world-reaching nation emblematized by the aquatic city of Lisbon. Lisbon is a maritime metropole that wields power because of the waters that flow outward from it in the form of the Tagus River and bring into its domains the *mar profundo* or vast ocean: "nobre Lisboa . . . a quem obedece o Mar profundo" (noble Lisbon . . . whom the vast sea obeys; III.57.i, v). Humanist Damião de Góis (1502–74), in his *Vrbis Olisiponis Descriptio* (Description of the City of Lisbon, 1554), remarks on the Tagus as a governing, monarchical force of the world: "quod hodierna die Tagus ipse per uniuersa oceani litora, in Africa, Asiaque, leges et instituta det, quibus ipsarum prouinciarum reges principesque, sponte uel coacti parent, tributaque Lusitanis soluunt" (In our day, this same Tagus sets forth the laws and norms on every coast of the Ocean, in Africa and in Asia. The kings and princes of these provinces subject themselves to these laws either freely or by force, rendering service to the Portuguese).[7] Through the Tagus River and the sea Lisbon reaches the world, *urbe ad orbem*.

The initial presentation of Portugal as a coastal nation, whose potency derives from its position on the threshold of land and sea and from whose shores mariners depart on voyages that create and solidify a global, historical order, coalesces with Camões's description of his own poetic voice and his invocation of the Muses. In the second stanza of canto I, Camões declares, "Cantando espalharei por toda parte, / Se a tanto me ajudar o engenho e arte" (In singing I will reach all parts, if my skill and my art aid me; I.2.vii-viii), after which he invokes the Tágides or nymphs of the Tagus River as a source of poetic inspiration:

> E vós, Tágides minhas, pois criado
> Tendes em mi um novo engenho ardente,
> Se sempre, em verso humilde, celebrado
> Foi de mi vosso rio alegremente,
> Dai-me agora um som alto e sublimado,
> Um estilo grandíloco e corrente,
> Por que de vossas águas Febo ordene,
> Que não tenham enveja às de Hipocrene.
>
> Dai-me hũa fúria grande e sonorosa,
> E não de agreste avena ou frauta ruda,
> Mas de tuba canora e belicosa. (I.4–I.5.i-iii)

(And you, my Tágides, created in me a new, burning art if ever in humble verses your river were happily celebrated by me; grant me now a high and lofty sound, a grand and flowing style; for your waters, Phoebus commands, will not envy those of Hippocrene. // Grant me a great and sonorous fury, and not one of a rustic reed or simple pipe, but of a loud trumpet of war.)

These lines, following the use of *espalhar* (to spread, to disperse), suggest an analogy between the poet's song and the movement of the waterways that extend across the earth, the web of rivers, oceans, and seas that are the basis of expansionist connectivity and Portuguese epic legacy. While classical myth held that poetic inspiration emanated from an aquatic source (Hippocrene, a spring on Mt. Helicon created by Pegasus's hoof striking the ground), here the fount of creativity is the Tagus.[8] Camões petitions the Tagus nymphs for a "fúria" (fury) that Edward Glaser argues is tantamount to an epic frenzy.[9] This comparison of epic register to the flow of water ("grandíloco e corrente" [grandiloquent and flowing]) has precedents in rhetorical treatises of antiquity. Hélio J. S. Alves studies the analogy between the sublime poetic style and currents of fluvial water, a pairing discussed by writers like Quintilian and Cicero.[10] The metaphor of the river in the *Aeneid*, according to Alves, is the ideal example of sublime language reflected in Camões's mention of the Tagus.[11] Yet I would add to Alves's argument the possibility that, with *corrente*, and with the Tagus as the principal aquatic gateway to the worldwide oceans, Camões is also referring to oceanic currents of water and in this way adapts his classical antecessors to his own maritime purpose. The poet's dismissal of the sound of rustic musical instruments (*avena, frauta*) as inappropriate to his project might also be understood as a reference to a domestic (i.e., nonoceanic) tradition of poetry that is being (temporarily) left behind. The distinction between fresh water and salt water is part of a Camonian aquatic symbolism in which fresh water is the domain of a land-bound poetry and salt water of epic action. In canto IV, when Gama's ships prepare to depart from Belém, Camões notes, "E já no porto da ínclita Ulisseia, / Cum alvoroço nobre e cum desejo / (Onde o licor mestura e branca areia / Co salgado Neptuno e doce Tejo) / As naus prestes estão" (And now, in the port of illustrious Ulysses, amid an auspicious tumult and with intent [where the waters of Neptune mix with the sweet Tagus and white sand], the ships stand ready; IV.84.i-v). The mix of salt and fresh water, or more specifically, the imminent reign of salt water, attends the shift in history that Gama's voyage creates. The contrast between fresh water and seawater is fundamental to geography, as basic as the distinction between land and water itself. In this regard, Camões is asking the Tágides to grant him a poetic register that is akin to the vast sweep of the currents of the sea, an oceanically thunderous speech. With its origin in the Tagus, such a register of poetic voice will spread and resonate like the sea, much as Adamastor's voice in canto V is superimposed on the roar of the ocean or Triton's blowing of the conch shell in canto VI resonates through the seas of the world. The sound of water, and sounds carried through water, create and consolidate an aural sphere of Portuguese influence around the globe.

With these equivalences between water and voice in mind, consider now how Camões inaugurates the action proper of his poem. After the petition to the Tágides nymphs as Portuguese Muses, and the dedication of the poem to the young king Sebastião (1554–78), an image of Gama's ship at sail on the high seas appears for the brief space of one stanza:

> Já no largo Oceano navegavam,
> As inquietas ondas apartando;
> Os ventos brandamente respiravam,
> Das naus as velas côncavas inchando;
> Da branca escuma os mares se mostravam
> Cobertos, onde as proas vão cortando
> As marítimas águas consagradas,
> Que do gado de Próteu são cortadas. (I.19)

(Already on the open ocean they sailed, cleaving the restless waves. The winds gently were blowing, and made the ships' sails billow; the sea was covered in white foam as the prows cut through the sacred maritime waters of Proteus's herds.)

Stanza I.19 is the epic *in medias res* device—Vasco da Gama and his fleet at this initial moment are in Mozambique.[12] They have already sailed from Lisbon around southern Africa and are halfway through the journey to India when the poem begins. The image of the ship moving swiftly and decisively across the sea propelled by auspicious winds is Camões's predilect icon of the full expression and plenitude of maritime might, with all its providential, cultural, and ethical directives. Camões's seaborne ship recalls a Virgilian precedent:

> Vix e conspectu Siculae telluris in altum
> vela dabant laeti et spumas salis aere ruebant. (*Aeneid* 1.34–35)

(Hardly out of sight of Sicilian land were they spreading their sails seaward, and merrily ploughing the foaming brine with brazen prow.)[13]

While the seaborne ship cleaving the water is common to both the Latin and Portuguese poets, there is a difference. In the Mantuan's poem, the ship sets the context for Juno's soliloquy that results in the storm that assails Aeneas and his crew. Camões's ship acts as a prelude to the Council of the Gods beginning in stanza I.20. Its stand-alone presence symbolically encapsulates certain ideas central to the entire poem. Consider some lexical details. The stanza begins adverbially with *já* (already), which in the Camonian epic idiom signals noteworthy action. The adverb engages our readerly attention, and modulates the narrative tone from the ceremonious (present in the immediately preceding dedication to the king) to the dramatic, a moment of present action. A sense of pronounced, forward movement emanates from these verses, partially a result of the first six lines that end in verbs or gerunds. The verbal constructions join the natural and artificial worlds into a maritime fleetness: air is brought to sails, water to prows, and the entire realm of the deep, inhabited by the herds of Proteus (sea creatures), buoys the ship and expansionist enterprise. The brisk verbs of nautical movement (*apartar* [to part, to rend] and *cortar* [to cleave]) suggest a forceful exercise of artifice over nature, a recruitment of the sea to human endeavor.[14] As ships move, they perform a primordial rending or parting of the waves of the seas "nunca dantes navegados" (never previously sailed; I.1.iii).[15] In this sailing over the sea's agitated waves, Gama's ships subjugate the realm of Neptune to the realm of King Manuel I. As the stanza draws to a close, verbs cede to adjectives: *consagradas* (sacred) and *cortadas* (cleaved) present seawater as the closing image of the *in medias res* moment, in which the consecrated waters of the gods are appropriated by Gaman vessels. The second appearance of the ship, some stanzas later following the Council of the Gods, marks a shift in focus from supernatural to divine actors: "Cortava o mar a gente belicosa / Já lá da banda do Austro e do Oriente. . . . / Tão brandamente os ventos os levavam, / Como quem o Céu tinha por amigo" (The bellicose company cleaved the sea, beyond the limits of south and east. . . . So smoothly the winds were carrying them, as if Heaven itself were an ally; I.42.iii-iv; 43.i-ii). Here the sea is the space of the confluence of supernatural will (established by the preceding resolution of the Council in favor of the Portuguese mission) and human agency, and the traversal of the ships over the water is a material manifestation of that confluence. The movement of the ship carves out the course of history and is a locus of supernatural consent and intervention in human affairs.

This image of the ship briskly propelled over the ocean's surface reappears frequently throughout the poem. For Camões, this nautical icon is not a static topos but rather a marker of noteworthy moments or episodes in Gama's voyage. In conjoining the image of the swiftly moving sea vessel to the *in medias res* convention, and by repeating that image regularly, Camões suggests that his poem begins over and over again throughout the course of its 1,102 stanzas. The nautical vignette Camões first employs in fulfillment of epic convention becomes an iterative principle of beginning. The repetition of the image of the ship at full sail infixes the directed, nautical movement of Vasco da Gama's ships into known and as-yet unvisited geographic spaces. This image lies at the epicenter of Camonian epic poiesis, since to navigate is to encounter, create, and know worlds, to narrate history, to write myth, and to prophesy the future. In its recursive presence, the *nau* on the high seas establishes the ceaseless, restless nature of oceanic expansion and its inevitability.

THE VIEW FROM THE DECK

Vasco da Gama's *naus* steer a course from the port of Belém to Calicut and back, a course that is an expression of Portuguese maritime authority. Camões frequently refers to Gama's vessels with their sharp prows (*agudas proas*) and their steerage (*inclinar proas*), so that the prerogative of expansion inheres in the movement and architecture of the fleet that "surges forward" (surge diante; II.74.v). Even when not stated explicitly, there is often an implicit presence of vesseled vision that directs the poetic narrative, an organizing perspective that surveys and apprehends the "novos mundos ao mundo irão mostrando" (new worlds [the Portuguese] will reveal to the world; II.45.viii).

The voyage made by Gama's fleet between 1497 and 1499 was the inauguration of the trade route between Portugal and India known as the *carreira da Índia* (India voyage). Throughout the fifteenth century, Portuguese trading interests in Africa motivated numerous Atlantic expeditions along the West African coast, and in 1488 Bartolomeu Dias was the first European to round the Cape of Good Hope. The India fleet under Gama's command as the *capitão-mor* (captain-major) was sent by Manuel I nearly a decade after Dias's voyage, with

Dias himself overseeing the preparations of Gama's ships. Gama's flagship was the *São Gabriel*. Gama's brother Paulo commanded the *São Rafael*, while Nicolau Coelho was captain of the *Berrio*. Interpreters who spoke Bantu and Arabic were part of the company. An onboard secretary, commonly identified as Álvaro Velho, produced an incomplete eyewitness account of the voyage, the *Roteiro da primeira viagem de Vasco da Gama*.[16] This document is the only surviving first-person account of the voyage.[17] By Camões's time the facts of Gama's expedition were well known, and the tight correlation between the details of the outbound trip to India in Velho and the itinerary narrated in *Os Lusíadas* suggests that Velho's narrative may have been one of Camões's sources.[18]

Velho's account is an example of the maritime textual genre of the *roteiro* (rutter). Generally, a *roteiro* is a record of a ship's journey between specified locales meant to serve as a guide to future navigators. *Roteiros* derive from medieval Mediterranean portulan charts, and record shoreline features, prevailing wind and water currents, distances and depths, and navigational dangers. They were frequently revised on successive iterations of the same journey.[19] While the purpose of the *roteiro* was pragmatic, in the Portuguese tradition it is a genre that also contains a variety of details unrelated to the technical aspects of a voyage. If some *roteiros* focus on the course and steerage of the ship in considerable technical specifics, others concentrate on geography and topography, flora and fauna, the customs and characteristics of peoples encountered, or the excursions of landing parties. In their differing registration of the realities of any one itinerary, *roteiros* are a mix of navigational guide, travel narrative, ship's diary, proto-ethnographic record, and historical chronicle. Velho's account, for example, provides a significant amount of information on trade and encounter between Portuguese and African and Indian populations largely because of the economic objectives of the voyage. As the pace of journeys to India and the Middle East increased in the sixteenth century, some *roteiros* incorporated learned discussions on a number of topics, such as the *roteiros* penned by João de Castro (1500–48). Castro was a military careerman and scholar who traveled extensively and who, in 1545, became the thirteenth governor of Portuguese India and its fourth viceroy. He left a substantial body of scholarly work, including three *roteiros*: the first on the voyage from Lisbon to Goa (1538), the second on the voyage from Goa to

Diu (1538–39), and the third on an expedition to the Red Sea (1541). Castro's rutters are far more than navigational guides, since they contain extensive disquisitions on the practice and theory of navigational science and allied topics that frequently dispute the findings of other scholars, pilots, and cosmographers.[20]

Whatever differences of content there may be in the surviving corpus of *roteiros*, or varying pragmatic or intellectual objectives, the nautical voyage is the structuring element in all of them and performs significant practical and symbolic work. *Roteiros* discursively reflect a conception of oceanic space that aligns with some points of Margaret Cohen's arguments on the chronotopes of the sea in novelistic fiction.[21] Cohen builds on Bakhtin's chronotope of the road, the "poetic dimension to the literary representation of space" in which "the representation of space always entails the representation of time . . . time and space are intrinsically connected."[22] Cohen argues that "the sea . . . has a particular affinity with narrative representations of space, which exist as movement as well, and which make evident space's dependence on temporal parameters, its intrinsic temporality," and that "space is experienced as movement."[23] *Roteiros* construe maritime space as movement with a pronounced, diurnal temporality; in recording the movements and temporary pauses of a ship's journey, *roteiros* characteristically parse those movements into daily entries. Daily, chronological time is the temporal building-block. The quick succession of daily entries, therefore, carries its own significance. The *Diário da navegação* (Diary of the Nautical Voyage) of Pero Lopes de Sousa, which records the voyage of the fleet of Martim Afonso de Sousa from Lisbon to Brazil in 1530, typifies the genre in its repetitive registration of weather, water currents, and navigational positions during the voyage.[24] On several occasions the handling of the ship in bad weather claims the writer's attention, although with scant technical or practical details. Sousa seems to be more interested in recording the experience of uncertainty and terror at sea than recording specific strategies to ensure the safety of the vessel. Such a protracted lingering over maritime dangers, and the reactions of the crew to these dangers, intensifies and amplifies the fretful consciousness of slowly passing daily time. What emerges is an awareness of diurnal temporality and the atomized, incremental movement of the ship through that temporality. The ship's movements, by extension, are not only defined by chronological time but also become the bearer of that time. In its plotted, repeated, and continuous movement the ship transforms the sea into a locus of forward-moving temporality. A stylus, the nautical vessel writes history onto maritime space and the terrestrial landscapes that maritime space reaches. Ships are seaborne clepsydras, clocking oceanic space and concatenating it into familiar temporal units. The chronotope of the sea as a lens through which to read *roteiros* reveals an underlying premise of the genre: while practical in their linking of time, forward movement, and oceanic space, *roteiros* construe navigation as a form of time making and of historical agency.

We noted that documents designated as *roteiros*, as well as other kinds of maritime texts such as books of seamanship (*livros de marinharia*), contain a considerable variety of details and focus on different aspects of a voyage or of nautical science, but all share the common denominator of a nautical route.[25] The nautical voyage is a structuring conceit in other genres, too, such as chronicles, even when there may not be the level of detail about nautical specifics that is found in *roteiros*. Gomes Eanes de Zurara's *Crónica de Guiné* (Chronicle of Guinea, finished in 1453 but with later additions) is the first chronicle dedicated to the Portuguese exploration of West Africa ("Guiné") south of Cape Bojador under the supervision of Prince Henry, "the Navigator."[26] Zurara records the capture of Black, sub-Saharan Africans for transport to Portugal for sale in the slave markets. The chronicler organizes many of the episodes in the chronicle (which are roughly equivalent to individual chapters) around individual nautical expeditions and, in doing this, creates a parallel between seafaring, the gathering of knowledge (one of the putative objectives of Prince Henry's African expeditions), and the office of the historiographer. Zurara establishes an association between nautical expeditions and "natural ordinance" (*natural ordenança*). For the chronicler, *natural ordenança* is part of a moral obligation to recognize the actions of those who "do well" (*bem fazer*), which in this case is Henry and the African expeditions. Zurara writes that there is a "natural semelhança" (natural resemblance) between the workings of nature and those deeds that are pursued for a moral good.[27] Just as the sun rises, illuminates everything on earth, and then returns to its cradle, or as rivers emanate from the sea, run their course, and return to the sea, so too does acknowledgment and recognition of *bem fazer* follow a natural cycle. Zurara's chronicle conscripts Henry's campaign into a militant Christianity and desire to know the world, a project to assess possible trade routes, to discover possible allies for Portugal (such as Eastern Christians), and to reconnoitre the strength of non-Christian Africans. Zurara insists on the naturalizing view of historical action and the ethos of the chronicler, for in his view history writing follows the dictates of the "rodas celestiaaes" (heavenly spheres). It is a sobering mentality when understood in the context of slaving raids and slave markets. In the Zuraran moral and cosmographic schema, seafaring figures prominently. The *Crónica de Guiné* registers the decisive oceanic turn of Portuguese history (glimpsed earlier in the first chronicle to bear Zurara's name, the *Crónica da tomada de Ceuta* [Chronicle of the Capture of Ceuta]). Seafaring is not incidental to but constitutive of that history. The movements and regular expeditions of ships, and the practice of seafaring generally, enact divine will and reflect the order of the universe.

The nautical expeditions recorded by writers like Zurara, Álvaro Velho, or João de Castro make seafaring an expression of imperial authority, regardless of the success or failure of any one individual expedition. While Zurara's account is retrospective and narrated in the third person, a *roteiro* is characterized by a first-person, eyewitness perspective. Such a perspective construes the ship as an eyewitness as well. A *roteiro* author establishes the nautical, eyewitness testimony in the following manner. There is, first, grammatical person and verbal tense. The present and future tenses are typical in descriptions of maritime landscapes in comments such as "You will see a shoreline" or "If you want to make port here you will need to . . ." Cohen observes that, in navigational guides, the present and future tenses are indicative of "action in the process of unfolding,"[28] and *roteiro* writers frequently situate themselves in such action through the vantage point of firsthand experience. The present and future tenses imbue these documents with a certain drama of encounter as worlds and peoples present themselves to the first-person eye, while this unfolding action also tacitly ascribes a continuous present to seafaring itself, an iterative enterprise that is never complete, always in process. The first-person perspective is inevitable, of course, because *roteiros* are accounts of actual voyages; it is either singular or plural (I or we), and is placed on deck, explicitly or implicitly. The shipbound perspective is characteristic of the *roteiro* if a future pilot is meant to correlate the observations in the document with what he sees on his

Epic Seas 59

own iteration of the same journey. The repeated, and repeatable, voyage was a constituent component of expansion and depended in large part on accurate *roteiros*. The action of *descobrimento* (discovery) was likewise dependent on nautical iteration. As Vitorino Magalhães Godinho observes, *descobrimento* in the early modern era had several meanings, chief among them the ability to sail a route to a predetermined port and return safely to the point of origin.[29] The recursive nautical voyages were a fundamental component of maritime expansion as an exercise of power.

The deck-bound gaze in *roteiros* is as integral to this genre of maritime text as the movement of a ship through aquatic space and chronological time. The details of any voyage and the ongoing, incremental accrual of knowledge and experience attained emerge in the *roteiros* through individual acts of seaborne seeing and often appeal to the visual imagination. Seaborne viewing pervades Manuel de Mesquita Perestrelo's sixteenth-century *roteiro* of south and southeastern Africa.[30] Perestrelo, an imperial voyager who saw assignments in Africa, India, and Indonesia, was a cartographer sent on a reconnaissance mission by King Sebastião in November 1575 to the South African coast in response to the need to improve knowledge of the sea route to India in the hopes of minimizing the danger of shipwrecks typical of that region.[31] Perestrelo departed from Mozambique and followed an east–west trajectory until he reached Good Hope in January 1576, and from there returned to Mozambique and then probably to Portugal in the same year. His *roteiro* provides detailed descriptions of the extensive coastline and its harbors, and includes eight sketches of coastal locales.[32] In the opening paragraphs, Perestrelo writes to Sebastião that he is able to speak of the people of the land based on what he saw and on his experience as a shipwreck survivor in the same region twenty years earlier. The peoples of southern Africa possess a "simplicidade e boa condição natural, disposta para se imprimir nela toda a doutrina do conhecimento de Deus e lei evangelica" (simplicity and good, natural character on which the entirety of the doctrine of the knowledge of God and evangelical law may be imprinted), and Perestrelo hopes that during Sebastião's reign "se lhe ha inda de fazer um tamanho serviço, como será chegar o som da sua palavra áqueles tão remotos e derradeiros fins da redondeza da terra, para salvação de tantas almas como puramente á mingua ali vivem perdidos" (a great service will be done such that the sound of His word will reach the remote and extreme ends of the round earth, for the salvation of so many souls which live there so utterly lost).[33] Perestrelo's cartographic, knowledge-gathering project is thus couched in the rhetoric of Christian imperialism and the authority deriving from his status as an eyewitness of remote populations. These comments reiterate the vast geographical reach of Sebastião's influence, an imperial realm sustained not only by the *verbum Dei* but by its aural propagation. Empire is partially comprised of a far-reaching acoustic sphere, an idea I will return to in chapter 4.

In accordance with the purpose of his document, Perestrelo infixes seaborne viewing of the coastline as the defining perspective in his text. The cartographer frequently notes that he writes his descriptions from the vantage point of someone who views the coast "de mar em fora," or "from out at sea." Consider this passage, which describes the coast represented in figure 2:

> Ao longo deste cabo, da parte do ponente, se pinta nas cartas um ilheu, chamado das serras, de que eu não dou fé. . . . quem estiver ao mar, verá estes dous cabos e não a terra da *ribeira*, de entre eles, na qual está uma malha grande de areia, e pelo sertão vai uma lombada de serra desta feiçam. (RAS 14; emphasis in original)

> (Along this cape, to the west, there usually appears on maps a small island named Serras, but I doubt its existence. . . . Whoever is at sea can see two capes, but not the shore between them, where there is a large sandy area; in the interior there is a summit of a hill that looks like this.)

Perestrelo's limning of this portion of the coast rests on his authority and experience as a cartographer, as is clear in his doubt registered regarding the existence of Serras Island. Perestrelo also questions early cartographic depictions of a river at Good Hope "por não darem autor de vista nem de escritura" (since they are not based on an eyewitness or written source; RAS 12). The carto-/chorographic eye observes the coast from on board a ship, and this eye represents the imperial reconnaissance of Sebastião.[34] While the practical aspect of Perestrelo's document requires such a vantage point, the repeated remark on the orientation of the viewer as "de mar em fora" establishes seaborne viewing as a basis of (scientific) authority. The sea-

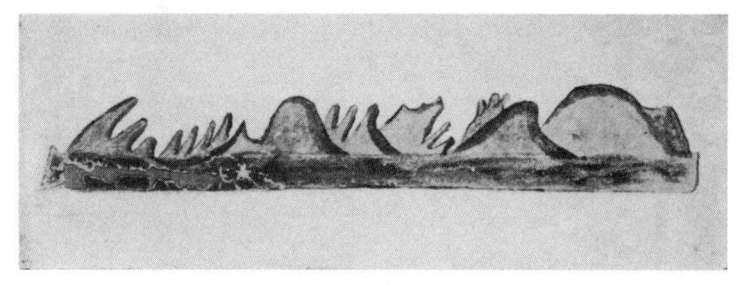

FIGURE 2. A detail of hills in the African landscape between Cape Agulhas and Cape Infante. From Manuel de Mesquita Perestrelo's *Roteiro da África do sul* (1576). Photograph: Houghton Library, Harvard University.

borne view is authoritative because it is one of the consistent perspectives in an expansionist surveillance of the world.

Perestrelo's and Velho's texts, then, are emblematic of the authoritative primacy of seaborne viewing that was part of the culture of *Os Lusíadas*. The seaborne vantage point appears iconographically in the illuminations in the British Library manuscript of João de Castro's *Roteiro do Mar Roxo* (Rutter of the Red Sea). The narrative portions of this *roteiro* describe the topography in the region of the Red Sea. These illuminations supplement the descriptions with a wealth of nautical imagery in the form of seaborne ships navigating coastal locales—one such illumination is seen in figure 3. The image depicts the strength of Castro's expedition by its many ships. These ships collectively create a pronounced directionality, since all their bows are oriented along the same vector. While the image on the one hand solidifies an intent of purpose and a bold exercise of seamanship, on the other it also emphasizes a seaborne perspective with regard to the ports and shoreline that occupy the upper half of the illumination. It is possible to think of the fleet as a collective of nautical eyewitnesses that inscribes naval vessels centrally in the authoritative rhetoric of *roteiros*.

By the mid-sixteenth century, nautical voyages and itineraries had become infixed in historiographic writing. Fernão Lopes de Castanheda's *História do descobrimento e conquista da Índia pelos Portugueses* (History of the Discovery and Conquest of India by the Portuguese, 1551, 1554) and João de Barros's *Décadas* (Decades, 1552, 1553, 1565) are two salient examples of how historians conceptualized history in a maritime key. Lopes de Castanheda (died 1559) spent ten

FIGURE 3. Illuminations of ships. From João de Castro's *Roteiro do Mar Roxo* (1543). Photograph: © The British Library Board (Cotton Tiberius MS D IX, f.22r).

years as an imperial administrator in Goa. João de Barros (1496–1570) traveled to Africa, held various appointments at the court of João III, and is best known as one of the leading Portuguese humanists of his day, who planned a vast history of Portuguese maritime expansion under the title *Décadas*, which was only partially completed at the time of his death. Both Lopes de Castanheda's and Barros's books count among Camões's sources and clearly exercised an influence on the poet's understanding of Portuguese historical action as oceanic in nature. In the prologue to his history, Lopes de Castanheda observes to João III (the dedicatee) that the Portuguese discovery and conquest of India is a superior history to that of the Greeks, Romans, and other "barbarians" (such as Semiramis or Alexander the Great) because those conquests were all pursued on land, while

> a da India foy feita por mar & por vossos capitães, & cõ nauegação dũ anno & doito meses & de seis ao menos: & não a vista de terra senão afastados trezentas & seiscentas leguas partindo do fim do Occidente & nauegando ate ho do Oriente sem verem mais que agoa & ceo, rodeando toda a Sphera, cousa nunca cometida dos mortais, nem imaginada pera se fazer.[35]

([the conquest] of India was achieved by sea and by your captains, and with a sea journey of one year, eight months [or six at the least], and not within sight of land but removed three and six hundred leagues, departing from the extreme West and sailing to the extreme East, without sight of anything but water and sky, circumnavigating the entire globe; something never attempted by mortals, nor even imagined as possible.)

The rhetoric of Portuguese exceptionalism marks an oceanic turn in world history that eclipses the ancients, a boast Camões also makes in the opening stanzas of his epic. In order to write the best history, Lopes de Castanheda notes, he went to India to the city of Goa, where the reward he worked to achieve

> foy saber muyto particularmente o que ate aquele tempo fizerão os Portugueses no descobrimento & conquista da India, & isto não de pessoas quaeisquer, senão de Capitães & Fidalgos que ho sabião muyto bem por serem presentes nos conselhos das cousas & na execução delas, & per cartas & summarios que examiney coestas testemunhas. (HDCI 2–3)

(was to know, in great detail, what until that time the Portuguese had achieved in the discovery and conquest of India; and I learned this not from just anyone, but from the captains and noblemen who knew this history well, having been present in the councils regarding these affairs and their execution; I also examined letters and reports in addition to these witnesses.)

The historian marries an aristocratic legitimation of his history to research method, all of it mediated through, and produced by, the authority of eyewitnessing. The work of gathering information and the examination of archival sources *in situ*, overseas, is another form of expansionist presence in India, is a correlate of the singularity of scale and significance of Portuguese discoveries and conquests worldwide, and acts as a guarantor of the content of the *História* that Lopes de Castanheda finished at the University of Coimbra after twenty years of research and arduous travels.

The story of Gama's 1497 voyage in Lopes de Castanheda and Barros takes on different configurations, which foreground each writer's understanding of oceanic history. Chapters 2 to 29 of Lopes de Castanheda's book 1 contain the history of this voyage. What is striking about the story in these pages is that it reads like a *roteiro*: even though the narrative voice is in the third person, there is a pronounced sense of eyewitnessing, and the journey, in the historian's pen, proceeds by daily increments. The parallels between the historical narrative and Velho's *Roteiro da primeira viagem de Vasco da Gama* suggest that Lopes de Castanheda consulted it as primary source, if not transcribing entire passages into his *História*.[36] The historian frequently begins chapters by referring to a ship's ongoing route (e.g., "prosseguindo por sua rota" [continuing on its course]) or to a specific nautical departure with a specified day and place. The recursive movements of ships determine Lopes de Castanheda's narrative divisions.

In adopting a structure characteristic of *roteiros* with their eyewitness perspective, Lopes de Castanheda makes certain claims about his book. The implicit yet discernible presence of the eyewitness confers an authority on the narrative, even if it is not Lopes de Castanheda's own witnessing. François Hartog argues, in the case of Herodotus's *History*, that the eye or autopsy of "I have seen" of a narrator provides a proof of claims, and that the ancient lexeme *histor* meant "witness" who knows by dint of having seen.[37] The importation of a *roteiro*'s eyewitnessing into a historiographic narrative imputes not only authority to the history but a more privileged register of authority that attends *nautical* eyewitnessing (recall Perestrelo's text). By writing in the mode of a *roteiro*, Lopes de Castanheda suggests that his authority is on a par with the view of the eyewitness, *roteiro* author. There is a conflation of traditional history writing with the nautically preeminent truth claims of *roteiros*.

João de Barros also includes Gama's voyage in his first *Década da Ásia* (Decade of Asia). Like Lopes de Castanheda, Barros dedicates his work to João III, and recognizes the terraqueous nature of the history he is about to recount as the "descobrimento e conquista dos mares e terras do oriente" (discovery and conquest of the seas and lands of the East).[38] There is not the tacit eyewitness presence in Barros's account of Gama's expedition that suffuses Lopes de Castanheda's version, although Barros does occasionally align the progression of his narrative by beginning some chapters with departures of the fleet, and others with notations about the continued movement of the nautical journey. If the nautical, observational perspective in Lopes de Castanheda's chapters on Gama lends the story an undeniable immediacy and authority, Barros's narrative rallies the nautical as well, but in a different manner. Chapter 2 of book IV describes Gama's departure from Lisbon, which Barros uses as a platform to include comments on the astrolabe and the science of celestial navigation as having begun with Prince Henry's expeditions to Guiné. Barros's scholarly discussion of nautical technology bestows an authority on both his history and Gama's voyage as participants in a scientific empiricism, only a century old, that reaches a culmination in the reign of João III.

I now turn to the seafaring frame of *Os Lusíadas*. Gama's voyage structures the action of the poem and concatenates the skeins of history, myth, and prophecy that delve into almost every corner of the Renaissance Portuguese imagination. Camões calibrates the overall narrative of the poem to the movement of Gama's fleet. The seafarers navigate the "mares nunca dantes navegados" (the oceans none had sailed before; I.1.iii),[39] and the poem acknowledges "as memórias gloriosas / Daqueles Reis que foram dilatando / A Fé, o Império, e as terras viciosas / De África e de Ásia andaram devastando" (the glorious memories of those kings who spread abroad faith [and] empire, and who toppled the vicious lands of Africa and Asia; I.2.i-iv). In a like vein, Álvaro Velho begins his *Roteiro da primeira viagem de Vasco da Gama*:

Em nome de Deus, Amem. Na era de 1497 mandou el-rei D. Manuel, o primeiro deste nome em Portugal, a descobrir, quatro navios, os quais iam em busca da especiaria, dos quais navios ia por capitão-mor Vasco da Gama, e dos outros: dum deles Paulo da Gama, seu irmão, e do outro Nicolau Coelho.[40]

(In the name of God, amen. In the year 1497 King Manuel, the first of that name in Portugal, sent four ships to make discoveries, in search of spices. Vasco da Gama was Captain-Major; his brother Paulo da Gama commanded another of the ships, and Nicolau Coelho another.)

Both Velho and Camões succinctly express three pillars of expansionist ideology and imperial self-justification: God, king, and sea. Velho anticipates Camões in that Gama's voyage is the realization of divine and monarchic authority in its ordered assembly of ships. As *capitão-mor*, Gama is the symbol and enactment of Portuguese maritime protagonism. He identifies himself and his crew in *Os Lusíadas* as a seafaring collective to the king of Melinde (Malindi) in East Africa: "[N]os recebes em paz, do mar profundo" (You welcome us in peace, from the deep sea; II.105.ii). The "mar profundo" as the realm of Gama's seafarers and the arena of Portugal's imperial enterprise also connotes a vastness or capaciousness of experience in reaching the spaces of the world that is unprecedented in history. The alliance between sea and collective (national) identity creates a new community of maritime actors on the world stage, the "gente marítima de Luso" (the maritime people of Lusus; I.62.i), whose formation and rise to preeminence is one of the histories recorded in the poem. This "gente marítima de Luso"—the true, corporate hero of *Os Lusíadas*[41]—leads Portugal into a new historical age, and Gama's forward-moving ships both inaugurate and are the emblem of this shift. Gama's voyage realizes, in part, the expansive "conquista do mar largo" (conquest of the wide sea; IV.66.viii); this oceanic *conquista* underlies the providential directive communicated to Manuel I in a prophetic dream in canto IV. In the dream, the Ganges River speaks to the king and announces his eventual victory in the East. Shankar Raman argues that the Ganges is "the very figure personifying the Orient" and "legitimates the Portuguese imperial project by offering a prophecy of its future."[42] I concur with the idea that the Ganges is a personification of the East, but would emphasize that this anthropomorphic figure is a body of (fluvial) water. Manuel's oneiric vision conflates India, the East, and, by extension, all of the spaces that Portuguese ships will reach into a single, aquatic figure, so that on waking, the king summons his advisers to prepare the "náutico aparelho" (nautical machinery; IV.76.v) in order to fulfill the otherworldly mandate. The Ganges as a course of water contained within the land confines of India represents the terrestrial conquest of the country, while the Indian Ocean as sailed by Gama is the sign of maritime supremacy.

So it is, for Camões, that the India enterprise is born. The authority that Gama possesses in the nautical logic of the poem is expressed in part as vesseled, seaborne vision. Like *roteiro* authors who "place the figure of the pilot at the forefront of the nautical narrative,"[43] so also does Camões place Vasco da Gama, whose first-person view presides over the voyage, at the front of the epic narrative. Gama's gaze, outward-looking from the deck of the flagship, *São Gabriel*, perceives and organizes into poetic narrative the phenomena that appear before the fleet. Gama's "scopic gaze," as Bernhard Klein terms it, is a central structural principle of *Os Lusíadas* because it "[casts] a seafarer as the principle of action and focalizer of the narrative."[44] The vessel-bound view is a nautical inflection of the first-person grammatical, eyewitness perspectives that pervade the poem.[45] Gama's role as the viewer-narrator underlies his and his ships' status as agents of history. Raman contends that "Camões's task was to *produce* history, to *re-present* an origin in history through which both the origin and a history following on its heels could be constituted in absolute terms."[46] In a similar argument, Fernando Gil states that "[Gama's] voyage gathers in history; the evocations of the history of Portugal occur as it proceeds."[47] I would add that the organizing gaze of Gama is central to the agentive relationship between nautical voyage and history; in this sense, Gama's journey not only gathers *in* history but also *enacts* history.

Through his deck-bound vision, Gama becomes conflated with the ship itself, a conflation of human and technological agency. This equation underlies books such as the *Livro de Lisuarte de Abreu* (The Book of Lisuarte de Abreu), perhaps the most striking example of the *memória das armadas* (memorial of fleets) nautical genre.[48] This book, compiled around 1563, is a lavishly illuminated manuscript that contains images of every Portuguese vessel that made the India voyage between 1497 and 1555, in addition to full-folio portraits of the more preeminent captains-major or political figures of Portuguese

India (see figs. 4 and 5). The ships are depicted with sails billowed by the wind, which imbues them with a sense of swift movement; as I noted above, the ship at full sail is Camões's predilect image of expansionist might and of the providential endorsement of Gama's thalassocratic enterprise. The coexistence in the *Livro* of portraits of noteworthy seafarers and imperial administrators and the iconographic depictions of individual vessels establishes ships and humans as co-protagonists of oceanic history and exploration. The miniatures of ships in the *Livro de Lisuarte de Abreu* grant seafaring vessels the same status of imperial subjectivity and agency as the men with their confident postures and attitudes. Moreover, the hundreds of images of *carreira da Índia* ships, in their visual repetitiveness, reflect and consolidate a unified, seafaring community, continuous through time, whose numeric abundance is testimony of a successful, concerted maritime endeavor. The iconographic proliferation of vessels asserts a seamless, expansionist protagonism that supersedes the occasional tragedy of a lost or doomed ship.

Several moments of deck-bound vision in *Os Lusíadas* establish its nautical and historical primacy. One occurs in the early stanzas of canto I, immediately following the Council of the Gods in which Venus, the patron goddess and protector of the Portuguese, secures support from the Council despite Bacchus's objections. After the Council, Camões returns his narrative to earth and to Gama's ships on the high seas as they unexpectedly encounter the inhabitants of Mozambique—the first encounter with a non-Western culture in the poem:

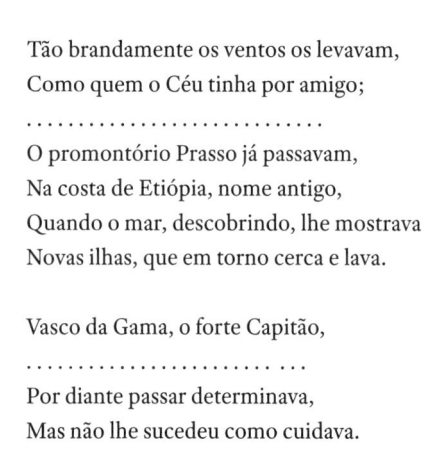

> Tão brandamente os ventos os levavam,
> Como quem o Céu tinha por amigo;
> ....
> O promontório Prasso já passavam,
> Na costa de Etiópia, nome antigo,
> Quando o mar, descobrindo, lhe mostrava
> Novas ilhas, que em torno cerca e lava.
>
> Vasco da Gama, o forte Capitão,
> ....
> Por diante passar determinava,
> Mas não lhe sucedeu como cuidava.

FIGURE 4. Miniatures of ships. From *Livro de Lisuarte de Abreu* (ca. 1563). Photograph: Houghton Library, Harvard University.

Eis aparecem logo em companhia
Uns pequenos batéis, que vem daquela
Que mais chegada à terra parecia,
Cortando o longo mar com larga vela. (I.43.i-ii, v-viii; 44.i, vii-viii; 45.i-iv)

FIGURE 5. Portrait of Vasco da Gama. From *Livro de Lisuarte de Abreu* (ca. 1563). Photograph: Houghton Library, Harvard University.

(So smoothly did the wind carry them along, as someone who had heaven for a friend // ... // they were already beyond the Prassum Promontorium on the coast of ancient Ethiopia, when the sea discovered and revealed new islands which it surrounded and bathed // ... // Vasco da Gama, the mighty Captain // ... // determined to sail onward, but matters did not happen as he expected. // There suddenly appears a group of boats [from the island that seemed closest to the mainland] sailing the wide sea at full sail.)

With the focus first on Gama's ships at the beginning of this passage, Camões repeats the sailing imagery of I.19, except that now, coming as they do immediately after the Council of the Gods in which Jupiter approves the voyage, the propitious nautical conditions are a sign of divine favor. Gama's forward-moving (and hence forward-looking) supervision underlies the expression "por diante"—it emphasizes the *capitão-mor*'s surveillance of the oceanic expanse in which the islands of East Africa appear. The scene assumes a deck-bound view of a flotilla of African boats or skiffs (*batéis*). "Eis aparecem" (I.45.i) suggests the flotilla's sudden emergence into a field of vision projecting outward from the deck of the flagship, therefore imaginatively placing Camões's readers squarely on board. The vessels swiftly come into full view as the scene continues:

> As embarcações eram na maneira
> Mui veloces, estreitas e compridas;
> As velas com que vem eram de esteira,
> De hūas folhas de palma, bem tecidas;
> A gente da cor era verdadeira
> Que Faeton, nas terras acendidas,
> Ao mundo deu. (I.46.i-vii)

(The vessels were swift, long, and narrow, and the sails were palm leaves tightly woven together; the crew was the very color that Phaëthon gave to the world in the burning lands.)

Camões describes the manner of dress of the Muslim sailors, the happy, raucous meeting with Gama on board Gama's ship, the convivial feast that followed, and the eager questions (in Arabic) to the Portuguese about the purpose of their voyage and what they hoped to find. The order of the description, with the boats coming first, followed by the observations on the physical and sartorial characteristics of unknown mariners, is strategic. It mimics a shipbound view of the horizon in which vessels appear first and then, as the boats move closer, their passengers. The narrative sequencing also reflects the immediate attention mariners might naturally give to the appearance of unusual sea vessels. The Portuguese reaction to the flotilla is *alegria* (joy), a telling sentiment, since it suggests that there could be no better indication of potential friends or allies than another navigationally minded people.[49] African seafaring would at first seem to be an indication of a shared disposition toward the sea that augurs well for the meeting with hitherto unknown peoples. Significantly, Christianity and non-Christian others meet through Portuguese *naus* and African *batéis*. Camões yokes the description of these African boats to African skin color with the reference to Phaëthon.[50] African skiffs coupled with their dark-skinned occupants conjoin non-Western seafaring to the mythic origin of racial difference.

At this point the seaborne scenario of encounter is positive in nature and leads to an apparently auspicious meeting on board Gama's flagship. The occupants of the African *batéis* beckon the Portuguese to approach, and they then enthusiastically board the *São Gabriel*. The *capitão-mor* learns from one of the "moors" (*mouros*), or inhabitants of Mozambique, that his people were originally foreigners (*estrangeiros*) in the place that is now their home.[51] The next day the ruler of Mozambique arrives at Gama's ship, an event that sparks curiosity among the Lusitanian sailors who scramble onto the *enxárcia* (ship's rigging) to watch the scene in wonder, noting the Africans' strange manners and the sound of their language. Camões creates a scene of the historic meeting of East Africa and Portugal by staging a collective, onboard viewing on Gama's ship. The company of unnamed mariners intertwined in the ship's architecture notionally makes Gama's vessel a collective witness of racial, religious, linguistic, and nautical alterity.

The auspicious atmosphere surrounding the contact between Portuguese and Africans, however, quickly deteriorates, as the king of Mozambique becomes suspicious of Gama's display of arms and firepower, a suspicion inflamed by Bacchus who descends to earth disguised as a *mouro*. The god fans the flames of hatred and fear by inducing the inhabitants of Mozambique to believe that the Portuguese are a band of thieves and murderers who have ravaged nearly the entire sea. This is what prompts the treachery of the "false pilot." Gama welcomes a Muslim pilot on board to help him navigate the Indian Ocean crossing,[52] but the pilot attempts to sabotage the expedition by steering it toward an ambush on Quíloa. Venus foils the plot by enlisting the winds to prevent the fleet's making port on the island, so the pilot's scheme fails. The false pilot foregrounds an important aspect of Gama's transoceanic navigation. The perfidy is enacted through outward signs of friendship on the part of the Mozambicans. The vocabulary Camões employs to describe these gestures of friendship—*mostras* (displays), *fingimento* (feigning), *figura* (guise or figure)—is semiotic in nature. These non-Christians are duplicitous sign-makers, and in this their treachery lies. Shankar Raman maintains that one of the persistent dangers the Portuguese face in Camões's epic is the danger of deception, which, for Raman, is the point of Bacchus's second attempt at destroying the fleet in Mombassa by disguising himself as a priest.[53] The episode of the false pilot and the episode of Bacchus as the false god function as a dyad. In the episode of the "falso Deus" at the beginning of canto II, Bacchus visits Mombassa disguised as a Christian and lures two of the *degredados* from Gama's fleet to shore.[54] There, Bacchus has erected a Christian altarpiece; he feigns piety so that the two emissaries from Gama's fleet will return to the ships with news of Christians, with the hope that more Portuguese will be enticed to come ashore where they will be attacked. If the episode rests on the simulacrum of Christianity in Bacchus's appearance and in the altarpiece as indicative of the misrepresentation inherent in idolatry posited by Raman, then the false pilot is equally treacherous and misrepresentative in his duplicity toward someone who relies on his nautical expertise. This is a sure sign of the insidiousness of the *falso piloto*. The Africans have betrayed navigation itself, and their demonstrated ability in seafaring only serves to magnify the extent of their perfidy. The rectitude of Christian seafaring stands in opposition to Moorish seafaring, just as idolatry stands in opposition to Christianity. Seafaring and Christianity are mutually constituting components of Camões's epic ideology.

NAVIGATION AND NARRATIVE

Gama's crossing of the Indian Ocean and arrival in India in canto VII occur after a long, historiographic peroration (begun in canto III) the captain-major delivers to a newfound ally (the king of Melinde in East Africa), a narrative that covers the history of Portugal and the origins of Gama's expedition. Gama concludes his history in canto V with the arrival on Melinde's shores:

> Até que aqui, no teu seguro porto,
> Cuja brandura e doce tratamento
> Dará saúde a um vivo e vida a um morto,
> Nos trouxe a piedade do alto Assento.
> ....
> Julgas agora, Rei, se houve no mundo
> Gentes que tais caminhos cometessem? (V.85.i-iv; 86.i-ii)

(Here to your safe port, in which a gentle and gracious reception can give health to the living and life to the dead, we were brought by the mercy of the high Throne. // . . . // Ask yourself now, King, if ever there was a people in the world who undertook such paths?)

This arrival and the conclusion of Gama's history make narrative and the nautical voyage coterminous. Story and ships make port simultaneously; history and historical narrative are forms of seafaring. Gama's rhetorical question to the king places his own voyage among the many *caminhos* he has just recounted, so that the routes of ships carve out the overall course of history. In the moments immediately preceding the commencement of his narrative in canto III the *capitão-mor* welcomes the king on board his longboat, explaining that the *regimento* of Manuel I prevents him from going ashore.[55] It is on this vessel that the king asks Gama to recite the history of his country and expedition. The historiographic account that is a discursive centerpiece of *Os Lusíadas* occurs, therefore, *in loco maritimo*. This pelagic location fortifies the relationship between Portuguese-Western historical agency and oceanic space in that not only is the sea the primary medium of history but it is also the condition and genesis of its telling. Gama's reference to Manuel's *regimento* is not incidental: by deferring to it, the maritime, historiographic narrative is invested with monarchic authority.

In his long recitation, Gama identifies the seaward turn of Portuguese history as beginning with the invasion of Ceuta under the orders of João I in 1415, a first step in the pursuit of oceanic routes that eventually extend through the Indian Ocean and to eastern Asia. When the *capitão-mor* describes the scene of his fleet's departure from Belém in July 1497, he tells of the sudden appearance of an aged man on the shore (the "Velho do Restelo," Old Man of Restelo) of venerable mien, who delivers an impassioned diatribe against imperial pursuits which are the result of a "vã cobiça" (vain lust) for fame. The Old Man excoriates Gama and his crew for leaving their homeland and foresees dangers, cruelties, and death as consequences of the vainglorious enterprise. He exclaims: "Oh! Maldito o primeiro que, no mundo, / Nas ondas velas pôs em seco lenho!" (Oh! Cursed be he who in the world was the first to launch dry wood on the waves! IV.102.i-ii). The imprecation repeats the famous condemnation of Horace in *Ode* I.3: "nequiquam deus abscidit / prudens Oceano dissociabili / terras, si tamen impiae / non tangenda rates transiliunt vada" (All to no avail did God deliberately separate countries by the divisive ocean if, in spite of that, impious boats go skipping over the seas that were meant to remain inviolate).[56] More contemporaneously, António Ferreira (1528–69) echoes the sentiment in one of his own odes.[57] The Old Man compares Portuguese seafarers to Prometheus, Phaëthon, and Icarus, a comparison that leads Christopher D. Johnson to conclude that Camões is "amplifying Horace's sentiments, while also explicitly comparing the ode's cast of overreachers, Prometheus, Phaethon, and Icarus, with their early modern imitators."[58] This argument recalls a line of criticism proposed by some scholars who find an anti-epic or anti-imperialist discourse embedded in Camões's poem.[59] In this view it follows that the Old Man of Restelo would damn those who first ventured forth in ships. Even if the epic/anti-epic binary risks oversimplifying the complexity of Camões's poem, the Old Man's harangue acknowledges an irrevocably lost simpler age. This "idade de ouro" (golden age), as Helder Macedo observes, is pastoral; its end was marked when trees were converted into ships, and its literary tradition professes moral values contrary to those of epic.[60] It is also possible to read the Old Man's imprecation as the swan song of a land-bound (and therefore superannuated) existence to what will become a riskier, seafaring gnosis of the world. If Gama and his crew were to heed the Old Man's words, this would quash adventurous daring (*ousadia* or *atrevimento*), the passionate impulses of Camonian epic exemplarity.

When Gama begins the story of his own voyage in his recitation to the king of Melinde, Camões once more employs the image of the ship at sail to mark another beginning in the narrative. With this moment comes a swift nautical surging forth:

> Estas sentenças tais o velho honrado
> Vociferando estava, quando abrimos
> As asas ao sereno e sossegado
> Vento, e do porto amado nos partimos. (V.1.i-iv)

> (These thoughts the venerable old man was speaking when we spread our wings to the serene and gentle wind, and from our beloved port set sail.)

Here, at the outset of canto V and at the midpoint of *Os Lusíadas*, the distant past cedes way to the seafaring imperative of the present, and Gama's voyage takes center stage as the matter of epic and historical narrative. The *capitão-mor* exercises a dual agency: he is the protagonist of the history being recounted as well as its epic narrator. Gama participates in a story that is already in the process of unfolding, a sort of experiential *in medias res*. As Gama concludes his story several stanzas later, Camões describes the attitudes of Gama's listeners:

> Da boca do facundo Capitão
> Pendendo estavam todos, embibidos,
> Quando deu fim à longa narração
> Dos altos feitos, grandes e subidos. (V.90.i-iv)

> (On the words from the mouth of the eloquent Captain all hung, drinking them in, when he ended his story of high deeds, great and noble.)

The adjective *facundo* (eloquent) to describe Gama is the same word Gama used a few stanzas earlier to describe Ulysses (V.86.iii-iv). Gama is naturally possessed of poetic prowess as befitting an epic traveler like Homer's king of Ithaca. He is a figure that conjoins poetry and maritime voyaging, the mariner-poet. At the end of canto V, Camões laments the absence of poet-warriors in Portugal like those of antiquity. This absence is the result of a national disregard of (epic) poetry and the literary memorialization of great deeds. Camões's voice is one of but a few in the poetic wilderness, but it is by dint of this that it is even more monumental as the singer of Gama's tale.

The departure of Gama's fleet from Belém at the opening of canto

Epic Seas

V brings the historical moment of the poem into synchronicity with its own chronology. Nautical movement sweeps through the initial stanzas of the canto, emphasizing the auspicious nature of the journey and its historical protagonism. As the first stanza sonorously and festively includes cries from the Belém shore of "Boa viagem!" (Have a good voyage) the ensuing strophes conjure a maritime fleetness:

> Já a vista, pouco e pouco, se desterra
> Daqueles pátrios montes, que ficavam
> ....
> Assi fomos abrindo aqueles mares,
> Que gèração algũa não abriu. (V.3.i-ii; 4.i-ii)

(Little by little, our sight was exiled from the hills of our homeland, which remained behind // . . . // And so we sailed, opening those seas that no generation had opened before.)

The shift in perspective, from shore to ship, neatly emblematized in the feet-on-shore positionality of the criers of "Boa viagem!" to the shipbound sailors, is key, since it situates the presiding optic on board and brings together nautical and narrative movement.[61] Camões infixes the nautical setting-forth grammatically in the narrative with a rapid succession of preterites and past participles that track the passage of the fleet along the points of its itinerary. "And so we sailed, opening those seas" Gama declares, and notes in the first lines of the next several stanzas:

> Passámos a grande Ilha da Madeira. . . .
> Deixámos de Massília a estéril costa. . . .
> Passámos o lemite aonde chega / O Sol. . . .
> Passadas tendo já as Canárias ilhas. . . .
> As Dórcadas passámos. (V.5.i; 6.i; 7.i-ii; 8.i; 11.i)

(We passed the great island of Madeira. . . . We left Massylia's barren coast behind. . . . We traversed the northern limit of the sun. . . . Having left the Canaries behind. . . . We passed the Dorcades.)

Ships and poem surge forward with an urgency and sense of direction and purpose. This celerity manifests the epochal nature of the voyage as the inauguration of a seafaring, historical order. The rapid series of preterite verbs quasi-paradoxically invests the narrative with an undeniable sense of the present, of action unfolding before our readerly eyes.

Once Gama's fleet has reached India, Camões temporarily pauses to express his growing fatigue at writing his poem and to lament the widespread "corruption and injustice in high places."[62] This contemplation is part of a Camonian practice of brief philosophical reflections that close some cantos. In this case, Camões's complaint attests, in Marina Brownlee's phrasing, to a "perspective of disillusion" that is one of the characteristics of the poem.[63] The poet's complaint begins:

> Mas, ó cego,
> Eu, que cometo, insano e temerário,
> Sem vós, Ninfas do Tejo e do Mondego,
> Por caminho tão árduo, longo e vário!
> Vosso favor invoco, que navego
> Por alto mar, com vento tão contrário,
> Que, se não me ajudais, hei grande medo
> Que o meu fraco batel se alague cedo. (VII.78)

(But oh how blind I am, that I, mad and reckless, should embark on such a long, arduous, and haphazard journey without you, Nymphs of the Tagus and Mondego! I beg your favor, since I sail on the high seas with a contrary wind; for if you do not help me, I am in great fear that my frail bark will soon founder.)

The eruption of Camões's first-person voice is recurrent in *Os Lusíadas*. Camões here fashions his poetic project as a dangerous sea voyage that imperils his own stamina. Camões's waning strength and his acknowledgment of the daunting magnitude of his enterprise become an enfeebled small vessel, a "fraco batel," in implicit contrast to the forceful and determined juggernaut of Gama's fleet. The stanza opposes two forms of subjectivity represented by boats and oceanic journeys: the collective, epic ship of Gama with its historico-mythological narrative, and the personal, lyric craft of Camões himself. As will be evident in the next chapter, the subject boat and nautical journeys of the lyric Camões contrast dramatically with the self-assurance and cosmic imperative of the epic undertaking. Epic ships and lyric boats make two very different kinds of existential and poetic claims.

Camões's first-person frail bark draws on a Petrarchan precedent. The image appears in the Italian poet's Sonnet 132:

> S' amor non è, che dunque è quel ch' io sento?
> ....
> O viva morte, o dilettoso male,
> come puoi tanto in me s' io nol consento?
>
> Et s' io 'l consento, a gran torto mi doglio.
> Fra sì contrari venti in frale barca
> mi trovo in alto mar senza governo.
>
> (If it is not love, what then is it that I feel? // ... O living death, O delightful harm, how can you have such power over me if I do not consent to it? // And if I do consent to it, it is wrong of me to complain. Amid such contrary winds I find myself at sea in a frail bark, without a tiller.)[64]

Petrarch finds himself in the throes of love and attempts to understand love's irrational nature. The poet describes the aimlessness and senselessness of love by claiming it is like being at sea in a fragile bark, sailing against the wind without a means of steerage. The contrary and paradoxical nature of love establishes a cognitive quandary that seeks resolution, and this is the impetus behind the movement of the sonnet from one verse to the next. The nautical metaphor of the helmless, frail bark is, in effect, the response to the preceding queries, and reiterates a sense of aimless, perilous voyaging. Since the poet is unable to resolve the contraries that confound him, the nautical metaphor stands as a moment of self-awareness, encapsulated in the reflexive construction "mi trovo" (I find myself). The *frale barca* signals a moment of failed cognition and reason, and hence constitutes a precarious subjectivity in the tenuous and fraught relationship between amorous experience and deliberate thought. The boat at sea without a tiller tosses and rolls without a compass like the mind of the poet at odds with his own intellection and with the world around him.

Camões's *fraco batel* appropriates the Petrarchan antecedent within the flow of epic narrative. Once more, navigation and narrative merge. "[N]avego por alto mar" denotes the act of composing the poem. The comparison of the composition of a (poetic) work to a nautical voyage dates to Roman antiquity, as Ernst Robert Curtius has shown.[65] Yet if Latin poets imagined that "the epic poet voyages over the open sea in a great ship, the lyric poet on a river in a small boat,"[66] in Camões's pen that metaphor is reconfigured. Camões the epic poet voyages over the sea in a small, fragile boat, one that is in danger of wreck and whose steerage falters, yet the *fraco batel* is no mere rehearsal of a literary topos. The contrary winds that assail the poet are not the irrational and paradoxical nature of love that confounds Petrarch but are, rather, the chaotic forces of a world in disarray. The misery and afflictions that beset the poet ("em tantos males") threaten his completion of the poem. The *fraco batel* is battered by the winds of a prevailing ill disposition or inability of Camões's contemporaries to rise above the pettiness of corruption and questionable ethics.

The beleaguered *fraco batel* anticipates the poet's reference to shipwreck in canto X, when, as Tethys identifies for Gama the locales in the East the Portuguese will eventually attain, she points out the Mekong River:

> Este receberá, plácido e brando,
> No seu regaço o Canto que molhado
> Vem do naufrágio triste e miserando,
> Dos procelosos baxos escapado,
> Das fomes, dos perigos grandes, quando
> Será o injusto mando executado
> Naquele cuja Lira sonorosa
> Será mais afamada que ditosa. (X.128)

(This calm and tranquil river will embrace the waterlogged poem from the woeful and miserable shipwreck, rescued from the storm-tossed shallows, starvations, and great dangers, when the unjust mandate will be imposed on one whose melodious lyre will be more famous than fortunate.)

Since Pedro de Mariz's introduction to the 1613 edition of Camões's poem, scholars have read this stanza as a reference to a shipwreck Camões himself suffered and from which he escaped by swimming as he clutched the manuscript of his epic.[67] The biographical authenticity of this wreck has long been debated, but it is ultimately irrelevant in the logic of the narrative. In the poem's nautical imaginary, the poet briefly shifts the narrative lens to his own subjectivity by expressing a relation of his imperiled body to shipwreck. For even though the waterlogged cantos are the text of *Os Lusíadas*, Camões has Tethys refer to his own posterity as that of a lyric, not epic, poet. In canto VII, and again in canto X, Camões transforms Petrarch's *frale barca* into a vessel of lyric subjectivity faced with the pressing weight of historical and epic enterprise.

However unsuccessful Gama's economic negotiations with the Samorim of Calicut turn out to be, with the fleet leaving the Malabar Coast abruptly to avoid further trouble, the sea journey itself was safely achieved. As I have been arguing, the successful exercise of maritime craft resides at the heart of the poem—voyages and narratives, although not without their moments of doubt and danger, reach the shore.

Another extensive account of travels composed in the late sixteenth century but not published until 1614 is Fernão Mendes Pinto's *Peregrinação* (Pilgrimage).[68] Mendes Pinto (1510?–83) was a Portuguese merchant-adventurer who spent over twenty years traveling through Africa, the Middle East, South Asia, China, and Japan. After his extensive sojourning, he returned to Portugal and, sometime between 1569 and 1578, composed the *Peregrinação*, a long tale that recounts a litany of Mendes Pinto's sufferings, misfortunes, and hardships abroad and is openly critical of Portuguese imperial activities and of the behavior of Mendes Pinto's fellow Portuguese in the East.[69] Like Marco Polo, Mendes Pinto is an astute ethnographic observer, linguist, and scholar, registering in his book's pages a wealth of detailed information about the peoples, cultures, geographies, and natural phenomena he encountered.

The author's criticism of empire, in Rebecca D. Catz's assessment, is one of the reasons the *Peregrinação* was not published during Mendes Pinto's lifetime—the world traveler was reticent to publish his tome because he criticized "every institution, sacred and profane, of his country" (TMP xxv). Literarily speaking, the book is sui generis. It is "a maverick book, an enigma to readers and critics alike" (TMP xxiii), because of the unusual authorial tone of criticism and cynicism with regard to the Portuguese and because the book does not fit squarely into a preexisting, generic taxonomy. By turns, the *Peregrinação* is an eyewitness travel account, historical chronicle, pirate narrative, slave narrative, geographical treatise, natural history, and shipwreck narrative. In one regard, the book is a compendium of the genres of prose writings of the day, much as Mendes Pinto himself inhabits several subject categories that were characteristic of early modern empire, such as traveler, trader, mariner, geographic or scientific observer, and slave. And while Portuguese military or diplomatic successes are part of the story, there is no overarching, celebratory or epic register to the tale, no embracing of the ideological mentality and machinery of imperialism.

Mendes Pinto begins his tale in this way:

> Quando às vezes ponho diante dos olhos os muitos & grandes trabalhos & infortunios que por mim passarão, começados no principio da minha primeira idade, & continuados pella mayor parte, & milhor tempo da minha vida, acho que com muita razão me posso queixar da ventura que parece que tomou por particular tenção & empreza sua perseguirme, & maltratarme. . . . Mas por outra parte quando vejo que do meyo de todos estes perigos & trabalhos me quis Deos tirar sempre em saluo, & porme em seguro, acho que não tenho tanta razão de me queixar por todos os males passados.
>
> (Whenever I look back at all the hardship and misfortune I suffered throughout most of my life, I can't help thinking I have good reason to complain of my bad luck, which started about the time I was born and continued through the best years of my life. It seems that misfortune had singled me out above all others for no purpose but to hound me and abuse me. . . . But on the other hand, when I consider that God always watched over me and brought me safely through all those hazards and hardships, then I find that there is not as much reason to complain about my past misfortune.)[70]

The opening salvo of the tale juxtaposes a long history of misfortunes throughout the author's life to the grateful acknowledgment that Mendes Pinto survived it all. Even so, the hardships and misfortunes define the content of the 226 chapters, so that, in one sense, the *Peregrinação* is negatively defined: survival of harsh misfortune was as much a matter of blind contingency or luck as skill or strategy. This explains the highly fragmented nature of the text. A reader can begin reading at virtually any point without the risk of losing the perspective of a plot or evolving story.

It is also possible to read the book for its seafaring or nautical content, although it must be kept in mind that sea journeys are only one component of the mix of experiences that Mendes Pinto records. A comparison of maritime voyages between Mendes Pinto and a text such as *Os Lusíadas* is instructive because it reveals fundamentally different views of seafaring. While the *Peregrinação* includes a number of successful Portuguese naval operations or descriptions of the author's travels on boats or ships, maritime peril and shipwreck are never far off. One example stands for many: I refer to the two-chapter account of a shipwreck Mendes Pinto and other Portuguese experienced on the Ilha dos Ladrões (Isle of Thieves) in China.[71] There, the Portuguese vessel was hit by a gale that blew the ship against the coast and dashed it to pieces:

> [O]rdenou a sua diuina justiça, que sendo ja passadas as duas horas despois da meya noite nos deu hum pegão de vento tão rijo, que todas as quatro embarcações assi como estauão vierão à costa, & se fizerão em pedaços. . . . [N]os fomos assi nùs & feridos meter num charco de agoa; no qual estiuemos atè pela menham, & como o dia foy bem claro, nos tornamos à praya, a qual achamos toda juncada de corpos mortos, cousa tão lastimosa & espantosa de ver. . . . Todos os que escapamos daquelle miserauel naufragio que atras deixo contado, andamos nùs & descalços por aquella praya, & por aquelles matos, passando tantos frios, & tantas fomes, que muytos dos companheyros, estando fallando huns cos outros cahião supitamente mortos em terra de pura fraqueza.[72]

(The good Lord, in the wisdom of his divine justice, ordained that at two hours past midnight we were struck by a wind of such tremendous force that all four of the ships were blown against the coast and dashed to pieces. . . . Those of us who survived . . . sought shelter, bleeding and naked, in some shallow pools where we managed to get through the night. In the morning we made our way to the beach and discovered that it was completely strewn with corpses. It was such an unbearably painful sight. . . . Those of us who survived the disastrous shipwreck I have described above wandered about the beach and through the woods, naked and barefooted, suffering from the extremes of cold and hunger to such a degree that many of our comrades, while talking to each other, suddenly dropped dead of exhaustion; TMP 98–99)

These passages, and other similar ones in the book, could have been lifted directly from the pages of Portuguese shipwreck literature. Mendes Pinto is a shipwreck storyteller, too, and his gratitude for surviving the horrors of wreck solely by divine grace characterizes some of the shipwreck tales of the sixteenth and seventeenth centuries. This attitude also characterizes Mendes Pinto's opening observations about his life's misfortunes, which constitute the matter of his book, so that the entirety of the *Peregrinação* in a general sense is a shipwreck narrative, where survival and the course of life are improvised affairs, barely grasped or pursued successfully in the face of adversity and of perilous shifts in fortune.

For Camões, sea journeys are organizational principles, providential manifestations, the course of history, demonstrations of seafaring skill, and enactments of a Christian, imperialist telos. For Mendes Pinto, sea journeys are but one form of experience or disaster and misfortune; they provide no overarching trajectory or structure of action, nor do they impart a hermeneutic unity to bind into meaning the components and years of a life spent in unresting travel.

A DIVINE ISLAND

In cantos IX and X of *Os Lusíadas*, Camões describes the homebound journey of the Lusitanian navigators. In Calicut, Gama unsuccessfully attempted to establish a formal and amicable trading alliance with the Samorim. Through the intervention of the Castilian-speaking Muslim Monçaide, friend to the Portuguese, Gama learned of a plot to destroy his ships and safely left the Malabar Coast. As the ships make the return voyage across the Indian Ocean, Venus, protector of the Portuguese, decides to provide the weary sailors with rest and pleasure by creating, in the remote reaches of the vast ocean, a "divine island" (ínsula divina; IX.21.iii) to be populated by nymphs who will seduce the Portuguese seafarers and provide them with a sumptuous banquet. There is music and festivity, a mass wedding between nymphs and mariners, and this Isle of Love episode ends with two prophecies—one sung by a siren and the other pronounced by Tethys—regarding future Portuguese actions and conquests in India, Africa, and Asia. The epic then draws to a close.

In a poem pulsing with love and desire of all kinds—human, divine, political, economic, cartographic, carnal—the Isle of Venus, together with a group of stanzas describing Eastern sexual deviance (or "amor nefando," nefarious love) is the most sustained treatment of Eros in all of the ten cantos. It conjoins the carnal and the cosmographic in ways that reveal the interdependencies between empire, gender, desire, and the poetic logic of aquatics that pervades almost every line of the poem.

Venus enlists the aid of Cupid to create the isle, located "no Reino de cristal, líquido e manso" (in the Realm of crystal, fluid and soft; IX.19.viii). For his part, Cupid wants Fame to be part of the Isle's rewards for the Portuguese. He gets to work creating the oceanic *locus amoenus* by shooting arrows into the sea:

> Despede nisto o fero moço as setas,
> Hūa após outra: geme o mar cos tiros;
> Dereitas pelas ondas inquietas
> Algūas vão, e algūas fazem giros;
> Caem as Ninfas, lançam das secretas
> Entranhas ardentíssimos sospiros. (IX.47.i-vi)

> (The fierce youth unleashes his arrows, one after the other—the sea moaned with the shots; some arrows directly pierce the unsettled waves, others twist and turn. The Nymphs fall; they emit the most ardent sighs from their innermost recesses.)

The creation of the Isle as a (violent) scene of penetration could hardly be more apparent. Cupid's arrows, like the prows of Portuguese ships that cleave the seas, enact a phallic penetration of the ocean that establishes seafaring and empire as a masculine venture, and the aquatic feminine, at least initially following Cupid's rain of arrows, is submissive. Once on the island, the mariners engage in an erotic chase with the nymphs who submit to the sailors' desires.

The openly erotic nature of this episode, with its celebratory and enthusiastic descriptions of the carnal dalliances of nymphs and seamen, has claimed the attention of scholars with an interest in gender and sexuality. A common reading of the episode is that it is Camões's injunction to King Sebastião, to whom the poet dedicates *Os Lusíadas,* to get to the business of producing royal progeny (Sebastião was unmarried and was known for his lack of interest in women). Yet the complexities of the episode, including the two prophecies relating to Portuguese history that bring it to a close, suggest other connections between desire and empire. Carmen Nocentelli finds intimations of sexual violence to be part of the island's landscape, and argues that "without the encounter between sailors and nymphs . . . there would be no properly imperial dimension to the poem. . . . The consummations at the Isle of Love . . . bespeak the importance of eros in both the semantics and the pragmatics of Europe's imperial expansion."[73] Nocentelli further argues that the marriages between sailors and nymphs acknowledge the intermarriage policy between Portuguese men and native Asian women that was characteristic of Portuguese expansion in Asia, and that the iconography of sexual violence on the Isle is a Camonian recasting of the rape of the Sabine women in the history of Rome.[74] With the brief inventory of Eastern *amor nefando* that precedes the description of the Isle itself, Nocentelli finds an identification of the East "as a site of sexual excess" that is also a recognition of "the disruptive potential of women's erotic agency" in that the ostensible link between erotic agency and masculinity is fragile, since in the instances of Eastern desire catalogued by Camões women are in control.[75]

Denise Saive likewise reads the episode through the lens of gender. Saive maintains that "love and desire in the epic poem affect masculinity and often suggest gender fluidity," and that there is an "anxious masculinity" on the Isle that "demonstrates a certain paranoia about losing control."[76] For Saive, Camões's inclusion of the myth of Actaeon criticizes Sebastião's lack of masculine behavior and interest in women, which made him a bad leader and threatened the independence of the Portuguese nation.[77]

Both Nocentelli and Saive find the assertive erotics of the Isle of Love unsettling, even threatening, entrenched forms of a masculine prerogative of desire and agency that is part and parcel of imperial expansion. In this regard, these arguments make the Isle of Love an island in the entirety of *Os Lusíadas* itself, since elsewhere in the poem masculine desire and agency coincide fairly easily within the practice of expansionist seafaring. The erotic engagements on the Isle of Love occur through the agency of water, which is where female power materializes. Cupid's eroticization of the sea with his arrows allows for seawater, in this episode, to carry a primarily sexual signification. The nymphs' seduction of and carnal submission to the mariners are amphibious: they happen in the woods of the Isle, as well as along the beach and in the water. Some of the nymphs swim as a form of enticement, while others dash among the trees or in the sand (see fig. 6). Aquatic submersion in this episode participates in the scenario of female erotic initiative studied by Nocentelli and Saive. But it also forms part of a larger preeminence of female power in the figure of Venus, who ensures the safety of her beloved Lusitanian seafarers. If the Isle of Love proffers bodily pleasures on the human level, then a supernatural, female agency that presides over Gama's voyage and the future transoceanic feats of Portugal is the most far-reaching and consequential exercise of female power. While seafaring and imperial expansion may be a masculine enterprise, in *Os Lusíadas* it is successful only because of the benevolent will of Venus and her coterie of sea nymphs. Were it not for Venus, Jupiter would not have shown favor to Gama's voyage on Olympus, the fleet would have been ambushed in East Africa in canto II, the storm would have sunk the ships in canto VI, and the homebound seafarers would have known no respite on their outbound voyage from India.

It is important to remember that the Isle of Love episode ends with prophecies pronounced by oceanic nymphs. There is a dramatic swerve from the historical circumstances and practices of Eros in imperialism to a cosmic perspective that ratifies Portuguese expansion as a global endeavor. After the siren delivers her predictions about future Portuguese exploits in India and of men not yet born (prophecies taught to her by Proteus), the sea goddess Tethys leads Gama to the top of a hill, where a globe of the earth, of mysterious manufacture, hangs in the air:

> Aqui um globo vem no ar, que o lume
> Claríssimo por ele penetrava,
> De modo que o seu centro está evidente,
> Como a sua superfície, claramente.
> ....
> Diz-lhe a Deusa
> ....
> "Vês aqui a grande máquina do Mundo,

FIGURE 6. The aquatic erotics of the Isle of Love. From Canto IX of the 1772 edition of Camões's *Os Lusíadas*, published by Miguel Rodrigues, Lisbon. Photograph: Houghton Library, Harvard University.

Etérea e elemental, que fabricada
Assi foi do Saber, alto e profundo,
Que é sem princípio e meta limitada." (X.77.v-viii; 79.v; 80.i-iv)

(Here a globe is in the air, a brilliant light passing through it making radiantly clear its center as much as its surface. . . . The goddess speaks to him. . . . "You see here the great machine of the world, ethereal and elemental, which was forged by the high and deep Wisdom which is without beginning or end.")

Tethys then enunciates a litany of future Portuguese actions and indicates their locations on the diaphanous globe.

The move from the siren's prophecy, inspired by submarine Proteus at the beginning of canto X, to Tethys's with the *máquina do mundo* traces a path that moves from the sea to the celestial heights and establishes the worldwide consequences of Gama's voyage and an expansionist teleology.[78] The use of prophecy in Renaissance heroic poetry, as James Nicolopulos observes, was "the construction of political and ideological legitimacy."[79] This legitimacy lends weight to Camões's vision of Gama's journey with its imperative of Christian expansion. The siren's and Tethys's prophecies not only provide a vision of people and actions to come as history unfolds, but both have marine origins and are incorporated into the structure of the universe in the form of the *máquina do mundo*. It is the culminating moment of the poem: as Hélio J. S. Alves argues, the *máquina do mundo* allegorizes the union of the Portuguese with the providential principle that governs the world.[80] As a sea goddess and the wife of Ocean, not only is it appropriate for Tethys to be the deity to reveal the world-machine to Gama, but the Apollonian view of the universe she grants is an extension of Gama's deck-bound gaze.[81] The horizontal surveillance of the seas from Gama's ship leads to a survey of the heavens and the earth. The goddess of the sea and the *capitão-mor*, in their joint witnessing of the *máquina do mundo*, cast Portuguese history and futurity within a decidedly maritime frame.[82]

The conclusion of the *máquina do mundo* episode on the Isle of Love proclaims a unity of the world's seas, an acknowledgment of the *conquista do mar*. Tethys's revelation of the globe to Gama consecrates the imperial ambitions of Portugal while also conferring the reward of fame, which is why the siren's and the sea goddess's prophecies are proffered on the Isle of Love. In the initial moments of her prophecy, Tethys calls Gama's attention to the "insanos mares" (untamed seas; X.91.v-vi) of the globe, seas that are divisive in their partitioning of the nations of the earth. At the end of her narrative, the sea goddess credits Gama for "[a]brindo a porta ao vasto mar patente" (opening the gate of the vast ocean; X.138.iv), for transforming divisive seas into a global, maritime connectivity, and for mobilizing the world's waterways as a principle of movement, power, and culture. The sea goddess concludes her prophecy by sending the now-refreshed mariners on their way home: "Podeis vos embarcar, que tendes vento / E mar tranquilo, pera a pátria amada" (You may set sail, for you have wind / and calm seas, to your beloved homeland; X.143.i-ii). The divisive, *insanos mares* now welcome Gama's fleet with their tranquility. And if congress with the nymphs on the Isle has threatened or at least temporarily unsettled erotic masculine agency, the cosmic consolidation of expansionist destiny evident in the *máquina do mundo*, and the calm, homeward-bound seas, might be Camões's indication that such anxious moments might be overcome by a reaffirmation of maritime enterprise in its most exalted mode. That is yet to be seen. The seas have been domesticated; they lie open for future expeditions. The goddess's final words inscribe Portuguese *navegação* into the cosmic harmony represented by the tradition of the *machina mundi*. Tethys tells Gama that the Portuguese are afforded a knowledge of future events because of the "mar, que já deixais sabido" (sea, that you now bequeath as known; X.142.iii).

3

Lyric Seas

Broadly speaking, it is possible to situate Camões's lyric within the culture of the "new poetry" of Iberia (and of Europe generally) that Richard Helgerson argues for in a study of the Spanish poet Garcilaso de la Vega (1501?–36). For Helgerson, the "new poetry" was a product of the valuation of vernacular languages as analogous to the status of Greek and Latin, an idea triggered by imperialism as a praxis that recalled the learning and greatness of imperial Rome: "Joining refinement in the national vernacular to the accomplishments of arms and government was the way to satisfy an expectation that never stopped thinking of Rome."[1] Based on a reading of one of Garcilaso's sonnets ("Soneto a Boscán desde la Goleta" [Sonnet to Boscán from Goleta]), Helgerson builds an argument that explores an explicit program of literary renewal in which the genre of the sonnet and the conflicting agendas of imperial ambition and devotion to love are constitutive of this new poetry.[2] In Helgerson's analysis, there is a definitional, causal connection between empire and the appearance of this new literature.

In a related vein, Leah Middlebrook studies Spanish imperial lyric as a poetry that develops the notion of courtly interiority and the chivalric subject. Middlebrook's imperial man is a noble and a fighter, and her idea of the "new lyric," like Helgerson's new poetry, places the sonnet at the center of this literary movement, a genre "which, in the second half of the [sixteenth] century, especially, became a virtual emblem of state and imperial power."[3] Both Middlebrook and Helgerson identify Garcilaso and Juan Boscán (1487?–1542) as founders of this poetry who "understood that the new lyric was a poetry of subjects."[4] Camões was an avid reader of Boscán and Garcilaso. As a participant in the new poetry and the project of creating a poetry of subjects, the Portuguese poet grants significant attention to the maritime subject, given his investment in oceanic travel and the sea as literary topics and cultural and historical realities. Like his Spanish counterparts, Camões also cultivated the sonnet as a preferred genre, but his lyric corpus that is part of the new poetry also includes elegies, songs, and eclogues. Petrarchan lyric was an influential predecessor for Camões, as was the case with so many Renaissance poets, so to understand how Camões appropriates and reformulates Petrarchan maritime conceits to his own poetic ends, we begin with a brief consideration of selected poems of the *Canzoniere*.

A small but notable group of lyrics in Petrarch's poetic corpus takes ships and seafaring as structuring conceits and metaphors.[5] We might think of nautical experiences and states of mind as constituting an aspect of Petrarch's "impossibility to give a stable figuration of the self," one of the numerous contemplations "on making the self the locus of singular and significant experiences . . . so obsessively bent on registering its variable moods."[6] More specifically, as Michelangelo Picone has argued, the metaphor of *navigatio* records a variety of inner experiences and philosophical and psychological states of a Petrarchan *nave dell' io* (ship of the self).[7] Consider, first, poem 80 ("Chi è fermato di menar sua vita"), a sestina that builds its nautical metaphor on the words *vita* (life), *scogli* (rocks), *legno* (ship), *fine* (end), *porto* (port), and *vela* (sail). With the pattern of lexical repetition characteristic of this genre, Petrarch moves between understandings of *vita* as the amorous life (here is one example of the topos of the *navigium amoris*, or love as a sea journey), the Christian afterlife, a sinful past, and the terrestrial existence of humankind, all of which may find salvation in the arrival at port.[8] Yet however polysemous Petrarch's *vita* may be, a key aspect of the nautical journey as the structuring metaphor in poem 80 is the steerage (*governo*) of the vessel. In the first stanza, the poet-mariner advises making port "mentre al governo ancor crede la vela" (while the tiller can still control the sail; PLP 180–81). Control of the vessel is tenuous. This fragile state establishes a tension that pervades the affective, spiritual, and philosophical movement of *navigatio*. In the second stanza, the poet speaks of his amorous life as a relinquishing of his control of the *legno*: "l'aura soave a cui governo et vela / commisi" (the soft breeze, to whom I entrusted both sail and tiller; PLP 180–81). Once the mariner is no longer a pilot (that is, once he abandons the exercise of nautical steerage), a waywardness ensues. Petrarch laments his wandering: "Chiuso gran tempo in questo cieco legno / errai" (Shut up a long time in this blind ship I wandered; PLP 180–81). *Errare* (to wander) can be understood as a morally bereft form of movement, if the poet is using the verb here with the meaning it carries in a passage of *De Vita Solitaria* (ca. 1356), according to Theodore J. Cachey Jr.[9] In poem 80, "errai" stands in opposition to the concerted movement toward an appropriate destination achieved through controlled, nautical directionality, and therefore invests pilotage with a moral dimension.

The surrender of control of the vessel appears in other poems as well. *Canzoniere* 235 ("Lasso, Amor mi trasporta ov' ir non voglio") presents the poet as entirely subservient to the force of love, carried into realms of emotion and existence he does not wish to enter. The poet's fragile or diminishing sense of self is the "weak bark" (*debile barca*) propelled by anguish. The sonnet concludes:

> ma lagrimosa pioggia et fieri venti
> d'infiniti sospiri or l'ànno spinta,
> ch' è nel mio mare orribil notte et verno
>
> ov' altrui noie, a sé doglie et tormenti
> porta et non altro già, da l'onde vinta,
> disarmata di vele et di governo. (PLP 392–93)

(but a tearful rain and fierce winds of infinite sighs have driven it, for in my sea now there is horrible night and winter // where it carries annoyance to others and nothing but pain and torment to itself, already vanquished by the waves, bereft of sails and tiller.)

Critical to my readings of Camões is Petrarch's emotional interiority as a sea, a maritime interiority. Moreover, the vessel, overcome by the waves and uncontrollable because of the loss of sails and tiller, evokes a loss of agency; the poet-mariner passively suffers the unwanted course of amorous sentiment.[10] Eventually the weak or frail bark transports suffering back to itself, so that it is both vessel and destination, an emblem of self-reflexivity.

Petrarch's nautical poems hence begin to establish maritime interiority as a dimension of Western lyric expression. Camões adapts and incorporates this interiority in several poems of the *Rimas*, and it is a distinguishing feature of the lyric inflection of the Camonian maritime subject. A few words on the use of "subject" are in order. Mary Malcolm Gaylord reminds us that there is a range of meanings of subject in critical discourses "which encompass the subject as protagonist of consciousness, cognition, feeling, verbal expression, syntax, and subject as theme and therefore as object of thought, speech, and writing."[11] Ross Knecht briefly summarizes the so-called egoist vs. anti-egoist debate, noting the contention between critics who ascribe a pure individuality or subjectivity to Petrarch and those who claim that no such coherent individualism is to be found.[12] In a study of subjectivity in seventeenth-century Spain, George Mariscal argues that early modern culture produced a variety of subjects through a range of discourses and practices, and that the postmodern "universal" or "bourgeois individual" is not the only possibility for understanding subjectivity in a historical context.[13] Mariscal argues that "all forms of subjectivity in any specific historical moment are the consequences of practices that make up the culture at large."[14] According to this argument, seafaring would arguably be one such practice that created subjects of different kinds. Political, religious, economic, and textual subjects were a result of a multifaceted and chronologically extensive seafaring endeavor. The "gente do mar" (people of the sea) are the most visible and recognizable form of a new class of historical actors implicated into a culture of writing.

Camões as a maritime lyric poet differs from Petrarch, although, predictably, there are parallels. Whatever claim that may or may not be made about Petrarch as an autonomous subject, both the Italian poet and the Portuguese poet are writing subjects and "protagonists of consciousness," to use Gaylord's expression. The historical circumstances of that protagonism, though, differ considerably. Both the author of the *Rime sparse* and of the *Rimas* were well traveled—Petrarch in Europe and Camões in Africa, India, and China.[15] In Petrarch's maritime poems, the sea and nautical travel do not make reference to biographical experience per se but rather are metaphoric or allegorical configurations of amorous, moral, and spiritual lives. Petrarch's seafaring conceits are consequently ahistorical, or at least apparently a-biographical. If travel through the Atlantic and

Indian Ocean spheres was a commonality in the lifetime of Camões and helped shaped his worldview, in terms of transoceanic voyaging Petrarch would have only been familiar with the expeditions to the Canary Islands in the fourteenth century. Petrarch wrote the *Itinerarium ad sepulchrum domini nostri Yehsu Christi* (Itinerary to the Sepulcher of Our Lord Jesus Christ) in 1358 in response to a request from his friend Giovanni Mandelli, who desired to take a journey to the Holy Land and wanted the poet to join him. Petrarch declined because of his fear of storms at sea.[16] The *Itinerarium* traces travel to the Holy Land from points in Italy and is a product of Petrarch the armchair traveler. Cachey explains that "the *Itinerarium* points the way toward modern travel and modern travel writing in which the self that writes 'I' becomes as much the subject of that writing as the landscape being traversed" and that "the incessantly wandering, incessantly writing Petrarchan subject conflates the planes of textual and territorial space in order to extend the range of the Petrarchan self and to authenticate the reality of that self by fixing it against the backdrop of cartographical-geographical space."[17]

If the *Itinerarium* conflates textual and territorial spaces from which Petrarch the traveling subject emerges, Camões's own oceanic travels are an important factor in the creation of an early modern maritime subject. Unlike Petrarch, who only glimpsed in the (re-)discovery of the Canaries what would later become a vast, European maritime enterprise, Camões wrote during a sustained national and Iberian imperial practice of seafaring, and this markedly differentiates his circumstances from those of his Italian predecessor. Camões's poetry thus connects with an established and national practice and history of maritime travel, both public and private. Camões's travels through and residence in most of the territories of Portuguese empire are registered in several of his lyric poems. Such references, quite apart from the question of biographical authenticity, create the outlines of a maritime personhood, or the poetic fiction of one. To such a subject there accrues a certain unity or autonomy of perspective and perception, since the idea of extrapoetic or biographical travels and experiences in the events and locales of imperialism consolidates the maritime poetic self. This does not presuppose that the subject encountered in the many poems of the *Rimas* is always the same, but rather that the historically grounded, lyric subject is one of the creations of Camonian poetics. Accordingly, for example, the figure of

Themistocles, protagonist of Elegy I and a stand-in for Camões that is purportedly based on the poet's own journey from Portugal to India, is a fiction that foregrounds the role of historical subjects in lyric poetry. The anachronism of the Athenian statesman and warrior who traverses the *carreira da Índia* is a cogent example of Camões's claim to historical subjects in imperial, seafaring contexts as the bases of a new culture of poetry.

THE SHIPWRECK SWIMMER

In the 1598 second edition of Camões's lyric poetry, we find the following sonnet:

> Como quando do mar tempestuoso
> o marinheiro, lasso e trabalhado,
> d'um naufrágio cruel já salvo a nado,
> só ouvir falar nele o faz medroso;
>
> e jura que em que veja bonançoso
> o violento mar, e sossegado
> não entre nele mais, mas vai, forçado
> pelo muito interesse cobiçoso;
>
> assi, Senhora, eu, que da tormenta
> de vossa vista fujo, por salvar-me,
> jurando de não mais em outra ver-me;
>
> minh'alma que de vós nunca se ausenta,
> dá-me por preço ver-vos, faz tornar-me
> donde fugi tão perto de perder-me.[18]

(As when of the stormy sea the mariner, weary, exhausted, saved from a cruel shipwreck by swimming, merely hearing mention makes him tremble in fear, // swears he will never return to the violent sea even if it be calm and tranquil, but then finds himself drawn to it again driven by a desire for fortune; // so lady, do I, who from the tempest of your sight flee to rescue myself, swearing never to endure such a storm again; // my soul, which never leaves you, rewards me with seeing you and compels me to return to where I was so nearly lost.)

Camões structures his contemplation on amorous torment as a comparison between the experience of shipwreck and the experience of love. While the analogy between love and stormy seas or navigation has lyric precedents in early modern Portugal in Garcia de Resende's *Cancioneiro Geral* (1516),[19] Camões's sonnet invokes survival of shipwreck in an emotional drama that results from the impulse of the lover who, to rescue himself from affective turmoil, flees the presence of the beloved only then to find himself drawn, irrationally and ineluctably, to her presence once again, to the brink of disaster. The simile of the shipwreck survivor equates amorous suffering with a sailor's willing return to a place of danger and possible wreck. Camões conflates love with maritime terror in the tercets by employing a vocabulary that superimposes the seafarer's world onto that of the afflicted loverpoet: the "tempest" (*tormenta*) necessitates an attempt at "rescue" (*salvar-me*) so as to avoid "loss" (*perder-me*). In Camões's time, *perder* (to lose) could be synonymous with "to suffer shipwreck."[20] In the course of the sonnet, what begins as a simile comparing the realms of shipwreck survivor and lover culminates as a metaphor in which the two realms of experience coalesce. The maritime and sentimental realms are interdependent; the (disastrous) movement of the mariner finds an analogue in the lover as a subject who travels through interior, tumultuous space. Camões summons the sailor's sea to speak of a more personal maritime space within himself, an inner ocean of affect that also harbors the possibility of shipwreck and perdition. Inner and outer voyages are mutually self-constituting.

The use of shipwreck here connects to a history of maritime disasters as part of Portuguese historical experience, and the conceit of the shipwreck survivor is part of a literary genealogy traceable to classical antiquity. One source of the shipwreck survivor that would have been familiar to the Portuguese poet is a brief passage in book 1 of the *Aeneid*. There Juno, in her hatred of the Trojan seafarers, convinces Aeolus to unleash fearsome winds to destroy the travelers. A violent storm besets Aeneas's fleet, and Orontes's ship is swallowed by the deep:

>ast illam ter fluctus ibidem
>torquet agens circum et rapidus vorat aequore vertex.
>apparent rari nantes in gurgite vasto,
>arma virum tabulaeque et Troïa gaza per undas. (*Aeneid* 1.116–19)

(but the ship is thrice on the same spot whirled round and round by the wave and engulfed in the sea's devouring eddy. Here and there are seen swimmers in the vast abyss, with weapons of men, planks, and Trojan treasure amid the waves.)[21]

Aeneas survives the tempest and reaches safe harbor in Africa with his weary crew. He scales a height to search for the other ships:

> Aeneas scopulum interea conscendit et omne
> prospectum late pelago petit. (*Aeneid* 1.180–81)

> (Meanwhile Aeneas climbs a peak and seeks a full view far and wide over the deep.)

Coming as it does after the terrifying storm at sea, Aeneas's scrutiny of the waters is a moment of self-possession and as such is an assertion of his heroic agency. Though exhausted, Aeneas maintains a presence of mind (suggested by the placement on high and his forward-looking surveillance of the water) that allows him to deliver an exhortatory speech to his companions not to despair and to press on to Latium. Aeneas's searching gaze testifies to his responsibility for the integrity of his crew and fleet. Virgil's scene thus assembles motifs that will reach Camões: terror at sea and shipwreck, survival of that terror, and the contemplation of the space of danger.

Camões's shipwreck survivor, then, is possibly a descendant of Virgil, but the survivor has migrated from the epic to the lyric register, from Aeneas's communal concern to an intensely private drama of the psyche. In the literary lineage I am tracing here, this shift in register has a plausible origin in Dante. Early in the *Inferno* (ca. 1304–7), after having fearfully come to himself in the dark wood, Dante glimpses the mountain whose summit is bathed in sunlight:

> E come quei che con lena affannata,
>   uscito fuor del pelago a la riva,
>   si volge a l'acqua perigliosa e guata,
> così l'animo mio, ch'ancor fuggiva,
>   si volse a retro a rimirar lo passo
>   che non lasciò già mai persona viva.

(And as he who with laboring breath has escaped from the deep to the shore turns to look back on the dangerous waters, so my mind which was still fleeing turned back to gaze upon the pass that never left anyone alive.)[22]

Robert Hollander recognized the parallel between Virgil and this moment in the *Inferno*, a parallel based on the common elements of the sea, the exhausted survivor, and the proximity of death by drowning.[23] Hollander notes that Virgil narrates a literal event, while Dante transforms it into metaphorical action as the *Commedia*'s first simile.[24] The maritime simile reflects the inward nature of Dante's journey; in the dangerous water Charles S. Singleton finds a symbol of the sinful life that Dante has left behind.[25] John Freccero reads the scene as indicative of Dante's complex movement toward conversion, where Dante's survival of a metaphorical shipwreck reflects a moral struggle in the figure of a drowning man, a common conceit in Dante's time.[26] For Freccero, Dante's shipwreck survivor arrives at a middle ground, having neither drowned nor reached port, and "from which he looks back, terrified, at the danger he has so narrowly escaped."[27] This comment, almost in passing, identifies a significant Dantesque innovation in the Virgilian scenario, one that will appear in Camões: unlike Aeneas, who looks forward over the sea, Dante instead turns back ("si volge," "si volse") to contemplate the site of maritime peril. In Dante, the simple act of turning, prompted by the fearful relief that grips the mind of the traveler, compels him to move forward on the journey that will constitute the *Commedia* and is thus a call to pilgrimage. Moreover—and this is an idea Camões reiterates—Dante shifts the burden of fatigue from the collective to the individual. While Aeneas rests from the travails of the storm at sea, he does so as representative of his crew. Dante's mariner, in contrast, is a lone survivor who does not arrive at safety in a ship, as do Virgil's seafarers, but as a body in direct contact with the water. The shipwreck survivor has become a shipwreck swimmer.[28] There is a dramatic presence of emotion in the shipless swimmer that is not present in Aeneas; the Trojan hero's calm moment of surveillance suggests a certain remove or distance from the trauma of shipwreck. The body in water compels a moment of heightened self-awareness and acts as a goad to the poetic subject's reflection on his own experience. The shipwreck swimmer, we might say, functions as a hermeneutic imperative. Dante scripts a quasi-epiphanic moment of intense realization as an emergence of a body from dangerous water.[29]

Petrarch's "Passa la nave mia colma d'oblio" (*Canzoniere* 189), one of the sonnets that, in Cachey's assessment, exemplifies the motif of shipwreck as a "signature theme" in the work of the author of the *Rime sparse*,[30] also marks an important moment in what would become the discourse of early modern colonialism, according to Roland Greene. Greene singles out this sonnet, which features the frustrated lover as a sailing ship, because it "epitomizes the poetic object that emerges out of a discourse of love [and] gets drawn into discourses of exploration and commerce."[31] Cachey reads shipwreck as a reflection of Petrarch's "anxieties about his place or lack of it in the world" and as an aspiration "for some provisional home or stable dwelling in the world."[32] Here is the poem:

> Passa la nave mia colma d'oblio
> per aspro mare a mezza notte il verno
> enfra Scilla et Caribdi, et al governo
> siede 'l signore anzi 'l nimico mio;
>
> à ciascun remo un penser pronto et rio
> che la tempesta e 'l fin par ch' abbi a scherno;
> la vela rompe un vento umido eterno
> di sospir, di speranze et di desio;
>
> pioggia di lagrimar, nebbia di sdegni
> bagna et rallenta le già stanche sarte
> che son d'error con ignoranzia attorto.
>
> Celansi i duo mei dolci usati segni,
> morta fra l'onde è la ragion et l'arte
> tal ch' i' 'ncomincio a desperar del porto. (PLP 334–35)

(My ship laden with forgetfulness passes through a harsh sea, at midnight, in winter, between Scylla and Charybdis, and at the tiller sits my lord, rather my enemy; // each oar is manned by a ready, cruel thought that seems to scorn the tempest and the end; a wet, changeless wind of sighs, hopes, and desires breaks the sail; // a rain of weeping, a mist of disdain wet and loosen the already weary ropes, made of error twisted up with ignorance. // My two usual sweet stars are hidden; dead among the waves are reason and skill; so that I begin to despair of the port.)

There is no shipwreck per se in this sonnet, only its possibility as suggested by the passage between Scylla and Charybdis. What bears noting is a pronounced equation between the ship and the poet's affective consciousness. Petrarch builds the association between ship and poetic subject first with the image of a *nave* whose cargo is forgetfulness, then enumerates a detailed inventory that links emotional states to the particulars of nautical architecture: oars are manned by thoughts; sighs, hope, and desire fill the sails; weeping, disdain, and ignorance are entwined in the rigging. The metaphor of the nautical journey as amorous travails in Iberia prior to Camões appears notably in fifteenth-century Valencian poet Ausiàs March's (1397–1459) "Veles e vents han mos desigs complir," which presents a union of amorous yearning and the fear of separation from the beloved by death and nautical journeying:

> Veles e vents han mos desigs complir,
> faent camins dubtosos per la mar.
> Mestre i Ponent contra d'ells veig armar;
> Xaloc, Llevant, los deuen subvenir
> ab llurs amics lo Grec e lo Migjorn,
> fent humils precs al vent Tramuntanal
> que en son bufar los sia parcial
> e que tots cinc complesquen mon retorn.
> . . . .
> Los pelegrins tots ensems votaran
> e prometran molts dons de cera fets
> . . . .
> Io tem la mort per no ser-vos absent,
> porquè Amor per mort és anul.lats

(Sails and winds will accomplish my desires, making dangerous paths across the sea. I see the mistral and the west wind take up arms against them; but the east and south-west winds will help them, with their friends the north-east and the south, humbly begging the tramontana to blow favourably on them, that all five may bring about my return. . . . All pilgrims together will make vows and will promise many votive offerings of wax. . . . I fear death because I do not want to leave you, for Love is cancelled by death.)[33]

March's amorous-nautical imagery is very much in the spirit of Petrarch 189 and turns, in Lola Badia's argument, on the troubadouresque *fin'amor* in which the winds steer amorous adventure in a depiction of the "timid lover."[34] The votive offerings envision a safe journey that is requitedness in love and presence in the mind of the beloved. March's "Així com cell qui es veu prop de la mort" (Like the man who finds himself close to death) likens the hopeless plight of the lover who seeks the solace of the beloved to a sailor in danger at sea who espies the refuge of port but who is unable to reach it. Like Petrarch, March enlists nautical imagery not in historical or biographic specificity but as a metaphor for reflecting on the nature of love and on the poetic subject's imperiled capacity to execute his own will.

The danger of shipwreck in Petrarch 189 is the threat to the possible loss of amorous agency. While the poet manages to maintain control of the vessel through the thoughts that move the oars and the sighs that fill the sails, in the final strophe the concerted exercise of reason and skill is gone and wreck is imminent. The shipwreck as a potentiality in *Canzoniere* 189 has, in the analogy at the center of "Como quando do mar tempestuoso," already occurred, leaving only the lone swimmer. If Petrarch's *Canzoniere* 189 is an expression of a maritime interiority, a precursor to Camões's sonnet, we should note a significant difference in terms of the equation between affective consciousness and ship: while Petrarch insists on the correlation between the states and expressions of amorous anguish and the architecture of the ship, Camões foregrounds a dissociative relationship between the poetic self and the ship in the form of the shipwreck swimmer. The shipwreck suggests a move toward self-annihilation, since the Petrarchan affinity between consciousness and ship, which does not disintegrate in poem 189, is in Camões pushed to the extreme with the wreck that results in the stranded swimmer. Camões's swimmer suffers an interior wreck, a loss of integrality. As a structure of consciousness and as the locus of poetic expression, Camões's maritime subject here and elsewhere depends on the explicit or implicit presence of a ship. There is an intertwining of subject and boat—a subject boat—in Camonian lyric, much as there is between epic subject and ship, as we saw in chapter 2.

The contact between body and water in the form of swimming is central to the analogy between the nautical and affective realms explored in the sonnet. Swimming is an intense, corporal mingling of the human and the oceanic, since, as Steve Mentz argues, "the sea touches human bodies most intimately through the halting and laborious art of swimming."[35] As a consequence of shipwreck, swimming is a survival tactic, a way toward safety.[36] But the immediacy of the contact of the body with water in Camões's sonnet is also analogous to the immediacy of emotional intensity and of lyric subjectivity. The lone, endangered, and terrified swimmer at sea emerges in "Como quando do mar tempestuoso" as a figure of the lyric poet with the first line of the sestet, "assi, Senhora, *eu*" (emphasis added). If we read the ship within the gendered logic that dominates Camonian representations of ships and seafaring, the poetic subject becomes a shipwreck swimmer after he casts off the ship as a rational, masculine structure, a form of uprightness that, once gone, allows emotional intensity. In Camões's poetic scenario, the ship is but a prelude to the wreck and to a moment of intense, lyric realization. As the shipwreck swimmer looks back at the wreckage, the journey to the horizon and essence of being occurs. The masculine subject becomes a lyric subject—contingent, naked, and wet. The possibility of metamorphosis and transcendence occurs in the fleeting seconds before the sea threatens to take one under, before the violence of the wreck culminates in flooded lungs.

Camões explores another interdependence of lyric speaking and swimming in "Seguia aquele fogo, que o guiava," his rendering of the Leander and Hero legend. This sonnet reads:

Seguia aquele fogo, que o guiava,
Leandro, contra o mar e contra o vento;
as forças lhe faltavam já e o alento,
Amor lhas refazia e renovava.

Despois que viu que a alma lhe faltava,
não esmorece; mas, no pensamento,
(que a língua já não pode) seu intento
ao mar que lho cumprisse, encomendava.

—Ó mar (dezia o moço só consigo),
já te não peço a vida; só queria

que a de Hero me salves; não me veja . . .

Este meu corpo morto, lá o desvia
daquela torre. Sê-me nisto amigo,
pois no meu maior bem me houveste enveja!

(Leander was following the fire that steered him against wind and current; as his strength and breath faltered, Love restored and renewed them. // As he felt his spirit fading away, he did not despair; but, in his thoughts [since his tongue could no longer move], he confided his intent to the sea, in hopes that it would comply. // "O sea," [the youth said to himself, alone,] "I don't ask you for life; only that you save Hero's, and that she not look upon me . . . // Turn this, my dead body, away from the tower over there. Be my friend in this at least, since you envy my greater well-being!")

The Hero and Leander story flourished among poets of the sixteenth century, with numerous renditions in European vernacular literatures in a range of genres.[37] Versions of the story go back as far as the ancient Greek poet Musaeus (whose "Hero and Leander" was only printed for the first time in the fifteenth century) and, famously, to Ovid's letters of Leander and Hero in the *Heroides*. The tragic fate of the young Leander, who repeatedly swam the Hellespont to be with the priestess Hero and who drowned on one such stormy crossing, clearly had an appeal for Iberian writers who were witnesses to the active years of maritime enterprise and to the personal tragedies resulting from oceanic travel. Jason McCloskey establishes a number of parallels between love and navigation in a study of Juan Boscán's *Leandro* (1543).[38] For McCloskey, navigational imagery allows Boscán to "participate in the rich poetic tradition that casts love in terms of the sea [and] make[s] the myth especially relevant to . . . the historical moment in which the story of Leander and Hero thrives throughout Spain and beyond."[39] The affinities between love and navigation help us to understand how a common literary theme took on new resonances in expansionist culture in the work of poets who explore alliances between maritime experience, the maritime imagination, lyric poetry, and subjectivity.

Boscán's Leander as swimmer, McCloskey argues, underwrites the metaphor of the body as a nautical vessel, an equivalence we also find in Ovid's *Heroides*.[40] In Camões's sonnet, the body/ship metaphor first presents Leander as the pilot of a vessel. The nautical verbs in the initial line of the poem (*seguir* [to follow] and *guiar* [to steer, to guide]) present Leander steering his body-ship toward Hero's beckoning flame. This *fogo* is as much a navigational beacon as the flame of love that compels Leander to swim in the first place and that rejuvenates his waning stamina.[41] The fire on the shore of Sestos, visible from Abydos, marks a significant geographical divide. The Hellespont, the boundary between Asia and Europe, would have had special significance for the Iberian sixteenth century, especially for a poet like Camões who might have read in the love of Hero and Leander an expansionist parable of desire to bridge East and West. Leander the pilot guides his body toward shore, and as he loses strength, his body becomes a moribund swimmer, a vessel beginning to wreck.[42] This decline is all the more pronounced because it stands in contrast to Leander's single-mindedness of amorous purpose.[43] The progression from pilot to swimmer is part of the navigational logic of the poem, as Leander's crossing is a movement toward death. Leander as pilot is as determined and bold as any epic navigator, and steerage is a gesture of confidence and daring, an attempted conquest of the maritime realm inflected by desire. With the shipwrecking body, Camões intensifies the correlation between love and death. Leander's strenuous and perilous swim is an expression of the magnitude of his desire, so much so that the capitulation to such a desire is ultimately self-annihilating, like the impulse of the shipwreck swimmer in "Como quando do mar tempestuoso" to return to the site of mortal peril.[44]

In his final moment, the shipwreck swimmer of "Seguia aquele fogo, que o guiava" relates water to voice. Leander's apostrophe to the waves figures prominently in scholarship on the Leander sonnet tradition in early modern Iberia. Antonio Alatorre, in a critical overview of the wide-reaching legacy of Garcilaso de la Vega's sonnet on the theme, contends that the Leander poems of Francisco de Sá de Miranda, Jorge de Montemayor, and Camões depart from the Garcilaso model because Leander in these three Portuguese poets explicitly acknowledges that he will arrive dead on the shores of Sestos, while Garcilaso's youth pleads to the waves to allow him to arrive alive.[45] Sá de Miranda's closing lines of Leander's declaration are "[M]as no haréis que allá no vaya. / ¿Vivo no queréis vos?, ¡pues iré muerto!" (But you will not prevent me from going. You don't want me alive? Then I'll arrive dead!).[46] For Whetnall, Sá de Miranda's

Leander "[replaces] the pathos of [Garcilaso's] Leander's plea to the waves with a pledge of witty defiance" and "invests Leander with a new dignity" that establishes the youth "as an exemplar of doomed but enduring love."[47]

Camões's Leander may also be considered in the same light in his apostrophe to the sea. Apostrophes, as Jonathan Culler writes, are addresses to absent or improbable addressees, to what is not a listener or to things not normally addressed.[48] They are poetic acts that demand critical attention, and more significantly, mark moments (indicated by the characteristic "O") in which voice establishes its poetic identity.[49] There is a poignance to Camões's Leander that arises not only from the tragic drowning but also from the death of voice. As Leander's body fails, so does his speech—and Camões takes care to note that Leander's tongue (the only body part explicitly identified) has been stilled. This marks an entirely inward turn of the apostrophe to the sea. Voice has been dyingly converted to thought or *pensamento*, a final form of Leander's isolation and removal from the world. Whetnall argues that only the Spanish poets Juan de Valdés and Hipólita de Narváez introduce a comparison between Leander and the lyric subject in their use of the pronoun *yo*. For Whetnall, Camões's Leander (as is the case with other poets) does not establish such a comparison in the apostrophe.[50] I contend, however, that the intensely personal nature of the apostrophe as a result of its utterance in the recesses of Leander's mind—Leander in effect speaks to himself under the rhetorical guise of an apostrophe—establishes a presence of the lyric subject. Leander's silent, inward voice is the death of (amorous) poetic speaking, much as his body is already dead ("este meu corpo morto") at the moment of the apostrophe.[51]

The Leander sonnets, in the pens of the Iberian poets, maintain the alliances between love and navigation as the presiding metaphor that allows Leander to embody nautical and amorous agency and passivity. The Greek youth begins as a pilot in control but ends as a swimmer at the mercy of the sea; his body is a steered, seaborne vessel and then a wrecked ship.[52] These forms of agency and passivity, borrowed from Ovid,[53] necessarily entail amorous transitivity: Leander is the lover and the beloved, the agent of love as well as its object in the waiting eyes and heart of Hero. Leander's apostrophe discursively enacts the tragic distance that will forever separate him from Hero.

Culler explains that an apostrophe creates a relationship between an "I" and a "you," between poetic subject and natural object, and that "[a] primary force of apostrophe is to constitute the addressee as another subject."[54] Leander's address to the sea hence establishes an I-you relationship with the Hellespont, one that fashions the sea as a substitute addressee for Hero. Such a rhetorical move dramatizes the apostrophe by construing it as a truncated form of amorous dialogue. Leander's sentiments will not be heard by Hero or by the sea; his plea of the mind is a silent moment of despair and desire for communication that will die with him. The Spanish poet Gutierre de Cetina, on the other hand, grants Hero her own sonnet in which the priestess sees Leander's corpse as it washes ashore in Sestos. In grief she throws herself from her tower, exclaiming as she falls: "Pues a mis brazos que llegase vivo / no quiso el hado, ¡oh sola mi esperanza! / espera, que a do vas te voy siguiendo" (Since fate determined that you were not to arrive safely to my arms [oh, my only hope!], wait then, for I follow you where you now go).[55] In granting Hero her own dying words, Cetina in effect completes the truncated dialogue begun by Leander's apostrophe to the water and admits Hero into the poetic drama of voice as it coincides with the moment of death.

In a sonnet by Diogo Bernardes, Leander speaks not once but twice, and in the second instance he expands the addressee of his apostrophe to include wind and sea:

Hai ondas! suspirando começou:
Mas dellas sem lhe mais alento dar
A fala contrastada a traz tornou.

Hai ondas (outra vez diz) vento, mar,
Naõ m'afogueis vos rogo, em quãto vou;
Afogaime despois quando tornar.[56]

("O waves!" he sighingly began; but because the waves did not grant him further breath, his words turned back on him. // "O waves" [again he said], "wind, sea, I pray don't drown me as I go, but later, when I return.")

Bernardes's inclusion of the wind in the final stanza magnifies the tragic uselessness of the youth's crying out: much as the water consumes and envelops Leander's body, so does the wind dissipate his voice. A negative relationship between wind and voice occurs in Camões's sonnet about a lovelorn fisherman:

> O céu, a terra, o vento sossegado . . .
> As ondas, que se estendem pela areia . . .
> Os peixes, que no mar o sono enfreia . . .
> O nocturno silêncio repousado . . .
>
> O pescador Aónio, que, deitado
> onde co vento a água se meneia,
> chorando, o nome amado em vão nomeia,
> que não pode ser mais que nomeado:
>
> —Ondas (dezia), antes que Amor me mate
> torna-me a minha Ninfa, que tão cedo
> me fizestes à morte estar sujeita.
>
> Ninguém lhe fala; o mar de longe bate,
> move-se brandamente o arvoredo;
> leva-lhe o vento a voz, que ao vento deita.
>
> (The sky, the earth, the wind blowing softly . . . The waves, spreading across the sand . . . The fish, suspended in the sea by slumber . . . The silence of night in quiet repose . . . // Next to the water rippled by the wind lies the fisherman Aónio, naming in vain the name he loves and weeping, since it can only be named. // "Waves," he says, "before Love kills me bring me back my nymph, whom you subjected all too soon to death." // No one answers. From afar the sea rolls in; the trees sway gently; the words he casts to the wind that same wind scatters.)

This nocturnal, maritime idyll is tranquil in its situation by the sea and funereal in the voice that dissipates on the wind, the name of the beloved merely a moment of ephemeral speaking, of something that fades irremediably into the past. It is possible to read this sonnet as Camões's lament (in the character of Aónio) on the purported drowning death of his beloved Dinamene,[57] who is the topic of another poem, which reads in part:

Ah! minha Dinamene! Assi deixaste
quem não deixara nunca de querer-te?
Ah! Ninfa minha! Já não posso ver-te,
tão asinha esta vida desprezaste!
....
Ó mar, ó Céu, ó minha escura sorte!

(Oh! my Dinamene! So it is that you left him who never ceased to love you? Oh! My nymph! I am no longer able to see you, so quickly did you disdain this life! // ... // O sea, o heaven, o my dark fate!)

In "Cara minha inimiga" (My sweet enemy), the poet promises that his "rudos versos" (crude poetry) will live as the epitaph to the beloved who was denied a burial in earth by the sea. Aónio's vocative in the first sonnet is in vain, his call merely the speaking of a name because it can be nothing more. His *ninfa* has been reduced to pure sonority, a name that is an empty, sonic vessel.[58] The only response to Aónio's address to the sea is the sound of the sea itself. The fisherman's voice dissipates and is carried off by the wind, a symbolic death that parallels his beloved's drowning in that Aónio's voice and his beloved nymph are now nothing but fading sound.

The plaintive and nullifying correlation between wind and voice appears again in Eclogue VIII, "Piscatória" (Piscatory), the Portuguese poet's appropriation of the piscatorial eclogue tradition originated by Jacopo Sannazaro (1458–1530).[59] Eclogue VIII arguably draws inspiration from Sannazaro's second eclogue "Galatea." In Camões's poem, the fisherman Sereno laments the unrequited love of Galatea while other fisherman cast their nets:

Os outros pescadores têm lançado
no Tejo as redes; ele só fazia
este queixume ao vento descuidado.

(Other fishermen have cast their nets in the Tagus; all [Sereno] was doing was complaining to the inattentive wind.)

Sannazaro's eclogue presents only the possibility that the fisherman Lycon's address to the wind is futile ("Verba irrita ventis / fudimus et vanas scopulis impegimus undas?" [Have we poured forth our words in vain to the winds and dashed our useless waves against the cliffs?]),[60] whereas Camões is resigned to that fact, since the wind is uninterested in Sereno's anguish. The fisherman's lamentations are bootless.[61] Sereno complains that his voice merely roils the waves of the sea: "Quantas vezes as ondas se encresparam / com meus suspiros!" (How often the waves have become choppy at my sighs!). Voice becomes part of a restless, maritime nature but is devoid of communicative power. Sereno's fisherman's boat is at the mercy of the sea: "[A] barca ao vento solta" (My boat is at the wind's mercy)—the wind-steered, lone boat is like Sereno's lone, plaintive voice that is cast upon indifferent winds. Boat and voice move mutely over the sea.

The sorrowful evaporation of voice is characteristic of the melancholy present in Camões's lyric contemplations on absent or distant love. If, as Roland Greene notes, wind is the carrier of unquenchable desire,[62] in "O céu, a terra, o vento sossegado" and Eclogue VIII wind silences desire, since it overpowers and dissipates voice. In Camões's Eclogue VI, the shepherd Agrário and the fisherman Alieuto meet in a seaside grotto and engage in a friendly, poetic contest (an amoebaean singing), and, by turns, extol the virtues of ancient, rural poetry and the "new maritime" style. As Maria de Lurdes Saraiva notes, the eclogue "opposes the bucolic style of the long-standing pastoral eclogue to the new rhythm of the piscatory eclogue" in which Camões's own oceanic experience finds resonance.[63] Through a series of set themes, the competing poets Agrário and Alieuto invoke terrestrial and maritime images, personages, and myths in their performance before fish and other sea creatures from the "glassy deep" (vítreo fundo) who listen mutely. Eclogue VI is a meta-eclogue, an eclogue on the new genre of piscatory eclogue in which Camões emphatically establishes the "nova lira" (new [lyric] poetry) as a genre not only of words but of sound. This new eclogue emerges patently from the realm of seaborne empire. Eclogue VI is dedicated to the Duke of Aveiro, whose actions at sea participate in a national, monarchic navigational presence "no mais remoto mar que o mundo viu" (in the most remote seas the world has ever seen) that Camões registers in the opening tercets. As Agrário comes upon Alieuto singing to his beloved (the sea nymph Lemnoria) he remarks that he was captivated by the "angélica harmonia" (angelic harmony) of the "som com que aqui cantas / a tua perigosa Lemnoria" (music with which you here sing to your perilous Lemnoria). This *som* is capable of overcoming and mollifying the roar of the "ondas horíssonas" (cacophonous sea). Agrário's reference to the "novo estilo" makes the piscatory eclogue something of a sweet, new maritime style, whose music will reverberate with Alieuto's "som de voz suave e terso" (sound of a mellifluous and disciplined voice). This lyric aurality in part distinguishes Alieuto's song from Agrário's landlocked pastoral. The piscatory genre is a new, oceanic way of singing and voicing the world of the sea.

We return once more to "Como quando do mar tempestuoso." If the threatening sea and its dangers have Petrarchan antecedents and are characteristic of mannerist literary expressions of the human voyage (according to Aguiar e Silva),[64] these tropes constitute only part of the semantics of shipwreck in Camões's time. Shipwreck was a regular and repeated experience of early modern Portuguese travelers.[65] The genre of Portuguese shipwreck literature emerged in the late sixteenth century. Most of these narratives were printed and sold as pamphlets. Stories of shipwreck spread rapidly throughout Portugal and the rest of Europe and became part of the fabric of legend. Many tales were famously anthologized and rescued from oblivion by Bernardo Gomes de Brito in 1735–36 under the title *História trágico-marítima* (Tragic History of the Sea), the seminal collection of Portuguese shipwreck narratives to this day. The ubiquity of shipwreck as part of oceanic expansion advocates for the status of shipwreck not solely as a type of experience but also as an icon or emblematic representation of maritime culture itself. Shipwreck is therefore at once literal and figurative and constitutes one of the facets of expansionist literary subjectivity. This dual nature of shipwreck—the porosity between the empirical or real and the metaphoric—would have been apparent to many of Camões's contemporary readers.

"Como quando do mar tempestuoso" is an exemplary instance of Camões's reworking of an international literary tradition to his own poetic ends. The quatrains establish the shipwreck swimmer simile, and, as in Dante, the survivor turns to contemplate the dangerous sea.[66] But unlike Dante, whose turn to the sea is visual, in Camões it is aural—hearing mention of the sea ("só ouvir falar nele o faz medroso" [merely hearing mention makes him tremble in fear]) occasions the turn toward it. The sea, danger, and shipwreck are stored in memory and are potentially ever present to the consciousness of the lover. The auditory action in the opening stanza contrasts with the visual gesture in the tercets, where the poet endeavors to escape his lady's gaze but returns to it, since seeing her again is itself a reward despite the emotional turmoil (and even perdition) that this return will likely occasion. Camões intensifies the antagonistic impulses of flight from, and the desire to return to, danger by assigning them to different senses: the ear punishes the shipwreck swimmer, the eye at once rewards and endangers the lover-poet. In the first tercet, a maelstrom of vision threatens to draw the poet irrevocably into the emotional deep. There is a connection to a depth of emotion that is unstable and contradictory, a mixture of pleasure and danger that Camões implies is an ineluctable condition of the lover. The backward glance of the shipwreck swimmer, and therefore of the poet-lover, effects the transition from life to death; it is tragic because it is enmeshed in the self-negating impulses of love.[67] Camões admits to an affective abyss that is irrational, a fascinated and sought relationship to disastrous depth. If the subject position in Camões is one of precariousness, where a single backward glance draws one quickly into death, then Camões's swimmer, through the immediate contiguity of body and water, manifests a similar precariousness that may, at any instant, give way to a descent into death. The close of the sonnet brings together escape and loss in the poet-lover-mariner who finds attraction in perdition and openly embraces the loss or sinking of the self. Lyrically, shipwreck creates a relationship between depth and self; it is a staging of a relation to the profundities of love, memory, and peril.[68] In Ode V, Camões compares the delight occasioned by his beloved's eyes to the relief of a ship after a tempestuous night:

> Nunca manhã suave,
> estendendo seus raios pelo mundo,
> despois de noite grave,
> tempestuosa, negra, em mar profundo,
> alegrou tanto nau, que já no fundo
> si viu em mares grossos,
> como a luz clara a mim dos olhos vossos.

(Never did the gentle dawn, on spreading its rays throughout the world after a terrifying night—stormy, dark, in the deep sea—delight so much the ship that found itself in heavy seas as the radiant light of your eyes did delight me.)

The nautical comparison organizes Camões's contemplation on the intensity of love as searing light through the dark, a chiaroscuro. The fear of the dark, tempestuous night and depths of the sea are a depth of emotion; there is a similitude between nautical vessel and poetic psyche.

The tension between shipwreck and desire, the escape from oblivion, and the compulsion to return to the sea appears in a sonnet by the Italian poet Bernardo Cappello (1498–1565), a poem Camões may have known. Cappello was a student and follower of Pietro Bembo and a friend of Bernardo Tasso, Torquato Tasso's father. The sonnet reads:

> Come nocchier, che sè perduto & uinto
> Crede; mentre dal uento, & da l'infesta
> Onda, che lo percote; & mai non resta;
> Si uede a forza, ou'ir piu teme; spinto;
>
> Et di color di terra il uiso tinto
> Chiama con uoce desiosa, & mesta
> Felice l'huom; cui la sua greggia desta
> Ne l'alba; & ricco il uillan scalzo, & scinto;
>
> Ne prima giunto si ritroua in porto,
> Ch' al suo legno rinoua arbore, & sarte;
> E ingordo d'arricchir periglio oblia;
>
> Tal io dal dolce ragionar accorto,
> Et da begli occhi, ond'Amor mai non parte;
> Tratto ritorno, ou'è la morte mia.

(Like a pilot, who has lost his way and believes himself to be conquered; while by the wind, and by the harmful wave that strikes him and never ceases, sees himself pushed, by force, where he most fears to go; // and with his earth-colored face calls, with a yearning and mournful voice, happy the man who wakes his flock at dawn and rich the unshod and half-clad peasant; // the moment he finds himself in the harbor and repairs the mast and riggings of his ship and, hungry to get rich, forgets danger— // So I, when I take notice of her sweet discourse and her beautiful eyes, whence Love never departs, quickly return to where my death lies.)[69]

Cappello, like Camões, builds his reflection on self-destructive love through a maritime simile, although here there is no shipwreck survivor but a storm-buffeted mariner who, once out of danger, feels compelled to return to the sea because of his lust for wealth. In Cappello and Camões, the exhausted yet greedy sailor knowingly seeks his death in the eyes of the beloved. Avarice (recall that the shipwreck swimmer is "cobiçoso") in the opening of Camões's sonnet finds a parallel in the idea of reward ("preço"), which is the enticing presence of the beloved that spurs the return to danger. There are classical precedents for this linking of greed and navigation. Horace, in his first ode, speaks of the trader frightened by the sea but who repairs his fleet, since he cannot live within modest means.[70] And in the introductory portion of the *Metamorphoses*, Ovid recounts the coming of evil after the golden age along with the "amor sceleratus habendi" (cursed love of gain), then observes that "vela dabant ventis nec adhuc bene noverat illos navita" (men now spread sails to the winds, though the sailor as yet scarce knew them).[71] While both Cappello and Camões echo this classical topos, in Camões the reference to material gain situates the poem within the economic dimension of Portuguese imperialism.

This publicly attested dimension of expansion—the interrelation of shipwreck, peril, and the quest for wealth—becomes a private, interior reality in the second half of Camões's sonnet. On the literal level the shipwreck swimmer is a figure of the Portuguese expansionist enterprise and its materialist underpinnings. But Camões then elaborates on this by taking Portuguese oceanic endeavor as a metaphor for the interior voyages of affect, and in so doing, equates two different forms of desire. There is an interpenetration of the public and the private in such a gesture, so that maritime pursuits shape an inner world—appealing, dangerous, and deadly. If we find in Camões's verses a presentation of love as a dark, cataclysmic force (a concept typical of Neoplatonic literary culture[72]), then the comparison of love to the expansionist desire for wealth grounds this Neoplatonic notion in historical specifics. Perhaps more significant is Camões's overlapping of materialist, imperial voyaging and the inner workings of personal desire that inflects the amorous, poetic subject with an ideological undercurrent, and, conversely, implicates lyric impulses in epic action. This straddling of two manners of desire against the backdrop of Portuguese maritime culture distinguishes Camões's poetic subject from the one we find in Cappello. As Camões's sonnet closes, the shipwreck swimmer records a hazardous depth of mind and emotion, an internal abyss.

So far I have considered how Camões's shipwreck swimmer equates maritime perdition with poetic interiority, and how the contradictory nature of love finds expression in the conundrum of the terrified shipwreck survivor who yearns to return to the sea. The swimmer's body in water becomes iconic of the lyric, maritime subject. Shipwreck and the maritime realm, therefore, promote an expression of poetic ipseity. Consider another sonnet in which Camões speaks of a visit to the temple of Love, partially quoted here:

> Amor, co a esperança já perdida,
> teu soberano templo visitei;
> por sinal do naufrágio que passei,
> em lugar dos vestidos, pus a vida.
> ....
> Vês aqui alma, vida e esperança,
> despojos doces de meu bem passado,
> enquanto quis aquela que eu adoro:
>
> nelas podes tomar de mim vingança;
> e se inda não estás de mim vingado,
> contenta-te com as lágrimas que choro.

(Love, with hope already lost, I visited your mighty temple; and in token of the shipwreck that I suffered, instead of my clothes I offered my life. // . . . You see here my soul, life, and hope, cherished remnants of my past happiness while I loved whom I adore: // with them you can take revenge on me; and if you still are not avenged, content yourself with the tears I shed.)

Garcilaso de la Vega presents a similar scenario in Sonnet 7:

> No pierda más quien ha tanto perdido;
> bástate, amor, lo que ha por mí pasado;
> ....
> Tu templo y sus paredes he vestido
> de mis mojadas ropas y adornado,
> como acontece a quien ha ya escapado

libre de la tormenta en que se vido.

Yo habia jurado nunca más meterme,
a poder mio y a mi consentimiento,
en otro tal peligro como vano;

mas del que viene no podré valerme,
y en esto no voy contra el juramento,
que ni es como los otros ni en mi mano.[73]

(Let him who has already lost so much lose no more; let suffice, Love, what I have already experienced; // ... // Your temple and walls are dressed and adorned with my wet clothes, as happens to him who has safely escaped the storm in which he found himself. // I vainly had sworn never again to place myself, through my own power and consent, in another such danger; // but of that danger that approaches I am defenseless and in so being I do not counter my oath, because such danger is not like the others I am able to control.)

Both poets describe Love's temple and speak of votive offerings, although, as Marimilda Rosa Vitali points out, Camões does not render thanks with the ex-voto of soaked garments for having survived the *naufrágio* but instead laments that his life has been saved and offers it as a potential object of divine vengeance.[74] And in contrast to the shipwreck swimmer in "Como quando do mar tempestuoso," in Garcilaso's sonnet the survivor absolves himself of self-contradiction by recognizing love as a danger unlike any other, so the contradictory impulses of Camões's love-afflicted subject are not submitted to scrutiny or rationalization, as they are in Garcilaso. Camões's sense of love's annihilating power in "Amor, co a esperança já perdida" takes form as a shipwreck, while for Garcilaso the mariner has simply escaped from a storm. Camões's "despojos doces" (cherished remnants) are the flotsam the poet sadly gathers from the wreck. In this sonnet's *naufrágio*, Camões formulates life and love as a continuous confrontation with the possibility of shipwreck.[75] The votive offerings, instead of clothes, are pieces of the poet's past, the ship of life that has fractured but that agonizingly endures and prompts the poet's meditation on time.

Finally, another of Camões's sonnets finds maritime peril configuring a reflection on the punishing vicissitudes of love. The first two stanzas are of interest:

> Busque Amor novas artes, novo engenho,
> para matar-me, e novas esquivanças;
> que não pode tirar-me as esperanças,
> que mal me tirará o que eu não tenho.
>
> Olhai de que esperanças me mantenho!
> Vede que perigosas seguranças!
> Que não temo contrastes nem mudanças,
> andando em bravo mar, perdido o lenho.

(Seek then, Love, new and inventive ways to kill me, and find new contempt; for you cannot rob me of hope, since you cannot take what I do not have. // Behold such hopes on which I live! See what perilous certainties! For I fear not change or contradiction, as I founder in the furious sea, my vessel lost.)

Here is also the mariner-lover. Camões ironically challenges love to devise new ways of sentimental destruction. In this challenge, the disabled vessel at drift on the rough, open seas relieves the poet of the fear of mutability and contention (an ironic gesture, since laments on an inevitable *mudança* in human life are a leitmotif throughout Camões's lyric). The vessel-less sailor stands for an affective ground zero, a state of numbness that Camões likens to a cognitive aporia in the closing tercet.[76]

The shipwreck swimmer, in his tenuous position on the surface of the sea, lives both the experience and the possibility of depth, and this underlies poetic contemplation and self-awareness. Sinking opens up realms of the self and of being; affect can be suddenly and terrifyingly abyssal, yet it is a danger the lyric subject finds unavoidably appealing, since in that potential of depth poetic selfhood lives. The voyage or movement downward is also the voyage in—sudden submersion and the imminence of the plunge mobilize the poet to write. This is one of the subjects that emanates from the lyric Camões: the endangered and terrified swimmer in his water-bound world.

THE SEAS OF EXILE

Camões's shipwreck swimmer, then, brings a tradition of the shipwreck survivor to bear on lyric subjectivity. The complexities of the relationship between Camões's maritime imaginary and the lyric self inform another group of poems that turn on exile. These poems most explicitly locate the poetic landscapes and poetic subjects in the geography and practices of seafaring. In the small but conceptually dense group of exile poems Camões expresses a philosophy and experience of being-in-the-world that in many ways stands in contrast to the telos of seafaring that permeates *Os Lusíadas* and the consolidation of a global, maritime sovereignty. Oceanic voyaging for lyric and epic maritime subjects produces different circumstances and consequences; in the exile poetry these consequences are largely existential. The poems I consider in this section also bear, to greater or lesser degrees, on the question of voice in the places and spaces of expansion. The poems are Elegies I ("O poeta Simónides, falando"), II ("Aquela que de amor descomedido"), and III ("O Sulmonense Ovídio, desterrado"); Songs VI ("Com força desusada"), IX ("Junto de um seco, fero e estéril monte"), and X ("Vinde cá, meu tão certo secretário"); and Sonnets 46 ("No mundo quis um tempo que se achasse") and 157 ("No mundo poucos anos, e cansados").[77]

Carlos Ascenso André notes that exile is an ambiguous and polysemous concept, with a range of meanings that include remove from a homeland, banishment (imposed or voluntary), and spatial or geographical displacement. It is as much a juridical, political, or social reality as it is a sentiment or psychological state.[78] Exile, in actual or imagined terms, involves distance, displacement, and movement, three conceits that shape Camonian exile, since it is primarily an experience born of oceanic errancy. It is possible to understand sea voyaging in lyric, as Maria do Céu Fraga suggests, as participating in the allegorical tradition of the *homo viator*, of life as a voyage.[79] However, in such a reading we need to be careful not to allow this allegorical tradition to divorce these poems from the historical culture of expansionist enterprise on which Camões's understanding of exile primarily depends.

It is noteworthy that in none of the poems does Camões explicitly call himself an "exile." Rather, the poet describes a condition and its consequences that sometimes are ontological but always fragmenting and existentially challenging. The one occurrence in which Camões applies a qualifier to himself that approaches the label of exile is in Song X, "Vinde cá, meu tão certo secretário," a jeremiad on adversarial fortune and amorous affliction, leitmotifs of Camões's lyric poetry. The poem contains a scenario of exilic wandering, since implacable fortune has forced the poet to travel the world as a soldier. The poet laments:

> Este curso contino de tristeza,
> estes passos tão vãmente espalhados. . . .
>
> agora, peregrino vago e errante,
> vendo nações, linguage[n]s e costumes,
> Céus vários, qualidades diferentes,
> só por seguir com passos diligentes
> a ti, Fortuna injusta.
>
> (This continuing course of sadness, these steps so vainly taken. . . . Now [I am] a traveler, aimlessly wandering, seeing nations, languages, and customs; many skies and different things, all to follow you, unjust Fortune, with diligent steps.)

The unwanted shift in destiny motivates Camões's self-identification as a *peregrino* (pilgrim, traveler), at once drawing on the Petrarchan vocabulary of exile and recasting that lexical heritage in a seafaring mode. For Petrarch, one understanding of exile is the sacred journey of *peregrinatio* that cannot conclude outside of paradise.[80] With *peregrino* it is probable that Camões means to establish an ironic tension between his own meanderings through the world and the idea of a committed journey with an edifying, perhaps even spiritual, objective and end. In doing so the poet depletes the term of its significance as a journey toward redemption or fulfillment within the bleak, existential narrative of the song, since the poet's life does not move toward fulfillment of any kind. There is no paradise glimpsed here, only the wanderings of a "feeble heart" (*fraco coração*) that vainly follows the memories of a happier past and over which the poet disavows control. The pilgrim-traveler of Song X is an unwilling sojourner through the world and through memory at the command of intractable destiny, whose "vain steps" do not move toward a moment of plenitude or consolation.

The conditions that define the *peregrino* in Song X underlie the Camonian fashioning of exile as an oceanic errancy that is an inherent condition of a seafaring culture—a recursive and prolonged experience of remove from the *pátria*, from a loved one, and even from a poet's own past. It is not a punitive experience from any juridical perspective (such as exile in Ovid), but is rather a *modus vivendi*, an unavoidable consequence of a nationally consecrated practice of seafaring. The sense of exilic wandering in Camões accrues from the poet's travels over time. Camonian exile is a mobile exile, a many-placed exile. Camões, living in the ceaselessly expansionist sixteenth century, might have made Petrarch's words his own:

> Compare my wanderings to those of Ulysses. If the reputation of our name and of our achievements were the same, he indeed traveled neither more nor farther than I. He went beyond the borders of his fatherland when already old. . . . I, begotten in exile, was born in exile.[81]

Camões addresses such extended travels in two sonnets that here serve as a prologue to the exile poems proper. The first is Sonnet 46:

> No mundo quis um tempo que se achasse
> o bem que por acerto ou sorte vinha;
> e, por exprimentar que dita tinha,
> quis que a Fortuna em mim se exprimentasse.
>
> Mas por que meu destino me mostrasse
> que nem ter esperanças me convinha,
> nunca nesta tão longa vida minha
> cousa me deixou ver que desejasse.
>
> Mudando andei costume, terra e estado,
> por ver se se mudava a sorte dura;
> a vida pus nas mãos de um leve lenho.

(In this world a certain time in life wanted to reveal if good came by chance or design; and, to verify if this was the case, resolved to make me Fortune's experiment. // But because my fate made it clear to me that it would not do for me even to harbor hope, never, in this overly long life of mine, did it allow me to encounter anything that I could desire. // Wandering, I traveled through customs, lands, and estates to see if my cruel fate would change; I entrusted my life to a small boat.)

The other is Sonnet 157, a poem dedicated to Pero Moniz, who presumably was a contemporary of Camões.[82] Although the postmortem persona of Moniz speaks the sonnet-epitaph, the parallels between it and Sonnet 46 make it difficult not to hear Camões's voice in its lines:

> No mundo poucos anos, e cansados,
> vivi, cheios de vil miséria dura;
> foi-me tão cedo a luz do dia escura,
> que não vi cinco lustros acabados.
>
> Corri terras e mares apartados,
> buscando à vida algum remédio ou cura;
> ....
> Criou-me Portugal na verde e cara
> pátria minha Alenquer; mas ar corruto
> que neste meu terreno vaso tinha,
>
> me fez manjar de peixes em ti, bruto
> mar, que bates na Abássia fera e avara,
> tão longe da ditosa pátria minha!

(I lived for few and exhausting years in the world, filled with harsh and vile misery; the light of day went dark on me early, for I did not live to see twenty-five. // I wandered distant lands and seas, searching for some cure or remedy for life. ... // Portugal raised me in my green and beloved Alenquer, but the putrid air in this earthen vessel // converted me into food for fish in you, savage sea, that roils by brutal and sordid Abyssinia, so far from my happy homeland!)

In both poems the lyric subject expresses itself from within the arena of the world itself. The concept of *mundo* in the early modern period, as Roland Greene notes, acquired meanings distinct from the medieval understanding of *mundus* as a unitary object of suspicion and disdain; beginning in the mid-fifteenth century, the totalizing concept of the world was becoming multiple and partial.[83] Ayesha Ramachandran similarly charts shifts in meaning in the sixteenth and seventeenth centuries, and, in discussing a passage in *Os Lusíadas*, comments on how Camões purposely blurs the distinction between understanding "world" as the geographic expanse of the earth subject to time and history and "world" as a figure for the entire cosmos as existing beyond time and encompassing all space.[84] Such a constellation of meanings invites comparison to the sense of *mundo* in these two sonnets, since the lyric subject invokes a personal history of maritime travel that, far from reflecting a consciousness of "world" as cosmic or subject to forces outside of time, serves to circumscribe, contain, and ultimately strand the poet in time and history.

"No mundo" evokes a sphere of experience and of disenfranchised placement that underlies the poet's existential despair. This despair arises from a tension between temporalities in each poem. In Sonnet 46, the time in the past ("um tempo") during which the poet was made the object of Fortune's trials does not delimit, agonizingly, the effects of such experiments in an overly long life. The world harbors a seemingly endless temporality. In Sonnet 157, the years of Moniz's young life, which were cut short, are characterized by fatigue and filled with misery. Both sonnets give testimony of a woeful, temporal plenitude, present in both a long life and one ended before the age of twenty-five. Within this time world, the subjects of the poems travel through the world of history and human circumstance in search of a change in fortune. In the far-encompassing *mundo* of "costume, terra, e estado" (Sonnet 46) and "terras e mares apartados" (Sonnet 157) the poet traverses a plurality of geographical and human diversity that results in no unified sense of *mundo*. The world is constituted of a fragmented multiplicity. Fortune remains implacable, unwilling to change, denying the speakers of both sonnets a futurity. In Song X, endless and miserable (expansionist) errancy causes a dissociation between poet, life, and world: "[F]altavam-me, enfim, o tempo e o mundo" (I was deprived of time and world). This disjunction between poet and world contrasts with the more monolithic, geographical thrust of maritime movement in *Os Lusíadas* that, in the end, produces a "mundo sabido" (known world).

It is the (futile) hope for a change in destiny that largely motivates seafaring travel in the lyric Camões. The "leve lenho" of Sonnet 46 is the central image of a life spent in aimless wandering—a feeble, vulnerable vessel subject to sudden changes in control and direction and, of course, to wreck. The endless oceanic voyages, bereft of destination, are the obverse of Gama's *naus* that instantiate the epic deed of global seafaring and Portuguese dominion over the sea. Sonnet 157's poetic subject is also a wanderer of "mares apartados" and whose (diseased) body is ultimately interred at sea; what was once the medium of the voyager's pointless movements has become the final devourer, a remote sea that deprives the youthful adventurer of repose in his homeland. The references to Portugal and Alenquer and the closing exclamation of the body's permanent remove from home contrast with Vasco da Gama's desire to be buried at home.[85] Such a desire in Sonnet 157 is denied to Pero Moniz, who is condemned to putrefaction at the bottom of a distant sea. This permanent and even ignominious form of a final, deathly exile reiterates the metaphoric equation between body and ship, as Moniz's body, filled with "putrid air" like the sails of a doomed vessel, wrecks and eventually decays under the waves.

Now, the five exile poems proper. For centuries, scholars have read these poems as documentary evidence of Camões's own purported life as an exile. In the first biography of the poet by Pedro de Mariz, "Ao estudioso da lição poética," Mariz raises the possibility that the poet was sent into exile because of an amorous involvement with a woman at court. Over half a century later, in the first of two posthumously published volumes of commentary on Camões's lyric poetry, Faria e Sousa identifies the woman as Catarina de Ataíde, the origin of the anagram "Natércia" in some of the lyrics.[86] No documentary evidence survives to confirm this supposed "official" exile of Camões. We do know, however, that the poet saw military service in Ceuta (the setting of Elegy II), resided for a time in Goa (where he supposedly composed Elegy I), visited Ternate (the likely setting of Song VI), and sojourned to the Red Sea and to Cape Guardafui, the locale of Song IX.[87] What these few biographical details establish is that Camões was no armchair traveler. Clive Willis notes that the poet spent a third of his life abroad.[88] This oceanic travel surely accounts, in part, for the pronounced vividness of oceanic experience in Camões's seafaring texts.

Elegy I, "O Poeta Simónides, falando," begins with a conversation between the Greek poet Simonides of Ceos (ca. 556–468 BCE) and his friend the preeminent Athenian statesman and naval commander Themistocles (ca. 524–459 BCE). Simonides offers to create an art of perfect memory for his friend, but Themistocles refuses it, saying that instead an art of forgetfulness would be much more welcome. For if someone is forced to leave his country by unjust Fortune, Themistocles asks Simonides, and if he is likewise compelled to endure a life of burdensome labor cheerfully, then what good is remembering the past unless it would be to cause anguish and pain? The unhappiness of the present is only exacerbated by comparison to the past. Following this exchange, the elegy narrates Themistocles's voyage to India from Portugal, a voyage parallel to Gama's journey in *Os Lusíadas*. The elegy ends with an encomium to life on land and to the agricultural vocation as preferable to the life of the seafaring soldier.

The opening exchange between the poet and the statesman establishes memory as the framing concept of the poem. In classical antiquity, the story of Simonides as the inventor of the art of memory was seminal in discussions of memory and appears in the works of Cicero and Quintilian.[89] What is notable in Elegy I about Simonides's "arte singular" (ingenious art) is the effect it would have on the Greek warrior, even though it would afford everlasting fame and glory:

> Bem merecia, certo, fama e glória
> quem dava regra contra o esquecimento
> que enterra em si qualquer antiga história.
>
> (The author of a means for saving the past from the pit of oblivion would surely deserve fame and glory.)[90]

There is a certain irony to Themistocles's rejection of Simonides's proposal given the ancient, oceanically wandering hero's *translatio* to the context of sixteenth-century seafaring. For however painful remembering the past might be personally for Themistocles, Simonides's art is tantamount to a historian's ideal. As a preeminent figure of public life, Themistocles would be in the position to remember his own life as part of a national history. His perfect memory would be the repository of a collective past. Yet he rejects this infallible remembering (which would be an epic achievement in and of itself) as a burden because his own, personal memory causes anguish. With the emphasis on personal affect, the consciousness and voice of Themistocles become decidedly lyric. In this scenario of memory and its tensions with individual emotions, Themistocles's ship differs markedly from Vasco da Gama's fleet: Gama's vessels witness and enact history, while the Athenian's *nau* is the stage for a voyage through personal time and history. Themistocles's speculative art of forgetfulness occasions the first aquatic and nautical image of the elegy, as the seafarer plaintively exclaims: "Ou, em pago das águas qu' estilei, / as que do mar passei foram de Lete, / para que me esquecera o que passei" (After all the waters I've wept, why weren't those I sailed of the Lethe, to make me forget what I've suffered?). The water of tears and the waters of the sea overlap as Themistocles rhetorically yearns to have sailed the mythic river of oblivion as a salve to unhappiness. The expanse of the ocean, a correlate of the intensity of the voyager's own lachrymose expressivity, establishes an inner ocean in tandem with the seas stretching from Portugal to India.

The sea voyage itself occupies the middle third of the elegy and includes key moments of Gama's journey recounted in the epic poem, such as the auspicious setting of sail, the doubling of the Cape of Good Hope, and a storm at sea. The circumstances of time and place, for Vítor Aguiar e Silva, confer on the poem an existential frame that motivates the expression of memories, the pain of love, and the desire for a tranquil, rustic life.[91] In Jorge A. Osório's reading, Camões develops an analogy between the difficult maritime journey and an interior dis-ease, born of a sense of absence created by the voyage itself.[92] Significantly, the transoceanic voyage activates *saudade* as a relationship to the sea and to the past that exile creates. Consider, for example, the shift of focus from the opening conversation between Simonides and Themistocles to the description of the sea voyage itself:

Já, Senhor, cairá como a lembrança,
no mal, do bem passado é triste e dura,
pois nasce aonde morre a esperança.

E se quiser saber como se apura
nũa alma saudosa, não se enfade
de ler tão longa e mísera escritura.

Soltava Éolo a rédea e liberdade
ao manso Favónio brandamente,
e eu já tinha solta a saüdade.

Neptuno tinha posto o seu tridente;
a proa a branca escuma dividia,
co a gente marítima contente.

O coro das Nereidas nos seguia,
os ventos, namorada Galateia
consigo, sossegados, os movia.

Das argênteas conchinhas, Panopeia
andava pelo mar fazendo molhos,
Melanto, Dinamene, com Ligeia.

(You see, my lord, how sad and bitter fond memory is in times of sorrow, since it's born where our hope has died. // And if you would know how a yearnful soul refines that memory, be patient as I tell my long tale of troubles! // Aeolus released his reins, freeing gentle and balmy Zephyrus, and I gave free rein to my yearning. // Neptune had taken up his trident and our prow sliced through the white foam, filling all the seamen with cheer. // The chorus of the Nereids came in our wake, stirring calm winds with beloved Galatea's aid. // Dynamene, Ligea, Melantho, and Panopea nimbly gathered the sea's silvery shells into bunches.)[93]

Themistocles sets sail for India as the wind blows auspiciously and the prow of the ship briskly cleaves the waves. But in the description of the oceanic voyage, the third-person, epic voice is joined to the elegiac first person. Whereas Gama's ships enact the imperative of expansion and consolidate a national identity based on seafaring, the Greek voyager's ship becomes, as the poem progresses, a sign of loss of community and of estrangement signaled by *saudade*. The inward resonances of the moment of departure perhaps explain why there is no direct reference to a ship in the first stanza to describe the voyage, since a ship evokes a forward-moving, collective endeavor. The gently blowing Zephyrs heighten the solitude experienced by the departing captain, so that the winds that propel vessels over the seas are here analogous to a natural, driving impulse that enjoins Themistocles to contemplate, melancholically, what is being left behind. This emphasis on wind aligns the retrospective, melancholic sentiment of the captain to the conditions of nautical movement. Camões suggests that only the act of setting sail can allow for an inner voyage of contemplation and reckoning, which is the content of the remainder of the poem. The shell-gathering Nereids who accompany Themistocles's ship, if they are part of a scenario of maritime harmony, as Maria do Céu Fraga asserts,[94] also contribute to a sense of oceanic solitude. In

Os Lusíadas, at one point Nereids likewise attend Gama's ships as they steer the fleet away from a Moorish ambush (II.19–23). These epic Nereids are a mythological figuration of the cosmic imperative of Portuguese expansion and collective identity (see fig. 7; this engraving from Rodrigues's 1772 edition of *Os Lusíadas* bears a resemblance to a woodcut in Sebastian Brant's 1502 edition of Virgil, in which mermaids accompany Aeneas's ship [fig. 8]). The nymphs who accompany Themistocles's exilic ship, however, bear witness to a potentially endless voyage of personal exile with no destination or end.

The elegiac Nereids are charged with a literary task when Themistocles asks them to memorialize him in verse on the banks of the Tagus should they ever return home, since he himself will presumably never again see the river's shores:

Ó claras Ninfas! Se o sentido
em puro amor tivestes, e inda agora
da memória o não tendes esquecido;

se, por ventura, fordes algũ' hora
aonde entra o grão Tejo a dar tributo
a Tétis, que vós tendes por Senhora;

ou por verdes o prado verde enxuto,
ou por colherdes ouro rutilante,
das Tágicas areias rico fruto;

nelas em verso heróico e elegante,
escrevei cũa concha o que em mim vistes:
pode ser que algum peito se quebrante.

E contando de mim memórias tristes,
os pastores do Tejo, que me ouviam,
ouçam de vós as mágoas que me ouvistes.

(O bright nymphs! If you've kept pure love in mind, not having let forgetfulness snatch it from memory, // and should you go where the great Tagus meets the sea, either to pay tribute to Tethys, the goddess you serve, // or to see the green fields it bathes, or to pick the rich fruit of gleaming gold mixed in with the river's sands, // there write down with a shell, in

FIGURE 7. Sea nymphs protectively guide Vasco da Gama's fleet. From Canto II of the 1772 edition of Camões's *Os Lusíadas*, published by Miguel Rodrigues, Lisbon. Photograph: Houghton Library, Harvard University.

FIGURE 8. Nereids accompany Aeneas's ship. From Sebastian Brant's edition of Virgil, *Publij Virgilij marōis opera* (Strassburg, 1502). Photograph: Houghton Library, Harvard University.

measured and well-turned verses, what you saw in me, that some breast may feel pity. // And may the shepherds there, who sadly remember hearing me, now hear from you the sorrows you heard from me.)

With his request, Themistocles asks the sea deities to become elegiac poets themselves. The lines of poetry to be written in the sand recall a long-standing tradition of inscribing elements of the natural world with words, thereby making nature a documentary archive or library of human experience, however ephemeral those elements or words might be.[95] Themistocles, in an ironic twist, has become a memory that will eventually be washed away by the fluvial waters of the Tagus. The future poem on the river's sands, in terms of the circumstances of its inscription, reflects the disavowal of memory that Themistocles desires at the beginning of the poem. In this way Themistocles will enter oblivion and will be freed from the pain of memory that he suffers in the elegy's opening lines. Themistocles's possible riparian memorialization, moreover, together with the reference to the nearby meadow, foregrounds a terraqueous natural setting. The Tagus estuary and its environs—a liminal space where meadows abut the sandy banks and the salt water of the ocean mixes with the fresh water of the river—symbolically encompass the transformation of a land-based literary culture into an oceanic one. This transformation, for the exilic Camões, also raises the specter of the loss of voice that is one aspect of Themistocles's projection of himself into the future as surviving only tenuously and temporarily in lines of sandy poetry. In this speculative scenario the nymphs, as couriers of the warrior's *saudade*, are akin to Ovid's *parve liber* (little book) in the opening lines of the *Tristia* as the emissary the poet dispatches to the home he has left.

After making his request of the Nereids, Themistocles fixes his gaze on the water:

> Elas, que já no gesto me entendiam,
> nos meneios das ondas me mostravam
> que em quanto lhe pedia consentiam.
>
> (Grasping my meaning from my looks, the nymphs made the waves swirl about to show me they would do my bidding.)

The sea itself has become a text the voyager reads, its undulations a mute, aquatic language. The waves are also the bodies of the Nereids themselves, figures of desire like the boats sailing the Tagus in Elegy III[96] that move in seductive and rhythmic fluidity, or *meneios*. The sea is a substitute for the body of the absent love the poet plaintively mentions early in the poem. Camões joins nautical movement and erotic loss through the movements of the sea.

The first-person, exilic consciousness of Elegy I defines itself by the emotional relationship to the past, or *saudade*. As Themistocles contemplates the sea from his ship prior to his address to the Nereids, he remarks:

Eu, trazendo lembranças por antolhos
trazia os olhos na água sossegada,
e a água sem sossego nos meus olhos.

(While I stared at the quiet waters, my memories serving me as blinkers, disquiet water filled my eyes.)

The poetic *eu* of these lines (and of the poem as a whole) is a mixture of the autobiographical and the fictive in the poetic persona of Themistocles, so that when the Athenian naval commander speaks, so does Camões. But Camões's conflation of autobiography and historical personages is also a moment of literary self-fashioning; as Helder Macedo claims, the figure of Simonides has a place in the poet's view of himself as both a poet and a warrior.[97] Camões stages a tension between the sea's tranquil surface and the disquieted, lyric consciousness as expressed in the restless water of the poet's eyes. As the ship travels further from Portugal, the rounding of Good Hope intensifies *saudade* ("[C]hegado ao Cabo da Esperança, / começo da saudade que renova" [When I reached that Cape where hope ended, my yearning was rekindled]).[98] Spatial displacement and travel activate *saudade* as an exilic emotion because it is premised on movement away from the *pátria* into the territories of empire and thereby renders all maritime voyaging as potentially *saudoso*. The elegiac and exilic sea voyage, with its *saudade*, is the obverse of the epic maritime journey.

While the epic voyage moves forward in time, enacting history through the concerted and measured movements of a ship, Themistocles's trip triggers a backward movement into time and memory. The Athenian's solitary, shipboard perspective does not enact a collective destiny (as does Gama's) but rather a separation and absence from country, maritime community, and even from the self in terms of the life that is left behind. The aquatic contemplation in Elegy I slows the forward movement of the narrative by causing a stasis that is reflected in Themistocles's "gesto imoto e descontente" (downcast, immobile face) as the voyage commences. *Saudade* lessens the sense of physical movement and heightens the ingress into individual memory, an inward, lyric sentiment that contrasts with the outward thrust of the epic emotion of *ousadia* (boldness or daring) touted in *Os Lusíadas*: a restless impulse to engage energetically with the external world and to mobilize a broad-ranging traversal through geographical space and consciousness of forward-looking time.

The coexistence of the sea voyage and Themistocles's woeful *saudade* suggests another dimension to the lyric subject boat. The ship mediates the Greek's relationship to the sea: only by being on board is poetico-philosophical contemplation possible. The vessel, in conjunction with the sea, creates the conditions for poetic reflection; in this the poetic consciousness maintains an associative relationship with the *nau*, quite distinct from the dissociative relationship caused by shipwreck in "Como quando do mar tempestuoso."

In Elegy I, the voyage to India includes, as in *Os Lusíadas*, a storm at sea as the ship rounds Good Hope. The tempest marks the transition from Themistocles's ruminations on the past and his remove from his beloved to the praise of the rustic life:

> Oh! lavradores bem-aventurados!
> Se conhecessem seu contentamento,
> como vivem no campo sossegados!
> . . . .
> Não vêm o mar irado, a noite escura,
> por ir buscar a pedra do Oriente;
> não temem o furor da guerra dura.
>
> Vive um com suas árvores contente
> . . . .
> Ditoso seja aquele que alcançou
> poder viver na doce companhia
> das mansas ovelhinhas que criou!

(How lucky those who till the soil! They don't know how happy they are, peacefully living off the land! // . . . // They don't face wrathful seas, black nights, for the sake of gems in the East; they don't dread the horror of war. // They live with their trees in contentment. // . . . // Happy the man who masters how to live in the sweet company of the gentle sheep he has raised!)

Such an encomium to the rustic life has antecedents in classical poets such as Horace, Virgil, and Tibullus, with Virgil's *Culex* being the most likely direct source here, as Richard Zenith has suggested.[99]

Camões appropriates the classical commonplace in order to compare, unfavorably, the life of the seafaring soldier to that of the husbandman. The "blessings of the shepherd" in *Culex* as counterparts to "dreams of wealth" (bona pastoris... somnia luxuriae)[100] are, in Elegy I, adapted to expansion, with its associated practice of material acquisition or "vaidade" (vanity). While Themistocles's praise of a life on land in part reflects a desire for a settled life in which natural needs are easily met, the verbs of these stanzas are all in the present tense, suggesting a rustic existence of continual present-ness unencumbered by memory of the past and therefore free of anguish. Such a life is like the rhythms of nature, which repeat through time but harbor no recollection of preterite states. Maritime voyaging is a cause for unhappiness in its relentless act of separating mariners from their *pátria* and in its irresistible call to ruminate on the past. It is a manner of enacting and perpetuating an existential or psychological dis-ease.

Cruel turns of love, fortune, absence, and the inevitable cycles of change that overturn pleasure and happiness underlie the anguish of exile in Elegy II, composed in the Moroccan city of Ceuta:

> Aquela que de amor descomedido
> pelo fermoso moço se perdeu
> que só por si de amores foi perdido,
>
> despois que a deusa em pedra a converteu
> de seu humano gesto verdadeiro,
> a última voz só lhe concedeu;
>
> assi meu mal do próprio ser primeiro
> outra cousa nenhũa me consente
> que este canto que escrevo derradeiro.
> ....
> Senhor, se vos espanta o sentimento
> que tenho em tanto mal, para escrevê-lo
> furto este breve tempo a meu tormento.
> ....
> Nem eu escrevo mal tão costumado,
> mas n'alma minha, triste e saüdosa,
> a saüdade escreve, e eu traslado.

Ando gastando a vida trabalhosa,
espalhando a contínua saüdade
ao longo de ũa praia saüdosa.

Vejo do mar a instabilidade,
como com seu ruído impetuoso
retumba na maior concavidade.

E com sua branca escuma, furioso,
na terra, a seu pesar, lhe está tomando
lugar onde se estenda, cavernoso.

Ela, como mais fraca, lhe está dando
as côncavas entranhas, onde esteja
suas salgadas ondas espalhando.

A todas estas cousas tenho enveja
tamanha, que não sei determinar-me,
por mais determinado que me veja.

(She who out of excessive love was lost for the beautiful boy who was lost in love for himself alone, // after the goddess turned her to stone so that of her human form only her voice remained; // so of my own ill nothing else is permitted me but this song that I write, at the last. // . . . // Sir, if the affection I have for such ill shocks you, to write it down I steal a brief reprieve from my pain. // . . . // And it is not I who writes such familiar anguish, but in my soul, despondent and mournful, the aching pain writes, and I translate. // I am whiling away my hard life spreading my continuous yearning along a nostalgic beach. // I see the unsettled sea, as with its furious din it resounds in the deepest recesses. // And with its furious white foam it takes over the reluctant land, extending itself into the caves. // The earth, as if the weaker of the two, surrenders her hollow viscera, where the salty waves spread. // I am overwhelmed with envy of it all, for I am unable to command myself, however determined I may be.)

The opening reference to Echo establishes voice as a presiding conceit of the poem. Echo's punishment by Juno for her garrulity was that she could not initiate speech on her own but was condemned to repeat only the final words of utterances spoken by others. Without a body, only Echo's passive voice remained. The dissolution of agency in speech informs Camões's appropriation of the classical story insofar as Echo's passive repetition of words is analogous to the poet's own voice in the form of his elegiac *canto* (song). This *canto*, the poet emphasizes, exists in written, not spoken form, something of a Petrarchan "effacement of speech into writing."[101] Camões's singing occurs mutely on the page and is not only a final act of poetic speech (and thus "derradeiro") but also a testimony of the passing of sound into written silence. The poet declares *saudade* to be the true author of the elegy. Camões merely acts as a transcriber or amanuensis, copying onto paper the dictates of an autonomous sentiment. In this way poetic composition, too, is deprived of a certain agency and is akin to a scribal echo.

Camões contemplates the loss of voice as a result of exilic desolation by creating a scene of (nonverbal) sound and acoustics on the Ceutan shore. It is along this littoral that the poet undergoes a continuous state of *saudade*; the shore also experiences *saudade*, a transferral to, or reflection of, the poet's state of mind in the maritime environment that is intensified in a thundering, littoral acoustics. As the poet contemplates the waves that wash over the shore, their restlessness evokes the emotionally unsettled life of the exile. The sound of water reverberating in the empty recesses of the beach and the sea's spreading of its foaming, roiling waters fills the poet's (and the reader's) ears with a "ruído impetuoso" (furious din). This roar of water, like the intensity of *saudade*, is a reification of *saudade* itself, an exteriorization of exilic longing like the "marítimas águas saudosas" (nostalgic maritime waters) of Song VI. *Saudade* and exile become sonically infixed into the maritime landscape. The sea speaks while the poet suffers in mute despair.[102] The oceanic clamor is evocative of the force of agentive voice the poet is in danger of losing in exile. Camões is envious of the sea's sonic prerogative and acoustic mastery over the shore and its recesses. The bulk of Elegy II is Camões's plaintive catalogue of experiences of endless change and remoteness, or "mudança e estranheza." Declaring that a life spent in pain and amorous suffering is what he is now forced to remember in exile on Africa's burning sands, Camões laments a continuous experience of change and being out of place in the world, in a new land among "estrangeira gente e estranha usança" (strange people and strange customs). Not even recalling stories of classical myth set in northern Africa is able to assuage or distract from his pain.

The analogy between water and voice reappears at the elegy's close:

> Porque se o duro Fado me desterra,
> tanto tempo do bem que o fraco esprito
> desampare a prisão onde se encerra,
>
> ao som das negras águas de Cocito,
> ao pé dos carregados arvoredos
> cantarei o que na alma tenho escrito.
>
> E, por entre esses hórridos penedos,
> a quem negou Natura o claro dia,
> entre tormentos ásperos e medos,
>
> com a trémula voz, cansada e fria,
> celebrarei o gesto claro e puro
> que nunca perderei da fantasia.

(Because if harsh Fate exiles me for so long from what is good that my weak spirit leaves the prison where it is confined, // to the murmur of the black waters of Cocytus near the dim groves I will sing what I carry written in my soul. // And, among those awful crags denied, by nature, the light of day amid bitter torment and fear, // with trembling voice, exhausted and cold, I will celebrate the bright and beautiful face that will never leave my mind.)

If the pain of long-standing exile is enough to occasion death, then only in the afterlife can poetic voice survive, only there is it durable enough to sing eternally. Camões loosely equates his otherworldly voice with the sound of the waters of Cocytus, establishing his song as forever moribund, forever resounding in the waters of gloom. Aquatic acoustics mark a Camonian, exilic dissipation of voice that becomes like the murmur of insensate water. The specter of Echo presides over a gradual loss of voice in the poet's world as one of the devastating consequences of exile.

The joint conceits of voice and water appear as part of the physical and psychological dimensions of exile in Song VI, in which Camões ponders the sepulchral destiny of voice in an unidentified locale in the East. The song begins:

> Com força desusada
> aquenta o fogo eterno
> ũa ilha lá nas partes do Oriente,
> de estranhos habitada,
> aondo o duro Inverno
> os campos reverdece, alegremente.
> A Lusitana gente
> por armas sanguinosas,
> tem dela senhorio.
> Cercada está dum rio
> de marítimas águas saüdosas;
> das ervas que aqui nascem,
> os gados juntamente e os olhos pascem.

(With unusual intensity, the eternal fire heats an island far in the East, inhabited by strange people where harsh Winter joyfully makes the fields green again. // The Lusitanian people, by exercise of bloody arms, rule over it. It is surrounded by a river of pleasing oceanwater; on the grass and plants that here grow, both cattle and our eyes graze.)[103]

The unusual intensity of the sun's heat in the East, a climatic alterity, is tempered by the natural and bucolic characteristics of the unnamed *ilha*. Camões conflates a traditional, pastoral setting with the oceanic geography and military practice of expansion. Empire generates exile, and its torment burns as fiercely as the Eastern sun. Deprived as he is of the sight of his beloved and turning to despair as a form of emotional protection, the poet's exile in a faraway land and prolonged errancy recall the two sonnets discussed at the beginning of this section, and has a precursor in Garcilaso de la Vega's Sonnet 3, whose opening stanza reads:

> La mar en medio y tierras he dejado
> de cuanto bien, cuitado, yo tenía;
> y, yéndome alejando cada día,
> gentes, costumbres, lenguas he pasado.

(With the sea between, I have left behind lands of whatever good that I, unfortunate one, used to possess; getting farther away every day, I have passed through peoples, customs, languages.)[104]

Fernando de Herrera compares the travels Garcilaso mentions to the wisdom gained by the heroes of antiquity, like Ulysses, who journeyed through distant geographical regions, cities, and peoples.[105] Yet unlike the Greek sojourner, the Spanish poet's travels and those of Camões occur within an expansionist culture that has brought peoples, customs, and languages into an Iberian cultural and political purview and promotes individual experiences of alienation and isolation. Garcilaso's wanderings that carry him away from his *señora* in this example of his "poetry of separation"[106] acknowledge experiences of ethnographic and linguistic plurality, but ones that, as in Camões's Sonnets 46 and 157, do not create a world of cohesive variety but rather an abiding disunity and existential placelessness.

Song VI comes to a close with an apostrophe to the river and the trees that populate the exile-scape, followed by a Petrarchan address to the *canção* itself:

Rio fermoso e claro,
e vós, ó arvoredos,
que os justos vencedores coroais,
e ao cultor avaro,
continuamente ledos,
dum tronco só diversos frutos dais;
assi nunca sintais
do tempo injúria algũa,
que em vós achem abrigo
as mágoas que aqui digo,
enquanto der o Sol virtude à Lũa;
porque de gente em gente
saibam que já não mata a vida ausente.

Canção, neste desterro viverás,
Voz nua e descoberta,
até que o tempo em Eco te converta.

(Clear and beautiful river and you, O groves that crown just victors, and maintain the peasant on his farm forever happy, from one single trunk many fruits you bestow; thus do you never feel any injury from time's passing, and the troubles I record here find in you shelter for however long the Sun illumines the Moon; generation to generation know that the absent life does not kill. // Song, you will live in this exile, unadorned and naked voice, until time converts you into Echo.)

The appeal to the river to receive and shelter the "mágoas que aqui digo" asks the landscape to receive the song so that exile transforms itself into a form of sound in plaintive sympathy with the natural world. The concluding echo that is the fate of the song is Camões's acknowledgment of his own death foretold in the tragic story of the myth, which will cause his singing to reverberate without a first voice, and will therefore become something of a sonic epitaph. So it is that, as in Elegy II and Song VI, Camonian exile, located in a particular landscape, produces a characteristic soundscape in the confluence of water, voice, and echo. The relationship to the external, acoustic world marks an unsettled, affective interiority that is part of the experience of *desterro*.

To speak of exile poetry in the Renaissance is necessarily to speak of Ovid, "the great Roman expositor of exile."[107] Camões does just that in Elegy III, "O Sulmonense Ovídio, desterrado" (Ovid, from Sulmona, exiled). Here, Camões addresses the Latin poet's exile in Pontus (Tomis), which is the subject of Ovid's *Epistulae ex Ponto*, and emphasizes the emotional hardships of this exile:

O Sulmonense Ovídio, desterrado
na aspereza do Ponto, imaginando
ver-se de seus parentes apartado;

sua cara mulher desamparando,
seus doces filhos, seu contentamento,
de sua pátria os olhos apartando;

não podendo encobrir o sentimento,
aos montes e às águas se queixava

> de seu escuro e triste nacimento.
> . . . .
> De suas fontes via estar nascendo
> os saüdosos rios de cristal,
> a sua natureza obedecendo.

> (Ovid, from Sulmona, exiled to the harshness of Tomis, contemplating his remove from his kin; // abandoning his dear wife and his sweet children, his own happiness and moving his eyes away from his homeland; // unable to contain his suffering, he lamented the sad and dark day of his birth to the mountains and waters. // . . . // From his eyes he saw sorrowful and homesick rivers of crystal flow, in keeping with his own nature.)

Camões imagines Ovid in plaintive remove from home, accompanied only by his Muse; exile is thus a precondition of poetic creativity.[108] This precondition also sees a "natural" disposition toward *saudade*, as Ovid's tears flow as "saüdosos rios de cristal." Camões's ascription of *saudade*—long renowned for being a uniquely Portuguese sentiment—to Ovid allows a commonality of sentiment and experience between both poets in their *desterro*. Elegy III turns on misfortune, a lost past, and the likely impossibility of recovering a happier life, one initially abstracted from the specifics of social or political circumstances that define the Latin's exile in both the *Epistulae ex Ponto* and the *Tristia*. Camões does not name the locale of exile, establishing only the distance from home by repetition of the deictic *ali* (there) in three stanzas. Then, the poet climbs a hill and expresses his anguish:

> dali me vou com passo carregado,
> a um outeiro erguido, a ali me assento,
> soltando a rédea toda a meu cuidado.

> Despois de farto já de meu tormento,
> dali estendo os olhos saüdosos
> à parte aonde tenho o pensamento.
> . . . .
> Vejo o puro, suave e brando Tejo,
> com as côncavas barcas, que, nadando,
> vão pondo em doce efeito seu desejo.

Ũas co brando vento navegando,
outras cos leves remos, brandamente
as cristalinas águas apartando.

Dali falo co a água, que não sente
com cujo sentimento a alma sai
em lágrimas desfeita claramente.

Ó fugitivas ondas, esperai!
que, pois me não levais em companhia,
ao menos estas lágrimas levai,

até que venha aquele alegre dia
que eu vá onde vós is, contente e ledo.
Mas tanto tempo quem o passaria?

(from there I go with heavy step to a high hill, and there I sit unleashing my cares. // After enough of my torment, I cast my longing eyes to where my mind wanders. // . . . // I see the limpid, soft, and murmuring Tagus, with concave boats that, in their swim, put their gentle will into action. // Some sail with a caressing wind, others with quick oars, gently cleaving the crystalline waters. // From there I speak to the water, which does not sense with what emotion my soul is reduced so cleanly to tears. // O fleeing waves, wait! for if you don't take me with you at least carry away my tears, // until that happy day when I go where you go, glad and content. But who could endure such a long amount of time?)

This passage designates the unspecified place of exile as intensely present in the poet's mind, and it is revealed to be in the poet's own country on the Tagus River within sight of Lisbon.[109] Camões remembers a time when the countryside was pleasant and flowery, and this memory creates a juxtaposition of temporalities: a present time of loss and decay and a previous time of growth. The temporal juxtaposition is dystopic in its effect on the poet, manifested through a concerted act of seeing ("estendendo os olhos saüdosos"). *Saudade* as a quality associated with the eyes marks an affective affinity to Ovid with the "saudosos rios de cristal" and, more importantly, establishes a moment of seeing as a kind of epiphany of the irrevocability of his condition. Through the "olhos saüdosos" the poet nostalgically views the place of happiness, now unattainable, and through them the exilic *ali* acquires both spatial and temporal plenitude. The eyes are a window onto the past and onto an anterior temporality, and the boats that sail gently on the waters of the Tagus are a central component of this spatiotemporal contemplation. The fluvial, nautical idyll is the existential fulcrum of the poem.

This nexus is apparent in the apostrophe to the water (absent in Ovid's exile poems), a moment of speaking in an otherwise silently contemplative text. The waves that lead to the Tagus as the carrier of the poet's tears are an acknowledgment of a previous state of being now irrevocably lost. The elegy ends with the poet wondering if Fortune will change his *estado* (estate) and his destiny. Exile has caused an ontological shift that is at the heart of the poet's despondence. The poet has been exiled from his former self.

One final example of the spatial, temporal, and ontological consequences of exile is Song IX, "Junto de um seco, fero e estéril monte," in which again Camões's own travels through the territories of expansion serve as a backdrop for his poetic rumination. Song IX recounts Camões's sojourn on Cape Guardafui on the Horn of Africa.[110] This is arguably Camões's harshest poem on the experience of exile, as the hostile and pestilential climate of the Cape weighs heavily on the poet assailed by sudden bouts of weeping as a victim of Fortune. The poet's recollection of his distant beloved lightens his burden somewhat. The song begins with a description of the forlorn hinterland:

> Junto de um seco, fero e estéril monte,
> inútil e despido, calvo, informe,
> da natureza em tudo aborrecido;
> onde nem ave voa, ou fera dorme,
> nem rio claro corre, ou ferve fonte,
> nem verde ramo faz doce ruído;
> cujo nome, do vulgo introduzido,
> é felix, por antífrase, infelice

> (By a dry, savage, and barren mountain, useless, naked, arid, misshapen, entirely abhorred by nature, where neither bird flies nor savage beast slumbers, nor clear waters run or spring gushes, nor green boughs sigh

gently, whose name, translated into the vernacular is happy, by antiphrasis unhappy)

The locale is a savage landscape of nothingness, situated by the sea:

> Aqui, no mar, que quer apressurado
> entrar pela garganta deste braço,
> me trouxe um tempo e teve
> minha fera ventura.
> ....
> Aqui me achei gastando uns tristes dias,
> tristes, forçados, maus e solitários,
> trabalhosos, de dor e d'ira cheios,
> não tendo somente por contrários
> a vida, o sol ardente e águas frias,
> os ares grossos, férvidos e feios,
> mas os meus pensamentos
> ....
> Aqui estiv' eu co estes pensamentos
> gastando o tempo e a vida
> ....
> Aqui o imaginar se convertia
> num súbito chorar, e nuns suspiros
> que rompiam os ares.
> Aqui, a alma cativa,
> chagada toda, estava em carne viva

(Here, where the sea, with intent, pushes its way into this gulf, I once was brought where fierce fate played out. // ... // Here I found myself passing sad days, sad, imposed, terrible, and solitary; arduous, filled with pain and anger, and having not only as my adversaries life, the hot sun and cold seas, the hot and malign heavy air, but also my own thoughts ... // Here I remained with these thoughts, wasting time and life itself ... // Here, thinking turned itself into sudden weeping, and into sighs that pierced the air. // Here, my thoroughly wounded soul was imprisoned in living flesh)

Cape Guardafui, a *locus horridus*, is perhaps a counterpart to Petrarch's windy and frigid landscape of solitude in *Canzoniere* 66

("L'aere gravato et l'importuna nebbia" [The burdened air and the importunate cloud]).[111] Here, as in Elegy III, the landscape of exile is infixed into the poetic consciousness with the repetition of an adverb (*aqui*), the first instance of which occurs as Camões shifts the narrative focus from a third-person description of the maritime, physical space to the first-person experience of that space. There is as well an attending shift of verbal tenses from the present to the preterite or imperfect as Camões describes his exile. The use of the exilic locative establishes a pronounced sense of spatial location, and as the poem proceeds the spatial "here" turns inward to designate a state of affect, in what Cleonice Berardinelli has called a movement of "progressive interiorization."[112] The retreat into the recesses of the mind and into the depths of emotion is the poet's response to a fate that has left his life "pelo mundo em pedaços repartida" (strewn in pieces around the world). The centerlessness of a lifelong wandering is intensified in the anguished and inhospitable fixity of *aqui*.

The turn inward to the topography of the mind brings with it an awareness of the space of *desterro* as sensorially punishing. The climatic conditions of Guardafui are aggressive to the poet, much as his own thoughts or *pensamentos*; the poet's mind and body are in conflict. This psycho-geographical inferno leads to an exclamation that brings sea, voice, and wind together:

> Oh! que este irado mar, gritando, amanso!
> Estes ventos da voz importunados,
> parece que se enfreiam!
>
> (Oh! how I wish I could calm this thunderous sea! These winds, perturbed by my voice, seem to lessen their force!)

This reference to the sea is a turning point of the poem. It marks the return to the present from the narrative of the poet's immediate past experiences on the Cape, and is prelude to the speculative relief that his *senhora*'s cognizance of him in the form of hearing the poet's voice would bring ("se esta triste voz, rompendo fora, / as orelhas angélicas tocasse" [if this sad voice, bursting out, should reach those angelic ears]). Unlike the voice in "O céu, a terra, o vento sossegado," which is dissipated on the wind, or the despondent poet of "Sôbolos rios que vão," who consigns his sad words to the wind ("[E]spalho / tristes palavras ao vento" [I scatter sad words to the wind]), here poetic voice exercises an effect on wind and sea. The intensity of suffering evokes a sympathetic reaction from the natural elements, as if the poet's pain were greater than the forces of nature. This extreme affliction is the inverse of the hypothetical relief the poet claims would result from even the slightest awareness of him by his *senhora*. There would be a transformation of torments into pleasant memories:

> Só com vossas lembranças
> me acho seguro e forte
> ....
> com que a fronte, tornada mais serena,
> torna os tormentos graves
> em saüdades brandas e suaves.
> Aqui, co elas fico.

(With just remembering you I feel strong and secure . . . and my countenance is more serene as deep torments turn into happy memories. // Here, I remain with them.)

Saudades are wistful, longed-for ruminations on the past. The move from *dor, ira,* and *tormento* to "saudades brandas e suaves" is the desired but impossible journey of Song IX, the unresolved tension between sentiment and memory that exile causes.

✳ 4 ✳

The Sunken Voice

The traversal of oceanic space is premised on a vast, horizontal maritime surface. Always bound to this horizontal travel is the possibility of sinking or submersion: for vessels, it is shipwreck, and for individuals, drowning. Much as navigation relies on the regulated and mensurate correlation of ship, sea, and compass, maritime danger draws back the curtain on the oceanic depths, on a disastrous verticality, a perilous alternate spatial axis. The menacing, life-extinguishing abyss is an aspect of the maritime imaginary. If the submarine depths might be thought of as spaces of deathly silence, even more inimical to human occupation than the volatile instability of the oceanic surface, depth can also, in sixteenth-century Portuguese accounts of seafaring, be a place of voice, of aural perception, of the sonic. More than simply a mute and mortal realm of the sea, the depths are also a conceptual locus of speaking and a domain of sound. In this chapter, by focusing on Manuel de Mesquita Perestrelo's narrative of the wreck of the *São Bento* (in 1554) and canto VI of *Os Lusíadas*, I consider the relationship between depth and speaking in the literary culture of seafaring. Perestrelo's *Relação sumária da viagem que fez Fernão d'Álvares Cabral, desde que partiu deste Reino por capitão-mor da Armada que foi no ano de 1553 às partes da Índia até que se perdeu no cabo de Boa Esperança no ano de 1554* (Concise Account of the Voyage of Fernão d'Álvares Cabral, Who Departed from This Realm as Captain-Major of the Fleet That Sailed to India in 1553 Until It Wrecked at the Cape of Good Hope in 1554)[1] ranks as arguably one of the most psychologically vivid of the Portuguese shipwreck tales, exploring in its pages the trauma of wreck and its haunting consequences, which include ghostly speaking, the terrified refuge to individual consciousness and memory, and disoriented and confused movement through geographical space. Canto VI of *Os Lusíadas*, for its part, is a transitional canto in Camões's poem with regard to both the voyage of Gama (it narrates Gama's crossing of the Indian Ocean following the encounter with the monstrous and spectral Adamastor and the rounding of the Cape of Good Hope) and the Portuguese relationship to the world's seas, which are here transformed into a realm of politico-cultural sovereignty. In *Os Lusíadas* and in Perestrelo's tale, voice and depth infuse the narratives and metaphoric logic as integral to the literary construction of seafaring with implications for the imperialist enterprise at large.

SPEAKING FROM THE DEPTHS

The earliest extant example of Portuguese shipwreck literature is the anonymous account of the wreck in 1552 of the great galleon *São João* on which traveled Manuel de Sousa Sepúlveda (ex-governor of India) and his wife and children.[2] Following the publication of this tale, shipwreck narratives flourished in Portugal as maritime voyaging became more and more of a daily reality of Portuguese seafaring culture. The dramatic and often gory details of wreck and survival in the pages of Bernardo Gomes de Brito's seminal anthology of Portuguese shipwreck narratives, the *História trágico-marítima* (Tragic History of the Sea, which includes Perestrelo's narrative) and in other, individual shipwreck tales clearly accounted for a large part of their appeal to the reading public.[3] Perestrelo's account of the wreck of the *São Bento* (*Saint Benedict*) stands out among the shipwreck narratives for its sheer drama and the gripping specifics of danger, terror, and survival. Perestrelo and his fellow passengers suffered a wreck on their voyage from Cochin to Portugal.[4] In the story of the *S. Bento* Perestrelo records his experiences during his castaway sojourn in the African wilderness near the Cape of Good Hope. The survivors negotiate the wilderness, search for food, and repeatedly fix their locations with maps or wander aimlessly through uncharted regions. The castaways are subjected to attacks by wild beasts, a blinding sandstorm, starvation, extremes of weather, and the deaths of several in their company. Encounters with indigenous peoples are fraught with anxiety, since the company is lost and at a decided disadvantage. Native populations and chieftains, according to Perestrelo, frequently exploit and abuse the hapless wanderers.[5]

In this story of tribulation and hardship we find private, emotional responses to shipwreck and its deleterious aftereffects. The *Relação* explores realms of sinking, both empirical and metaphoric. Throughout, there is a notional speaking from the depths, as shipwreck causes many forms of depth: spatial depth (sinking or drowning), psychological depth (memory and recollection), and affective or emotional depth (despair, torment, fear, and solitude). As is characteristic of the shipwreck genre, the imminent threat of sinking appears in the opening pages. The crew fears that the vessel might soon "ir ao fundo" (sink to the bottom) as the distressed *S. Bento* begins to ship water. This loss of controlled surface movement is the first incursion into the deep:

> uma onda que de muito longe vinha levantada por cima das outras todas em demasiada altura . . . e foi o ímpeto e peso dela tamanho que quase nos soçobrou daquele primeiro golpe . . . Após este mar veio outro que, conquanto não foi tamanho como o primeiro, achou já a nau tão aderrada que quase a acabou de meter debaixo da água. (RSV 224)

> (A wave approached from quite a distance, very high above all the others . . . and the impact was so great that we almost capsized from that first hit. . . . After this wave there was another, though not quite as large as the first, but the ship was keeling over so much it almost sank.)

From here it is not long until the vessel wrecks. Perestrelo tells us:

> A este tempo andava o mar todo coalhado de caixas, lanças, pipas e outras diversidades de coisas que a desventurada hora do naufrágio faz aparecer. E andando tudo assim baralhado com a gente, de que a maior parte ia nadando à terra, era coisa medonha de ver, e em todo o tempo lastimosa de contar, a carniçaria que a fúria do mar em cada um fazia, e os diversos géneros de tormentos com que geralmente tratava a todos. (RSV 232)

> (The sea was covered with boxes, lances, barrels, and many other things that the unfortunate hour of shipwreck causes to appear. Everything was floating among people, most of whom were swimming to shore. It was an

awful thing to see and to relate—the severe injuries to each one and the various forms of torment the sea inflicted on all.)

The "unfortunate hour of shipwreck" (desventurada hora do naufrágio) signals a shift from the descriptions of maritime labor in the initial pages in which the crew diligently endeavors to save the beleaguered ship to a manner of measuring time; it identifies both a specific moment in time and a type of experience emanating from that moment. In the desperate attempts to control and maintain the *S. Bento* afloat prior to the wreck, time is measured by the mariner's clock—Perestrelo refers to the four- (*quarto*) and half-hour (*relógio*) intervals of working the pumps. With the "hour of shipwreck" the measured clock essentially disappears, since it is irrelevant to the demands of survival. There is a sinking of hourly units of time that is substituted by less temporally dependent vital necessities and affective experience. The hour of shipwreck tags an elastic understanding of the shifting consciousness of time as a result of disaster.

One of the effects of this alternate temporality is the sudden and dramatic focus on the individual psyche and on individual bodies. Bodily hardships are subject-intensifying in that they foreground the individual and separate the individual from the collective. To a large degree, the community of a seaborne vessel, postwreck, disintegrates. Perestrelo notes the self-absorption of his shipmates once on land, while at the same time he allows his own perceptions and emotions to emerge in the course of the narrative. For Perestrelo, who is both a shipwreck author and a survivor, pain and terror cause a retreat into the self, into a depth of mind and emotion. There is a tension between Perestrelo's desire to tell his story and his stated desire to avoid the particulars of human misery as he renders trauma into history. The author worries that emphasis on unpleasant details might diminish his credibility as a writer, yet he also frets over his responsibility as a reliable chronicler of events. Perestrelo does not shy away from fearsome and terrible specifics as he lingers over the "diversos géneros de tormentos" (various forms of torment) visited on the company. This sense of a heightened first-person consciousness predicated on emotional and personal perspectives establishes a writing subject that is self-ish, quasi-lyrical in its emphasis on the first-person private life. Perestrelo comments on the personal nature of his account when he writes, "[D]irei o que alcancei na experiência de meus trabalhos, sem acrescentar nem diminuir a verdade do que se me oferece a contar" (I will relate what I achieved through the experience of my hardships, without adding or diminishing the truth of what is to be told; RSV 219). As survivors begin to experience the inhospitable terrain of southern Africa, rain, lack of shelter, hunger, and misery force each person into his or her own minds. At first, the trauma of shipwreck, and the sight of the destroyed vessel, cause a physical stasis in that the passengers find it difficult to leave the scene of the wreck:

> cada um dos que o entendiam, entre si conta como quão pouco apercebimento começava tão comprido, incerto e perigoso caminho, e quão certo tinha acabar nele à pura necessidade e desamparo, posto que dos outros perigos escapasse, sem falar palavra, levando a fantasia ocupada nesta angústia e os olhos arrasados de água, não podíamos dar passo, que muitas vezes não tornássemos atrás para ver a ossada daquela tão formosa e mal-afortunada nau. (RSV 242)

> (Each one of us, thinking to himself, understood how blindly we had undertaken such a long, uncertain, and perilous journey, and how certain it was that we would end our days on this journey out of pure want and deprivation, for however many other dangers had been averted, without saying a word and with our reveries filled with anguish and our eyes filled with tears, we couldn't take one step forward; how many times did we keep turning back to contemplate the skeleton of that beautiful and doomed ship.)

The inability to leave the scene (both mentally and physically) is part of the inward turn of the shipwreck experience, a nostalgic impulse to an immediately past and traumatic event that prevents forward movement.[6] This inward turn of survivors and their affective experience of time (such as the nostalgic contemplation of the remains of the ship) contrast with the external action of *caminhar* (to walk, to march), which is the principal mode of measuring time in the tale. For the cartographically trained Perestrelo, protracted hardships, the difficulty in knowing or recording chronological time accurately, and the incursions into memory and fear triggered by shipwreck all hinge on experiences of unbounded or unplotted space.

The seaborne community that faces varying degrees of dissolution once disaster has struck appears most dramatically in the guise of a maritime labor force during the intense moments of handling a storm-struck or foundering vessel. Typically, the Portuguese narratives begin with descriptions of how crews attempt to control and minimize damage. These descriptions usually include a proliferation of technical terms relating to sails, rigging, and the architecture of the ship. As Steve Mentz notes, "Mariners respond to shipwreck with skilled work" and "Maritime labor provides a language for understanding crisis."[7] The nautical details that accompany the urgent exercise of seamanship in situations of peril are first instances of maritime suffering. The iteration of nautical detail and the (ultimately) futile exercise of seamanship establish a sense of fatigued tribulation and infix the beleaguered mariner into the very architecture of the ship; the ship's body, and the mariner's body, become mutually self-referential. As spars, masts, and helms splinter, and as sails are torn to shreds, so too do the bodies of sailors and passengers suffer extreme injury. These specifics of maritime labor receive comic treatment in a sixteenth-century play by Portuguese playwright Gil Vicente (ca. 1465–ca. 1536), the *Triunfo do Inverno* (Triumph of Winter). The play was first performed in 1529 to celebrate the birth of Princess Isabel, daughter of King João III and Catherine of Austria. The play centers on Winter's boastful exercise of its powers, which includes a verbal duel with a shepherd as well as the unleashing of storms to afflict ships traveling the *carreira da Índia*. As is typical of Vicente's farces and comedic plays, characters are largely representatives of social and vocational types who have distinct manners of speech that are characteristic of their status or labor class. In Vicente's play, the pilot of a ship and a more knowledgeable *marinheiro* (sailor) dispute, during a storm, how to best manage the vessel. The scene includes two other shipmates, one of which is an apprentice seaman (*grumete*). Vicente paints a comically chaotic scenario in which the crew does not know the names of the sails or rigging, nor how to steer the vessel. The ship's pilot is farcically ignorant of African geography as the ship traverses the sea near Guinea. The playwright lampoons the exercise of maritime labor in a storm, and registers incompetence as a historically verifiable cause of shipwreck.[8] Tragic causality and comedy overlap in the Vicentine scenario and present a parodic portrait of maritime skill that we never find in the shipwreck narratives: for all their inability to save a vessel from disaster, shipwreck authors do not question the expertise or capabilities of the crew. The maritime storm in a play that moves from winter to spring and includes various components of the "order of nature" and the "hierarchical order of the universe"[9] suggests that maritime storms and peril had become a paradigmatic form of Portuguese affliction. The seaborne experience of fear had, by the first quarter of the sixteenth century, become part of the Portuguese allegorical imagination and of the cycles of nature.

Following the moments of maritime labor and the disabling of the vessel in the *S. Bento*, the survivors at last arrive on shore. There, they find a terrain of steep ridges and deep valleys comparable to the crests and troughs of waves. They must negotiate a landscape that alternates vertiginously between height and depth:

> E indo desta maneira fazendo muitos pousos, chegámos ao alto do cabeço, onde achámos tudo bem diferente do que cuidávamos, porque não tão-somente não vimos povoação, mas ainda quanto descobríamos com os olhos, era cercado de vales tão baixos e serras tão altas, que estas confinavam com as estrelas e aqueles com os abismos. (RSV 242)

> (And proceeding in this fashion we had to rest many times; and we arrived at the top of the hill, where we found everything considerably different from what we were expecting, because not only did we find no village, but that which we could see with our own eyes was surrounded by valleys so deep like the depths, and mountains so high that they touched the stars.)

The castaways then deliberate as to which route they should take in order to find villages and shelter. Some decide to venture "pela meia ladeira daqueles montes, assim como o rio corria" (halfway up the slopes of the mountains, following the course of the river; RSV 244), while others wander "pelas cumeadas deles, até que de alguma descobrissem parte por onde a pudessem atravessar" (through the mountain peaks, so far as they might lead until a suitable crossing point could be discovered; RSV 244). Perestrelo summarizes these experiences of wandering by noting:

> E como continuamente trouxéssemos a vista espalhada por aqueles outeiros a ver se descobríamos alguma gente ou povoação . . . vimos da outra banda um fumo . . . por haver quatro dias que, chovendo sempre, não ces-

The Sunken Voice

sávamos de andar, sem caminho nem carreira, pelos altos e baixos daqueles matos. (RSV 244)

(And as we continuously kept a wide lookout from those hilltops to see if we could discover people or a village ... we [finally] saw smoke rising from the other side of the river ... for it had been four days, with incessant rain, that we did not cease our march, without road or route, across the peaks and valleys of those jungles.)

The dynamic of depth and height plays itself out in the marchers' attempt to gain a cartographic perspective on the landscape of hardship, to situate themselves within a geographical space in a way that identifies desired coordinates, such as other people or villages. The uses of *caminho* (road) and *carreira* (route) here are telling. While the terms are used synonymously, Perestrelo indicates the absence of a predictable or governable road or path with an implied point of destination. *Caminho* and *carreira* are also nautical terms, indicating the route of a ship or the overall trajectory of a maritime voyage. The nautical route has been transferred to land, but just as shipwreck does violence to the completion of a sea voyage, so does the aftermath of shipwreck make it difficult to trace discernible and repeatable courses across land. When castaways walk or plod through space, the pedestrian travel bears a cartographic intentionality: it is the only way to traverse and track space, and therefore to map, however provisionally, the arena of survival.

Most of the time, the concerted act of *caminhar* fails in that it does not provide a working knowledge of the landscape or location but merely heightens disorientation and the reality of being lost. The regular scaling of peaks by members of the company, as opposed to those who prefer to remain at a lower vantage point on the slopes and follow the course of the river, dramatizes the attempts to gain an Apollonian, cartographic perspective on the expanses of Africa. Such a perspective would have been of primary interest to the cartographer Perestrelo. The lower perspective along the banks of the river corresponds to a position on an itinerary map, which lacks the expansive surveillance of the Apollonian gaze.[10] Perestrelo suggests that he and his companions attempt to regard Africa as a map, and that part of the trials of survival is to read that map correctly and to plot coordinates. The frustrated attempts at cartographic observation lead the author to remark at one point that "caímos no erro que fizéramos em deixar a fralda do mar, porque além de nos parecer que ele próprio se mostrava mais doméstico e conversável para nossas necessidades, que as asperezas do sertão, achámos também pelos penedos . . . muitas ostras e mexilhões" (we made the mistake we had made before leaving the shore, because apart from seeming to us that it was very much more domestic and amenable for our needs than the hardships of the interior, we also found among the rocks . . . many oysters and mussels; RSV 249–50). In the experience of disaster Perestrelo finds the presence of the ocean more domestic (it is more historically and cartographically familiar) than the South African wilderness.

There is, then, a negotiation of geographic space in the narrative of the *S. Bento* and a shuttling between cartographic specificity and disorientation. Much of the drama of this tale is the result of the constantly frustrated attempts to move in one, discernible direction owing to a landscape that shifts inhospitably between height and abyss. The survival march through southeastern Africa fails to map or trace repeatable routes because those attempts are deprived of an organizing, Apollonian perspective and are beset by a multitude of disorienting contingencies. In a sense, until they are rescued at the narrative's end, the crew and passengers of the *S. Bento* are always in the depths, *no fundo*.

As Perestrelo paints it, hostile African space is always an embodied space punctuated by the presence of (European) bodies, and it emerges into narrative view partly because of this embodiedness. Shipwreck leaves in its wake an insistent corporeality, unavoidable with the regularity of distressing bodily experiences. Perestrelo's expression "recear em extremo" (to fear in the extreme) establishes the shipwreck experience as one of pushing limits. The first expression of shipwreck as a limit case is the immediate fracturing of the community by the wreck of the ship. Individuals are on their own to sink or swim, and the collectivity of a seaborne vessel is violently fractured. Community can be reestablished, but it is characteristically tenuous and splintered by individual necessities. The individual person *in extremis* seeks the safety and solace of the company of fellow passengers while forced into the solitude of unprecedented fear.

This embodied space of wreck and survival becomes apparent as dawn of the second day on African soil breaks:

E tanto que ela começou de esclarecer, partimos caminho da praia a buscar alguma roupa com que nos reparássemos, a qual achámos toda coberta de corpos mortos, com tão feios e disformes gestos que davam bem evidentes mostras das penosas mortes que tiveram, jazendo uns por riba, outros por baixo daqueles penedos. (RSV 234–35)

(And as soon as morning began to break, we set off from the beach in search of any clothing we might find to cover ourselves. The beach was completely covered in dead bodies, so disfigured and appalling that the terrible deaths they had suffered were very evident; some lay above the rocks, and others below.)

This is the initial, haphazard placement of bodies in the African landscape. The locations above and below the rocks on shore initiates a conceit of the body in sunken or lowered positions that is a physical correlate of a state of abjection. As the tale nears its end, Perestrelo calls attention to the degraded state of the castaways, who, after walking in circles for weeks, were famished and reduced to skin and bones, where each survivor "representava a imagem da morte muito mais propriamente que coisa viva" (looked more accurately like the image of death than anything alive; RSV 296). Throughout Perestrelo's pages, as throughout those of other shipwreck narratives, an abject or abyssal, disoriented subject—one problematic inflection of the expansionist subject—comes into view through the depiction of mangled or tormented bodies, another of the consequences of the "unfortunate hour of shipwreck."

The spaces through which the survivors move, in addition to being defined by insistent contingency, are also partially defined by sound. These shipwreck spaces are a soundscape. A disastrous sonority suffuses Perestrelo's story in which sounds and an aural consciousness perform different functions. Wes Folkerth notes in his study of Shakespeare that "the acoustic environment is always experienced within specific cultural contexts";[11] in shipwreck narrative, that cultural context is expansionist seafaring and empire. Bruce R. Smith avers that a soundscape consists "not just of the environment that the listener attends to but of the listener-*in*-the environment."[12] I would like to think about how Perestrelo listens and hears in the environment of shipwreck.

Perestrelo inscribes an aural attentiveness into his account. Survival can depend on sounds. The first such moment occurs when all on board the foundering ship are convinced that their demise is imminent:

> [P]edíamos perdão uns aos outros, despedindo-se cada um de seus parentes e amigos com tanta lástima como quem esperava serem aquelas as derradeiras palavras que teriam neste mundo. Nisto andava tudo ... ouvindo-se também de quando em quando algumas palavras lastimosas. (RSV 228)
>
> (Everyone begged forgiveness from each other, each of us saying farewell to parents and friends with the heartache of one who expects those to be the last words uttered in this world. This was the sole occupation of everyone ... and, from time to time, many pitiful words were heard.)

The use of the impersonal "ouvindo-se" (were heard) identifies a generalized, nonindividualized hearing, as the sinking ship was permeated by human speech, the "pitiful words" Perestrelo chose not to record. There is in this moment only a certain inflection of speaking and hearing, a shipboard sound of despair and sorrow, wordless words. Perestrelo's ear hears only a mournful din. Since hearing is one manifestation of the body that absorbs, the author seems to suggest, by not identifying the words heard, the sound inundated the passengers involuntarily like the waves that swamped the decks and threatened to send the ship to the bottom. Hearing is one form of forced passivity that is characteristic of the experiences of wreck and survival, much like being acted upon by the hostile forces of nature.

Although, according to Perestrelo, God's intervention temporarily saves the imperiled ship, it eventually breaks apart, leaving each person to survive by swimming to the relative safety of the shore. In these moments of despair, Perestrelo notes that "nos iam as ondas botando à terra, soando neste tempo, por todas as partes, um confuso, alto e miserável grito, com que todos a uma voz pedíamos a Nosso Senhor misericórdia" (the waves pushed us toward shore, while everywhere there resounded a confused, shrill, and miserable cry, as all of us with one voice called on Our Lord for mercy; RSV 230). The soundscape of disaster is now an anguished, anonymous, and ubiquitous chorus, a diffuse echoing and reverberation (indicated by the verb *soar*, "to [re-]sound") that attends the futility of maritime labor. Perestrelo terms this confused and chaotic resonance a *pranto* (lament):

Acontecido tamanho desastre, os que dele nos doíamos e estávamos de uma e outra parte do rio, levantando um pranto que atroava as concavidades daquela ribeira, com muita tristeza e lacrimosos soluços nos espalhámos pela praia. (RSV 262)

(With such a disaster which afflicted us all, we on both sides of the river raised a mournful cry that resonated in the caves of the shore, and with much sadness and pitiful sobs we dispersed along the shore.)

The relationship of survivor to landscape in the experience of shipwreck is in part sonic, as the spaces of Africa and the seashore become a sounding board of suffering, a dispersal and loss of bodies accompanied by a collective and anonymous dispersal of voice, like the legend of Echo.

One of the more dramatic moments of shipwreck sonority occurs at night once the survivors have reached land. They hear strange voices in the night:

Posto que o conselho do sábio seja que as coisas de admiração e espanto, ainda que verdadeiras, sejam antes de passar caladas, que de contar com risco de serem mal cridas, atrevo-me a dizer uma, pelas muitas testemunhas com que posso alegar: e é que, assim esta noite, depois que fomos recolhidos, como a outra atrás passada e as mais que neste lugar estivemos, quando era já bem cerrada a noite, ouvíamos claramente brados altos no lugar onde se a nau quebrara, que por muitas vezes gritavam, dizendo "A bombordo, a estibordo, arriba," e outras muitas palavras confusas, que não entendíamos, assim e da maneira que nós fazíamos quando, já alagados, vínhamos na força da tormenta que nos ali fez encalhar. O que isto fosse, nunca se pôde saber de certo, somente suspeitámos que ou a nós se representava aquilo nos ouvidos, pelos trazermos atroados dos brados que continuamente naquele tempo ouvíamos, ou eram alguns espíritos malignos que festejavam o que de alguns ali poderiam alcançar. . . . Mas qualquer destas que fosse, o certo é que foi, ou ao menos a todos pareceu sê-lo: porque, posto que ao princípio cada um cuidasse que a ele só se representava aquele espantoso som, e pela dificuldade que nisso havia não cresse ser verdade, a continuação do tempo fez perguntar uns aos outros se ouviam o mesmo; e afirmando todos que sim, assentámos, segundo as horas, escuro e tempestade das noites, ser alguma coisa das que dito tenho. (RSV 237–38)

(Though the wise man's counsel is that marvelous and fearful things, even if true, should be passed over in silence since in their telling they might be disbelieved, I will dare to tell one of them, given that there were so many witnesses to vouch for it: so it was that that night, after we had gone to bed [like the previous night and all the others while we were in that place], we clearly heard, well into the wee hours, voices shouting from the place where the ship had wrecked. Over and over they cried "to starboard! to larboard! aloft!" and other confused words we couldn't understand, all in the manner we had cried when, already foundering, we were forced to land there by the force of the storm. Whatever that was was never known for sure; we suspected that the noises were something we already had in our ears since we always heard cries and screams during that time, or they were evil spirits who rejoiced at those who had fallen under their spell.... But whatever the cause was, it is certain that it occurred, or at least so it seemed. For although each person at first thought that he was the only who heard this strange sound, and because it was so strange could not believe it to be true, as time went on all were asking one another if they heard the same thing. Everyone said yes, and given the hour and the darkness and storminess of the night, we concluded it was a result of one of the causes I have already mentioned.)

The ghostly voices in the night are the voices of the doomed passengers and many of the survivors, a sonic aftereffect of wreck, or an "acoustic ghost," as Dominic Pettman might call it.[13] What is noteworthy about Perestrelo's description of the disembodied voices, the "espantoso som," is that they are "coisas de admiração e espanto" (wonderful and fearful things), aural mirabilia. The ears, and not the eyes, are the site of the marvelous, the fearful, and the wondrous.

Perestrelo is unable to make sense of these voices; he and his companions never arrive at a clear understanding of the auditory phenomenon. The chaotic, sensorial environment of wreck strains the credibility of Perestrelo's narrative as much as it frustrates the attempt to listen (as distinct from hearing), to exercise aural discernment in the soundscape of the African shoreline. What Perestrelo implicitly addresses here is the discriminatory capacity of his—and his companions'—ear. Perestrelo uses the verb *representar* (to represent) to characterize the relationship of sound to the ear. The ear is not simply receiving sound passively, since there is a cognitive effort to interpret that sound. The "representation" of sound suggests that there is a problematic, mimetic issue at hand—an instance of aural mimesis—that Perestrelo wants to record. While Perestrelo is able to discern a few words ("A bombordo, a estibordo, arriba") there are many other "palavras confusas" (confused words) he is unable to make out. In *On Things Heard*, a short treatise on the production of sounds by humans, animals, and objects, with comments on the scale of clarity and distinctness of different kinds of sounds, pseudo-Aristotle links levels of exertion in speaking to the clarity of the voice:

> For voices which are rather harsh and slightly confused and have not any very marked clearness are the fitting accompaniment of outbreaks of passion and of advancing years, and at the same time, owing to their intensity, they are less under control; for what is produced by violent exertion is not easily regulated, for it is difficult to increase or decrease the strength of the sound at will.[14]

In the Aristotelian tradition, as Susan Boynton et al. explain, violence is inherent to sound,[15] so the physical exertion of the maritime labor Perestrelo identifies as the context of the phantasmal clamor ties the violence of shipwreck to the violence of sound. Ancient grammarians such as Donatus proposed a distinction between sounds "capable of being represented in writing (because they are 'distinct'), and those that are not (because they are indistinct or 'confused')."[16] This distinction corresponds to two categories of human voice, *vox distincta* and *vox confusa*.[17] Even if the erudite Perestrelo had no direct knowledge of the grammatical tradition, his "palavras confusas" aligns with the distinction between distinct and inarticulate speech, which is here part of the soundscape of maritime disaster.

The observation that the ghostly voices are the voices of the passengers makes a claim about the land- and soundscape the survivors inhabit. If many of the speakers are still living, there is a temporal and bodily discontinuity in the space of wreck: voices resound on a sort of delay as disaster separates speakers from their own articulations. Smith notes that "as the inhabitants of a certain geographical space, a *speech* community also constitutes an *acoustic* community."[18] The narrative provides witness to a (Western) speech community in a foreign locale. The spectral voices are the sonic debris of shipwreck. Put another way, speaking becomes temporarily a form of loss, a leftover.

The nocturnal echoes are part of a larger crisis that shipwreck visits on time, space, and systems of order. The words with no speakers begin to lose their intelligibility as the words themselves signal a breaking apart of a discourse of (triumphant) imperialism. The ghostly voices reflect a loss of control over nautical technology and constitute a dimension of the disturbing experience of shipwreck in that the survivors seem to haunt themselves. The imbrication of language and sound in imperial culture is not limited to this narrative, however. As I have argued elsewhere, Pero Vaz de Caminha's *Carta* (Letter, 1500) on the finding of Brazil by the fleet of Pedro Álvares Cabral contains references to the sounds of spoken language in the arena of Euro-Amerindian encounter. Spoken Portuguese, as opposed to the "chatter" of Tupi, establishes a linguistic dimension to the sphere of imperial power.[19] In Perestrelo's spectral scenario, the coherence of the sphere of language momentarily dissolves, in that the Portuguese language itself becomes a ghost in the geography of empire. If the phantasmal voices are one dimension of shipwreck under an imperial aegis, the attention to voice and acoustics to maintain the integrity of the survival community is another. As the castaways seek asylum in the dryness of the jungle one night, they keep track of one another by the sounds of their voices: "[E] fazendo um corpo com as vozes, ao som delas nos tornámos a ajuntar perto do pé da rocha" (We called out and made a body of our voices, and by the sound of them gathered together near the rock; RSV 248). Cries of pain as the survivors trod the harsh landscape serve the same purpose. The maintenance of community—always threatened by the difficult terrain or indigenous peoples—can thus be predicated on acoustics and the deliberate act of listening (the selective use of the ear) and not simply hearing as a survival tactic.[20]

CAMÕES'S MARITIME ACOUSTICS

From the sounds and soundscape of shipwreck in Perestrelo's tale we move to canto VI of *Os Lusíadas*, which narrates the final leg of Vasco da Gama's voyage across the Indian Ocean and the sighting of Calicut. With the exception of the first four stanzas, this canto takes place entirely at sea, the only such canto with this distinction. It is also a noisy canto, filled with human and nonhuman sounds and reverberations. It is a canto of ascents and descents, of movements from the supernal to the abyssal. The various scenarios narrated throughout canto VI move from the seafloor to the celestial heights, and the traversal of vertical space is one of the canto's organizing conceits. Camões inscribes a contemplation on the symbolic nature of the sea here, and the canto ultimately presents a new vision of the ocean. From its initial stanzas, canto VI bears testimony to a new understanding of the oceanic worldspace traversed by Gaman vessels in the poetic logic of *Os Lusíadas*.

As the canto begins, Gama is impatient to recommence his voyage after his stay in Melinde, despite the hospitable celebrations and banquets offered by the king. Gama's eagerness to depart emblematizes the restlessness of the expansionist enterprise itself and the irresistible call to the sea. Once Gama is en route, an infuriated and desperate Bacchus descends from Olympus to the sea as he realizes that heaven was "determinado / De fazer de Lisboa nova Roma" (determined to make Lisbon a new Rome; VI.7.i-ii). As the mythic conqueror of India, Bacchus is the foe and antagonist of the Portuguese, broodingly envious of the seafarers' potential to eclipse his fame. The god attempted unsuccessfully to destroy the Portuguese fleet in canto II by inciting hatred and distrust of the Lusitanian mariners among the inhabitants of Mombassa; now comes his final attempt to obstruct the Portuguese expedition. Bacchus asks Neptune and other sea deities to unleash a storm to sink Gama's fleet. The battle for control of the ocean looms.

In stanza 8, Bacchus descends to earth and enters the sea on his mission to secure the allyship of Neptune, and in so doing casts this canto into its oceanic mode. Camões describes Bacchus's watery descent:

> No mais interno fundo das profundas
> Cavernas altas, onde o mar se esconde,
> Lá donde as ondas saem furibundas,
> Quando às iras do vento o mar responde,
> Neptuno mora e moram as jucundas
> Nereidas e outros Deuses do mar, onde
> As águas campo deixam às cidades
> Que habitam estas húmidas Deidades. (VI.8)

(In the hiddenmost recesses of the deepest caverns where the sea hides, there from which the waves issue with a great fury when the sea responds to the anger of the winds, live Neptune and the delightful Nereids and other gods of the sea, where the waters make space for the cities inhabited by these wet deities.)

In these eight verses, Camões infuses the narrative with aquatic depth and sonority. Haroldo de Campos was one of the first readers to note the onomatopoetic quality of the phoneme *nd*, which pervades the stanza and evokes the sound of waves.[21] Occurring at the moment of Bacchus's descent into the sea, the onomatopoeia conjures not only the sound of the sea but the sea as heard from beneath the surface. Camões plunges the narrative underwater as Bacchus dives. The repeated *nd* enlists the ear—it is the rhythmic pounding of the waves heard from underwater, the heartbeat of the sea. So within the first stanzas we are not only *on* the sea but *in* it as Bacchus descends to the bottom. In a study of the ocean in Shakespeare, Dan Brayton argues that "the depths represent an otherness that cannot be intellectually or linguistically domesticated."[22] By contrast, the incursion into the Camonian depths initiates a process of transformation of the sea in that, with the eventual failure of Bacchus's plot, the abyss becomes part of the Portuguese aquatic imagination, a symbolic appropriation of all oceanic space, horizontal and vertical, that Camões's poem records. This notional domestication of the deep is a spatial conceit with a pronounced aural dimension. Sound performs an adhesive function as it binds together a world-encompassing, maritime gnosis. Camões claims the totality of marine space as the medium of a new historical and epistemological regime. Hearing the ocean from beneath is the first step in displacing the ancient gods from the sea, the representatives of old configurations of knowledge about the ocean prior to the navigational advancements in knowledge of the world made possible by Portuguese seafaring.

With Bacchus's aquatic descent, Camões reveals a similarity between the god and the Portuguese, for Bacchus, too, is a discoverer of unknown realms ("Descobre o fundo nunca descoberto / As areias ali de prata fina" [(Bacchus) reveals the ocean bottom never discovered; the sands there are of fine silver; VI.9.i-ii]), much as the Portuguese are discoverers who sail the "mares nunca dantes navegados" (the seas never before navigated), announced in the third line of the poem. There is a melancholic sympathy between Bacchus and the angry sea that will soon assail Gama's fleet. Throughout the poem

Camões refers to the undomesticated sea as "mar irado" (irate sea), an expression that invests the worldwide ocean with a furious and melancholic disposition prior to its submission to Portuguese governance. Much as the Portuguese supplant Bacchus as the mythic conqueror of India, so too do they banish the old maritime gods of the oceanic depths when the attempt to destroy Gama's fleet fails.

When Neptune agrees to convene the demersal council at Bacchus's behest, Triton summons the marine deities to the sea god's palace by blowing on his conch shell:

> Na mão a grande concha retorcida
> Que trazia, com força já tocava;
> A voz grande, canora, foi ouvida
> Por todo o mar, que longe retumbava. (VI.19.i-iv)

(A huge, twisted conch [Triton] held in his hand, blowing on it with all his might; the great, bellicose sound was heard through the whole sea, resounding far and wide.)

Camões invests Triton's conch blast with the status of voice (*voz*). The shell speaks and reverberates through the whole sea. In the convocatory shell trumpet there is a speaking and an implied hearing. The reverberation of the sound through the world sea recalls the voice of Adamastor in canto V, which seems to emanate "do mar profundo" (from the deep sea; V.40.vi), much as it also recalls Camões's own voice when the poet states in the opening stanzas, "[C]antando espalharei por toda parte" (By singing I will reach the world's every part; I.2.vii). Both Camões's voice and Triton's call sonically travel the sea.[23] The poet uses the same adjective, *canora*, to describe Triton's voice and the exalted, booming register of epic voice that he seeks from the Tagus Muses. The oceans are consequently pathways of sound and voice and an arena of contest between Gama, his crew, and the marine gods. All of these individual or collective speakers stake their own claims: Camões claims the ocean, once and for all, as the basis of national and poetic identity infused with a Christian, imperialist ethos, and Triton inaugurates the final attempt of the pagan gods to retain the sea as their own domain. Oceanically situated and perpetrated sound is proprietorial because it makes an assertion of ownership. There is no mistaking that, despite the *governo do mar* being incrementally realized by Gama's fleet across the ocean's surface, the depths are still, at the beginning of canto VI, under the governance of the old gods. Recall that at the end of his encounter with Gama in canto V, Adamastor departs "cum medonho choro" (with a terrifying cry; V.60.i), and "cum sonoro / Bramido muito longe o mar soou" (with a thunderous wail that resounded far through the sea; V.60.iii-iv). The sea-wide resonance that accompanies Adamastor's disappearance becomes indistinguishable from the roar of the ocean itself as the monster, in a dying gesture, recognizes the Portuguese entrance into the until-then hallowed and guarded oceanic realms. Given Camões's description of Triton as a "mancebo grande, negro e feio" (enormous youth, black and ugly; VI.16.vii) with a monstrous and grotesque appearance, it is possible to think of Triton as a submarine version of sorts of Adamastor, who equally seeks to safeguard a marine sovereignty.

The conch blast, then, announces and consolidates a sense of place and unity of purpose if we adopt "sense of place" as Steven Feld and Keith H. Basso propose the idea when they note that soundscapes and acoustics are constitutive elements of place.[24] The political association of sea deities is such a unity of purpose, since they assemble for a single objective: to hear Bacchus's petition, which the god begins by addressing Ocean: "E tu, padre Oceano, que rodeias / O Mundo universal e o tens cercado" (And you, Father Ocean, who surround and encircle the universal world; VI.27.v-vi). Through the vengeance-seeking deity, Camões acknowledges an antiquated, oceanic dominion of the pagan gods and a cartographic fallacy—the globe-encircling river Ocean of medieval T-O maps. Gama's journey exposes this long-lived conception as obsolete. Bacchus construes the Portuguese intrusion into the maritime realm as a sacrilege that threatens to raise them to the level of the gods and to relegate the gods to human status, a sort of euhemerism in reverse. The god of wine succeeds in his petition, and the collective resolution among the oceanic deities is that there will be no more mariners on the sea. We read that Proteus is on the verge of making a pronouncement ("algũa profunda profecia" [some profound prophecy; VI.36.iv]) but is prevented from doing so by Aeolus's unleashing of the winds. The unspoken prophecy, whatever it was going to be, originates in the marine deep. It is an aborted rising up of fate from the saltwater abyss, but given that the observation directly follows the gods' resolution that there be no more sailors on the sea, the prophecy might well have contravened this resolution by forecasting the ultimate destiny of the Portuguese as governors of the sea, perhaps a prolepsis of oceanic sovereignty as represented by the *máquina do mundo* episode in canto X. If this is so then Proteus's interrupted announcement would have been "profound" in the sense of a teleological fulfillment, one of the semantic dimensions of the Camonian *profundo*.

Next, the narrative suddenly rises to the surface, from the council in the submarine depths to the night watch on Gama's flagship. To fend off sleep, the crew decides to tell a story: Leonardo (hapless in love, who will eventually find erotic fulfillment on the Isle of Love) suggests a love story, but Fernão Veloso insists that the story be bellicose to reflect the nature of their India-seeking mission. Veloso tells the story of the Doze de Inglaterra (Twelve of England), a medieval tale of chivalry in which twelve Portuguese knights travel to England to defend the honor of twelve English maidens. Veloso's recitation of the tale on the eve of Gama's arrival in India is significant. As Sara V. Torres argues, the tale assigns ethical and chivalric qualities to sailors, extends chivalry "to new naval and mercantile contexts," and is a locus of chivalric values in the epic poem.[25] If we understand Veloso's story as infixing (medieval) chivalric values into the naval and mercantile world of the poem, those values are nonetheless secondary to the practice of seamanship. Veloso's tale is, after all, an entertainment, an imaginative incursion into a distant past in order to while away the dead hours of the night. If the story is inspiring to the sailor-listeners—certainly plausible given its celebration of Portuguese chivalric prowess—then it is also appealing in its past temporality, removed from the circumstances and demands of onboard duties. And it is precisely a juxtaposition of temporalities that brings Veloso's story to an end: the sudden, shrill sound of the boatswain's whistle jolts the crew back into the present as strengthening winds announce the onset of a storm:

> Eis o mestre, que olhando os ares anda,
> O apito toca: acordam, despertando,
> Os marinheiros dhũa e de doutra banda.
> E, porque o vento vinha refrescando,
> Os traquetes das gáveas tomar manda.

"Alerta (disse) estai, que o vento crece
Daquela nuvem negra que aparece!" (VI.70.ii-viii)

(Here, now, the boatswain, who was watching the skies, blows his whistle; the mariners quickly awake and spring to their posts on all sides. And, because the wind was freshening, the boatswain orders the men to reef the fore-topsails. "Get to it," he cried, "the wind is growing stronger out of that black cloud!")

The scenario becomes one of urgency and clamor:

O céu fere com gritos nisto a gente,
Cum súbito temor e desacordo;
Que, no romper da vela, a nau pendente
Toma grão suma de água pelo bordo.
"Alija (disse o mestre rijamente),
Alija tudo ao mar, não falte acordo!
Vão outros dar à bomba, não cessando;
À bomba, que nos imos alagando!" (VI.72)

(In this terror and tumult everyone pierces the sky with cries and shouts; for as the sail was shredded, the keeling vessel shipped much water. "Lighten the ship," the boatswain sternly ordered, "everything overboard, everyone together! Some of you to the pumps, keep at it; to the pumps! We're foundering!")

The cries that lacerate the heavens are a sudden, auditory thrust upward, followed by a quick descent back to the deck of the ship with the orders of the boatswain. The sound of the whistle in stanza 70 marks the beginning of the storm episode and auditorily foregrounds it. The whistle is an aural vocative that points to a moment of hermeneutic importance. It compels us to pay attention to sound as sound, to reimmerse ourselves in a soundscape that the poet builds in this canto. Such a sonic imperative aligns with Angela Leighton's observation that "the sound effects of poems are part of what they are about."[26] The mariner's whistle also exercises a central role in the storm scene of Vicente's *Triunfo do Inverno*. Like Camões's storm, Vicente's begins with the whistle:

Apito: Pi pi pi pii.[27]

The whistle sounds regularly throughout the storm portion of the play. Vicente accords it the discursive status of a character, indicated by the designation *apito* and by the fact that none of the other characters in the scene are identified as blowing it. The *apito*, in the flow of dialogue, possesses its own voice. This is consonant with Gil Vicente's practice in other plays of granting nonhuman sounds their own place in formal, theatrical speech. In Vicentine theater, dogs bark, cats meow, and mariners' whistles blow in the regulated metrics of *redondilha maior*. The infixing of nonhuman sounds into the prosody of theatrical speaking imbues those sounds with an enunciative status. They are manners of speaking, like their human counterparts, in Vicente's aurally verisimilitudinous world. In the *Triunfo do Inverno*, the whistle functions not only as a warning of danger but also calls attention to the tragicomic human interaction with nature through the mediation of maritime labor. Vicente's lampooning of nautical knowledge and competence makes the repeatedly heard *apito* something of a sonic punchline, which accentuates the comedic, seaborne mayhem. It can be understood, and heard, as a funny, not alarming, sound.

Scholars typically note that the storm sequence in *Os Lusíadas*, initiated by the whistle and lasting for twenty-one stanzas, rehearses a commonplace in epic poetry and has many antecedents.[28] Hélio J. S. Alves relates the storm in classical texts to the formation and demonstration of virtue in the epic hero, while Michael Murrin reads it as a conglomerate of accounts of storms during Gama's voyage and the Southwest Monsoon.[29] Yet in Camões's *poetica tempestas*, the storm more immediately participates in the recently emerged genre of Portuguese shipwreck literature. The maritime chaos, the desperate maneuvering of the endangered ship, and the references to nautical architecture could all be taken directly from the pages of the *História trágico-marítima*. The shipwreck genre inflects canto VI's storm with a pronounced, contemporary Portuguese literary resonance.

Sonically, the storm is the most cacophonous episode of the poem. As it begins, after the urgent piping of the whistle the mainsail is shredded by the wind. Passengers and crew cry out in terror, and the continuous presence of the perilous winds puts the sound of wind everywhere. As the storm rages, the halcyon birds sing their woeful song, while thunder peals and lightning flashes. The waves of Neptune, and the ships on them, seem to reach the clouds one instant while heading toward the very bowels of the deep the next. If, for example, in the cries (*gritos*) of the crew we find another instance of maritime labor "in its noisy manifestation" as a confirmation of the "common sailor's centrality to the entire process" of imperial expansion and national definition,[30] in this episode it is the sonic sphere of tempestuous, maritime noise that is of importance. David Novak reminds us that the word "noise" is etymologically linked to ships, since the Latin root is *nausea* from the Greek *naus* (ship): "The reference to seasickness captures the basic disorientation of the term: noise is a context of sensory experience, but also a moving subject of circulation, of sound and listening, that emerges in the process of navigating the world and its differences."[31] Camões's noisy episode stages a contentious interaction between gods, nature, technology, and humans. It is a final battle that marks a shift in orders of knowledge about the world that the poem celebrates. For Ramachandran, "the crossing of the oceans from Atlantic to Indian is a national victory for Portugal, but more importantly it represents a conceptual breakthrough in global understanding."[32] This epochal turn in part motivates the poetic representation of dizzying shifts in perspective, from the heights to the abyss as the storm rages. At one point, for example, Camões directs the focus of his narrative downward to the dolphins that seek refuge from the tempest in underwater caves, or describes the sands of the seafloor (following Ovid) that are stirred to the surface in the roiling waves.[33] Here is both a storm and a seaquake. While there is no katabasis in the poem following the classical model of a descent to the underworld, there is a visual, submarine katabasis with this plunge into the depths and the arenaceous upsurge from the ocean floor. The descent acquires a psychological dimension when, in despair, Vasco da Gama sends a prayer heavenward in his plight—a dramatic, discursive movement from the abyssal to the supernal. In his prayer, Gama refers to Paul's shipwreck, and this links the present affliction on the sea to biblical instances of maritime despair. As Rodrigo Toromoreno has argued, one of the likely subtexts of Gama's supplication is Psalm 130, the "De profundis."[34] For Toromoreno, Gama's personal voice becomes the public or collective voice of the Portuguese.[35] Gama's prayer is another voyage, this one from the depths of despair to the heavens. Voice is a traveler of vertical space. The dynamic of movement upward from the deep is the movement that consolidates fate and a new historical order.[36]

This consolidation becomes evident in the manner that the storm subsides. Following Gama's prayer, the noise (howling wind, humming sails, and thunder) continues briefly until Venus, suspecting that the storm is one of Bacchus's machinations, "dece ao mar aberto" (descends to the open sea; VI.86.v) and commands her nymphs to adorn themselves with roses and make personal entreaties to the gods. The supplications work, and as the storm abates, India appears before the fleet: "Já a menham clara dava nos outeiros / Por onde o Ganges murmurando soa" (Now the bright morning broke over the hilltops, through which the murmuring of the Ganges echoes; VI.92.i-ii). The land of India enters the poem visually and sonically. The sound of the gentle flow of Indian water is aural testament to a Portuguese, expansionist inhabitation of an aquatic worldspace.

The sonority that pervades canto VI, then, engages our ears as a way of foregrounding a pivotal moment in the poem and in history. The sonorous, acoustic dimensions of *Os Lusíadas*'s water worlds create an immediacy of experience, a now-ness, a supplanting and rendering obsolete of a fossilized epistemological past. The Camonian sea is noisy—this is the sea of epic contest, the privileged locus in which gods, humans, and nature meet and clash. Following canto VI, the *mar irado* (irate sea) becomes domesticated and calm. The storm marks a transition in the conceptual flow of the poem. In Virgil and Lucretius, for instance, storms "allude to physical processes on the largest scale and to the most general aspects of the relation between man and nature."[37] The storm here might well be considered a mise-en-scène of the Portuguese negotiation of nature and destiny as symbolized by the Greco-Roman gods. In commenting on the spatial dimension of Camões's poem, Klein argues that

> the poetic narrative of the historic voyage posits a basic epistemological premise at its outset, which is one of abstract but uncertain knowledge: the Portuguese seafarers in the poem know even before their ships are launched that there is a world out there beyond the oceans. . . . The set-up already resembles a sea-chart in kind: there is a framework, only no content; a hypothesis, but no certainty. Navigating within this imagined map means to fill in its blank surface as you go along, not to have your

course readily charted at the start of the voyage. The most prominent cartographic narrative in *The Lusiads* . . . follows just this logic of completion through piecemeal accumulation—a slow, inductive approach to an imaginary state of final plenitude.[38]

Katharina N. Piechocki studies cartographic ideas in relation to Gama's passage into the Indian Ocean as one of the scientific advances recorded in the poem.[39] These cartographically inflected studies claim a shift in orders of knowledge that Gama's journey represents. There is a quasi-protean transformation of the world, a new outline of knowledge and space delineated by Gama's ships and his seaborne enterprise.

ACKNOWLEDGMENTS

Over the years it took to write this book, many people helped and encouraged the project in a number of ways. I initially brought several ideas from these pages to the classroom, first at the University of Toronto and then at Harvard University, and my students at both universities unfailingly provided insight, clarification, counterarguments, and inspiration. I tested ideas—rejecting some and honing others—in conference papers, lectures, and workshops. I thank the following individuals for their invitations to present work in progress at their respective institutions: Roland Greene, Stanford University; Pedro Schacht Pereira, The Ohio State University; Michael Armstrong-Roche, Wesleyan University; the graduate students of the Department of Romance Languages and Literatures at the University of Michigan for the invitation to speak at the Annual Charles F. Fraker Conference in 2010; the Center for Medieval and Renaissance Studies at the University of California, Los Angeles, for the invitation to deliver the Rebecca D. Catz Memorial Lecture in 2011; the Center for Reformation and Renaissance Studies, University of Toronto; K. David Jackson, Yale University; Joachim Küpper, Dahlem Humanities Center, Freie Universität Berlin; Daniel J. Paracka, Division of Global Affairs, Kennesaw State University; Robert Davidson, Director of the Northrop Frye Centre, Victoria College at the University of Toronto, for the invitation to deliver the Annual Northrop Frye Centre Lecture in 2017; Marina Brownlee, Princeton University; Neil Safier, Brown University, for the invitation to deliver the 2018 Annual Gulbenkian Vasco da Gama Lecture at the John Carter Brown

Library; Antonio Arraiza Rivera, Wellesley College; and António Matias Coelho, Casa-Memória de Camões in Constância, Portugal. To all of these friends and colleagues, my profound thanks.

Apart from these welcome institutional occasions, many individuals have supported this project with their interest, inquiries, and enthusiasm. They have been sources of scholarly stamina with their intellectual generosity. At Harvard, I have been fortunate to rely on the friendship and astute critical sensibilities of Daniel Aguirre-Oteiza, Homi Bhabha, Bruno Carvalho, Mary Gaylord, Sean Gilsdorf, Luis Girón-Negrón, Mariano Siskind, and Diana Sorensen, all of whom took an interest in aspects of this book and offered encouragement and feedback. Maria Aida Batista, Rafael Burgos-Mirabal, James F. Burke, David Fernández, João R. Figueiredo, Nicholas Jones, Manuela Marujo, Kenneth Mills, Ricardo Padrón, Nancy Ratey, Dylon Robbins, Ricardo Sternberg, Rodrigo Toromoreno, and Ted Young, in one way or another, provided support or references that drove completion of the book forward. The librarians of Robarts Library and the Thomas Fisher Rare Book Library at the University of Toronto, and of Widener and Houghton libraries at Harvard, cheerfully assisted with research. In the final stages of manuscript preparation prior to production, I relied on the efficient help of Caio Cesar Esteves de Souza, a doctoral candidate at Harvard, who smoothed many technical issues. I continue to draw ideas and inspiration from the learning collaboration that began in 1978 with Wayne J. Redenbarger. In recent years, until his passing in 2019, my graduate school teacher and doctoral supervisor Joaquim-Francisco Coelho asked just the right questions about the book at just the right times. Jill Coelho and Anita Coelho have offered friendly hospitality and dinners that have done much for my spirits. I'm very grateful to Vincent Barletta and Steve Mentz, the readers of the manuscript for the University of Chicago Press, for their thoughtful, generous, and critically rigorous evaluations. Their recommendations for revision helped me improve arguments and avoid blunders; they will recognize most of their suggestions and ideas in these pages. Any infelicities of interpretation or fact are mine alone. Randy Petilos of the Press has been a superb editorial guide, and has encouraged this book from the moment I first mentioned it to him some years ago. My late father, Josiah H. Blackmore II, had a love of ships and the sea that inspired almost every sentence of these chapters. Conversations with my mother, Joyce, have revealed many fun details about Dad's Navy service and seafaring years. My sisters, Anne Paris and Judith Dann, figure in the book's existence, too, and the newest members of the family, Cole and Claire Wessels, are happy reminders of the positive force of the future.

To one and all, *muitos abraços*.

Early versions of some of the arguments in this book appeared as follows: portions of chapter 1 as "Portuguese Scenes of the Senses, Medieval and Early Modern," in *Beyond Sight: Engaging the Senses in Iberian Literatures and Cultures, 1200–1750*, edited by Ryan D. Giles and Steven Wagschal (Toronto: University of Toronto Press, 2018), reproduced by permission; portions of chapter 3 as "The Shipwrecked Swimmer: Camões's Maritime Subject," *Modern Philology* 109.3 (2012): 312–25, © 2012 by The University of Chicago, all rights reserved; and portions of chapter 4 as "The Sunken Voice: Depth and Submersion in Two Early Modern Portuguese Accounts of Maritime Peril," in *Shipwreck in Art and Literature: Images and Interpretations from Antiquity to the Present Day*, edited by Carl Thompson (New York: Routledge, 2014), reproduced by permission of Taylor and Francis Group, LLC, a division of Informa PLC.

NOTES

INTRODUCTION

1. There are various opinions as to the identity of the king targeted here. Frede Jensen holds that it is Alfonso X of Castile and León (reigned 1252–84); *Medieval Galician-Portuguese Poetry: An Anthology* (New York: Garland, 1992), 540. Graça Videira Lopes maintains that it was Sancho IV (Alfonso X's son and successor, reigned 1284–95, and under whom Paio Gomes was *almirante-mor* or admiral major), "Cantigas Medievais Galego-Portuguesas," accessed March 17, 2021, https://cantigas.fcsh.unl.pt/.

2. Diogo Bernardes, *Obras completas*, vol. 2, ed. Marques Braga (Lisbon: Sá da Costa, 1946), 283, 288.

3. *Rhythmas de Lvis de Camoes. Diuididas em cinco partes. Dirigidas ao muito Illustre Senhor D. Gonçalo Coutinho* (Lisbon: Manoel de Lyra, 1595); *Rimas de Lvis de Camões. Accrescentadas nesta segunda impressaõ. Dirigidas a D. Gonçalo Coutinho* (Lisbon: Pedro Crasbeeck, 1598).

4. Stuart B. Schwartz, "The Economy of the Portuguese Empire," in *Portuguese Oceanic Expansion, 1400–1800*, ed. Francisco Bethencourt and Diogo Ramada Curto (Cambridge: Cambridge University Press, 2007), 19–48, at 26.

5. The unilaterally triumphalist reading of the poem is not without its problems. For a brief treatment of some of the milestones of criticism on *Os Lusíadas*, see Vincent Barletta, "The *Lusiads* Affect: Standing in the Middle of the Sea," in *A Companion to World Literature*, vol. 3, ed. Christopher Lupke and Evan Nicoll-Johnson (Hoboken: John Wiley and Sons, 2020), 1469–79.

6. Bernhard Klein, "Camões and the Sea: Maritime Modernity in *The Lusiads*," *Modern Philology* 111.2 (2013): 158-80, at 164.

7. Bernhard Klein, "Mapping the Waters: Sea Charts, Navigation, and Camões's *Os Lusíadas*," *Renaissance Studies* 25.2 (2010): 228–47, at 232.

8. Maria Vitalina Leal de Matos, "O mar em Camões," *Oceanos* 23 (1995): 54–65, at 63.

9. Hélio J. S. Alves, "Poesia oceânica: Camões, da navegação ao naufrágio, ante o

precedente de Corte-Real/Oceanic poetry: Camões, Seafaring to Shipwreck, Faced with Corte-Real's Precedent," *Limite: Revista de Estudios Portugueses y de la Lusofonía* 13.1 (2019): 53–81, at 54.

10. Joyce E. Chaplin, *Round about the Earth: Circumnavigation from Magellan to Orbit* (New York: Simon and Schuster, 2012), 9.

11. I use "connectivity" simply as a way to designate the emergence of the "governo do mar" in *Os Lusíadas*. Cross-cultural encounters in early modernity studied under the terms "connectivity" and "disconnectivity" are topics of historiographic debate; see Zoltán Biedermann, "(Dis)connected History and the Multiple Narratives of Global Early Modernity," *Modern Philology* 119.1 (2021): 13–32.

12. John Villiers maintains that early Portuguese navigational skills were unreliable, even after the gathering of information in declination tables, charts, and sailing directions, in the designs of ships and rigging, and in nautical instruments, so that, in the period under discussion here, "Portuguese navigation remained a remarkably hit-and-miss affair" ("Ships, Seafaring, and the Iconography of Voyages in the Age of Vasco da Gama," in *Vasco da Gama and the Linking of Europe and Asia*, ed. Anthony Disney and Emily Booth [Oxford: Oxford University Press, 2000], 72–83, at 76).

13. Margaret Cohen, *The Novel and the Sea* (Princeton, NJ: Princeton University Press, 2010), 9–10, 12; Steve Mentz, *Shipwreck Modernity: Ecologies of Globalization, 1550–1719* (Minneapolis: University of Minnesota Press, 2015), xxxiii.

14. Francisco Contente Domingues, "Vasco da Gama's Voyage: Myths and Realities in Maritime History," *Portuguese Studies* 19 (2003): 1–8, at 5–6.

15. David Quint, *Epic and Empire: Politics and Generic Form from Virgil to Milton* (Princeton, NJ: Princeton University Press, 1993), 87.

16. *Metaphysics*, trans. W. D. Ross, in *The Complete Works of Aristotle: The Revised Oxford Translation*, vol. 2, ed. Jonathan Barnes (Princeton, NJ: Princeton University Press, 1984), 1552–1728, at 1552.

17. João de Castro, *Tratado da Sphæra; Da Geografia; Notação Famosa; Informação sobre Maluco*, ed. A. Fontoura da Costa (Lisbon: Agência Geral das Colónias, 1940), 30–31.

18. Shankar Raman, *Framing "India": The Colonial Imaginary in Early Modern Culture* (Stanford, CA: Stanford University Press, 2002), 36.

19. In a parallel vein, Dan Brayton argues for "the constitution of a subject born of a relationship with a watery globe" in Shakespeare, an "oceanic subjectivity" that, in Brayton's argument, is associated with oceanic vastness and benthic depths (*Shakespeare's Ocean: An Ecocritical Exploration* [Charlottesville: University of Virginia Press, 2012], 75). The maritime subject I argue for appears gradually (such as the historical actors in Zurara's chronicles) but quickly becomes a constant presence in Iberian writers and thinkers in early modernity.

20. Roland Greene, *Unrequited Conquests: Love and Empire in the Colonial Americas* (Chicago: University of Chicago Press, 1999), 14.

21. Klein, "Camões and the Sea," 171.

22. For these and other biographical details, see Luis Nuno Sardinha Monteiro, "Fernando Oliveira's Art of War at Sea (1555): A Pioneering Treatise on Naval Strategy," *Naval War College Review* 68.4 (2015): 94–107.

Notes to Pages 9–21   177

23. Fernando Oliveira, *Liuro da fabrica das naos* (Lisbon: Academia de Marinha, 1991), 62; hereafter cited as LFN with page numbers.

24. Fernando de Oliveira, *Arte da guerra do mar: Estratégia e guerra naval no tempo dos descobrimentos* (Lisbon: Edições 70, 2008), 49.

25. Oliveira, *Arte da guerra do mar*, 51.

26. Robert Foulke, *The Sea Voyage Narrative* (New York: Routledge, 2002), 9.

27. Steve Mentz, "Introduction: Wet Globalization; The Early Modern Ocean as World-System," in *A Cultural History of the Sea in the Early Modern Age*, ed. Steve Mentz, vol. 3 of *A Cultural History of the Sea*, 6 vols., ed. Margaret Cohen (London: Bloomsbury Academic, 2021), 1–23, at 6. For Claire Jowitt, Craig Lambert, and Steve Mentz, exploitation of the world's oceans was crucial to the development of a globalized, and therefore modern, world ("Introduction: Oceans in Global History and Culture 1400–1800; Expanding Horizons," in *The Routledge Companion to Marine and Maritime Worlds, 1400–1800*, ed. Claire Jowitt, Craig Lambert, and Steve Mentz [London: Routledge, 2020], 1–29, at 2).

28. *Oxford Latin Dictionary*, ed. P. G. W. Glare, 2nd ed., vol. 1 (Oxford: Oxford University Press, 2012), 820.

29. Sidney I. Dobrin, *Blue Ecocriticism and the Oceanic Imperative* (London: Routledge, 2021), 12, 21.

30. Melody Jue, *Wild Blue Media: Thinking through Seawater* (Durham, NC: Duke University Press, 2020), 3, 16.

31. Quint, *Epic and Empire*, 7–9.

32. David Quint, *Virgil's Double Cross: Design and Meaning in the* Aeneid (Princeton, NJ: Princeton University Press, 2018), 50.

CHAPTER ONE

1. Details vary somewhat between the two versions but the basic story remains the same. The title in Portuguese is *Navegação de S. Brandão*; citations are from *Navegação de S. Brandão nas fontes portuguesas medievais*, ed. Aires A. Nascimento (Lisbon: Colibri, 1998), cited as NSB with page numbers.

2. Elsa Maria Branco da Silva, ed., "Conto de Amaro," in *Navegação de S. Brandão nas fontes portuguesas medievais*, ed. Aires A. Nascimento (Lisbon: Colibri, 1998), 243–81, at 246.

3. Albrecht Classen, *Water in Medieval Literature: An Ecocritical Reading* (Lanham, MD: Lexington Books, 2018), 78.

4. Margaret Cohen, *The Novel and the Sea* (Princeton, NJ: Princeton University Press, 2010), 15.

5. The Anglo-French version, by contrast, contains a lexicon of nautical terminology based on the kinds of vessels that would have been known in northern Europe; see William Sayers, "The Maritime and Nautical Vocabulary of *Le Voyage de saint Brendan*," *Neophilologus* 97 (2013): 9–19.

6. Martina Kado's comment on the ship in nineteenth-century literary narratives, specifically in Melville, applies as well to Brendan's *Voyage*: "A crew is taken on a vessel, and a hierarchical social and technical architecture is set up as this compound traverses

water space to perform a mission" ("The Ship as Assemblage: Melville's Literary Shipboard Geographies," *Atlantic Studies* 15.1 [2018]: 40–61, at 41). While there is no nautical or technical hierarchy present on Brendan's ship, there is a hierarchical social and spiritual structure that the voyage itself emphasizes and consolidates.

7. Kado, "The Ship as Assemblage," 41.

8. *Crónica dos feitos notáveis que se passaram na conquista da Guiné por mandado do Infante D. Henrique*, vol. 1, ed. Torquato de Sousa Soares (Lisbon: Academia Portuguesa da História, 1978), 43. For the possible identifications of Brendan's Isles with islands encountered in fifteenth-century European and Portuguese sea voyaging, see Jacques Paviot, "L'imaginaire géographique des decouvertes au XVe siècle," in *La Découverte, le Portugal et l'Europe: Actes du Colloque, Paris, les 26, 27 et 28 mai 1988*, ed. Jean Aubin (Paris: Fondation Calouste Gulbenkian; Centre Culturel Portugais, 1990), 141–58.

9. Christopher L. Pastore, "Knowledges: Constructing the Early Modern Ocean, 1450–1700," in *A Cultural History of the Sea in the Early Modern Age*, ed. Steve Mentz, vol. 3 of *A Cultural History of the Sea*, 6 vols., ed. Margaret Cohen (London: Bloomsbury Academic, 2021), 25–51, at 28.

10. See Samuel Eliot Morison, *Portuguese Voyages to America in the Fifteenth Century* (Cambridge, MA: Harvard University Press, 1940), 15–18.

11. Svat Soucek, "Islamic Charting in the Mediterranean," in *History of Cartography*, vol. 2, bk. 1, ed. J. B. Harley and David Woodward (Chicago: University of Chicago Press, 1992), 263–92, at 271. Martin Behaim, who resided for a time in Lisbon, included the Paradise island of St. Brendan on his globe (Valerie I. J. Flint, *The Imaginative Landscape of Christopher Columbus* [Princeton, NJ: Princeton University Press, 1992], 39).

12. The anonymous author of the fragmentary *Arte de trovar* (Art of Poetry), contained in the *Cancioneiro da Biblioteca Nacional de Lisboa* (one of the three main manuscript testimonies of the *cantigas*), presents the generic distinction between the *cantigas de amigo* and the *cantigas de amor* as one based on gendered voice: "E porque algūas cantigas i há en que falam eles e elas outrossi, per én é bem de entenderdes se som d'amor, se d'amigo: porque sabede que, se eles falam na prim<eir>ra cobra e elas na outra, <é d'>amor, porque se move a razon d'ele (como vos ante dissemos); e se elas falam na primeira cobra, é outrossi d'amigo; e se ambos falam en ūa cobra, outrossi é segundo qual deles fala na cobra primeiro" (And because there are *cantigas* in which both men and women speak, it is good to ascertain if they are *cantigas d'amor* or *cantigas d'amigo*. Know that if men speak in the first verse stanza and women in the next, it is a *cantiga d'amor*, because his speaking determines the song, as we said before; and if women speak in the first stanza, it is a *cantiga d'amigo*. And if both men and women speak in a stanza, it depends on who speaks first in the stanza; *Arte de trovar do Cancioneiro da Biblioteca Nacional de Lisboa*, ed. Giuseppe Tavani [Lisbon: Colibri, 1999], 41). Yet, as Vincent Barletta emphasizes, it is not simply the gender of the voice that distinguishes a *cantiga de amigo* from a *cantiga de amor*, "but rather *who speaks first*" in a "temporal sequence of a performative speech event" and a dynamic of turn-taking ("Songs of Stance," in *Portuguese Literature and the Environment*, ed. Victor K. Mendes and Patrícia Vieira [Lanham, MD: Lexington Books, 2019], 79–92, at 86–87; emphasis in original). However, *dialogic* cantigas between men and women

are few in the extant corpus, so that the gender of the voice in a given song remains an adequate generic distinction.

13. Graça Videira Lopes, "Galician-Portuguese as a Literary Language in the Middle Ages," in *A Comparative History of Literatures in the Iberian Peninsula*, vol. 1, ed. Fernando Cabo Aseguinolaza, Anxo Abuín Gonzalez, and César Domínguez (Amsterdam: John Benjamins, 2010), 396–412, at 400.

14. João Zorro's poems, for example, explicitly establish military service as a reason for the absence of the *amigo*.

15. This conjoining of nostalgia and yearning for an absent lover and the sea is one of the distinguishing characteristics of the Galician-Portuguese poetic tradition (Stephen Reckert and Helder Macedo, "Cinquenta cantigas de amigo," in *Do cancioneiro de amigo*, 3rd ed., ed. Stephen Reckert and Helder Macedo [Lisbon: Assírio e Alvim, 1996], 71–247, at 142).

16. "Pela ribeira do rio / cantand'ia a dona virgo /d'amor: / 'Venhan'as barcas polo rio /a sabor'" (Along the riverbank the virgin woman was singing of love: "Let the boats come along the river in pleasure") appears to imply that when the boats arrive, along with the *amigo*, the singer will no longer be a virgin. The *ribeira* as a site of sexual congress is more explicit in this *cantiga*: "Pela ribeira do rio salido / trebelhei, madre, com meu amigo; / amor hei migo, / que nom houvesse; / fiz por amig'o / que nom fezesse" (On the bank of the risen river I frolicked, my mother, with my friend; would that I didn't have the love that I do; I did for my friend what I shouldn't have done). *Trebelhar* (to play, to frolic) carries a sexual meaning, with the agitated, high waters of the river amplifying the scenario of erotic contact. On *trebelhar*, see Jensen, *Medieval Galician-Portuguese Poetry: An Anthology* (New York: Garland, 1992), 501, and Eugenio Asensio, *Poética y realidad en el cancionero peninsular de la Edad Media*, 2nd rev. ed. (Madrid: Gredos, 1970), 43–44. Erotic contact as suggested by lexical allusions is the topic of Rip Cohen, *Erotic Angles on the* Cantigas d'Amigo (London: Department of Iberian and Latin American Studies, Queen Mary, University of London, 2012), although Cohen does not study the *barcarolas*.

17. "Cantigas Medievais Galego-Portuguesas," accessed March 17, 2021, https://cantigas.fcsh.unl.pt.

18. Paio Gomes, a Galician nobleman, was named *Almirante do Mar* (Admiral of the Sea) between 1284 and 1286, but was relieved of the title by Alfonso X for unknown reasons (Jensen, *Medieval Galician-Portuguese Poetry*, xciv-xcv).

19. Asensio, *Poética y realidad*, 41; Jensen, *Medieval Galician-Portuguese Poetry*, 537.

20. Reckert and Macedo, "Cinquenta cantigas de amigo," 154. These scholars read the entire *cantiga* as chronicling the *amiga*'s witnessing of the ship's departure until it disappears from sight.

21. Other similarities to *cantigas de amigo* are the poem's parallelistic structure, the vocabulary referring to the woman as *velida* and *formosa*, and the setting in nature ("Cantigas Medievais Galego-Portuguesas," accessed March 17, 2021, https://cantigas.fcsh.unl.pt).

22. Carolina Michaëlis de Vasconcelos, ed., *Cancioneiro da Ajuda*, vol. 2 (Halle a.S.: Max Niemeyer, 1904), 478. Michaëlis de Vasconcelos singles out the waves as consonant with the poet's beating heart, which, for her, is the poetic interest of this poem.

23. On Codax's *cantigas* as a linked sequence, see Giuseppe Tavani, *Ensaios portugueses: Filologia e linguística* (Lisbon: Imprensa Nacional-Casa da Moeda, 1988), 305–13, and Charmaine Lee, "La *chanson de femme* attribuita a Raimbaut de Vaqueiras, *Altas undas que venez suz la mar*," in *Studi di filologia romanza offerti a Valeria Bertolucci Pizzorusso*, vol. 2, ed. Pietro G. Beltrami, Maria Grazia Capusso, Fabrizio Cigni, and Sergio Vatteroni (Ospedaletto [Pisa]: Pacini, 2006), 865–81, at 872–74.

24. Pilar Lorenzo Gradín, *La canción de mujer en la lírica medieval* (Santiago de Compostela: Universidade de Santiago de Compostela, 1990), 201; Anne-Marie Quint, "O mar na lírica medieval galego-portuguesa," in *Actas do quinto congresso da Associação Internacional de Lusitanistas, Universidade de Oxford, 1 a 8 de Setembro de 1996*, vol. 3, ed. T. F. Earle (Oxford-Coimbra: Associação Internacional de Lusitanistas, 1998), 1321–29, at 1327.

25. Vicenç Beltran, *La poesía tradicional medieval y renacentista: Poética antropológica de la lírica oral* (Kassel: Edition Reichenberger, 2009), 105; Egla Morales Blouin, *El ciervo y la fuente: Mito y folklore del agua en la lírica tradicional* (Madrid: José Porrúa Turanzas; Potomac: Studia Humanitatis, 1981), 224–25, 229; Celso Ferreira da Cunha, *O cancioneiro de Martin Codax* (Rio de Janeiro: Departamento de Imprensa, 1956), 92–95; Gradín, *La canción de mujer en la lírica medieval*, 211; Vasconcelos, *Cancioneiro da Ajuda*, vol. 2, 893n4; Luz Pozo Garza, *Ondas do mar de Vigo: Erotismo e conciencia mítica nas cantigas de amigo* (A Coruña: Espiral Maior, 1996), 78, 81.

26. Pozo Garza, *Ondas do mar de Vigo*, 121.

27. Frede Jensen, *The Earliest Portuguese Lyrics* ([Odense]: Odense University Press, 1978), 68.

28. Reckert and Macedo, "Cinquenta cantigas de amigo," 147.

29. Maria do Rosário Ferreira argues for a universal and symbolic equation between water and the feminine, and that it is possible to identify a feminine desire to fuse with water, even as a stylized form of drowning (*Águas doces, águas salgadas: Da funcionalidade dos motivos aquáticos na Cantiga de Amigo* [Porto: Granito, 1999], 50–51, 56).

30. Translation by Richard Zenith, "Song of Clean Shirts," "Cantigas Medievais Galego-Portuguesas," accessed March 17, 2021, https://cantigas.fcsh.unl.pt.

31. See Blouin, *El ciervo y la fuente*, 99; Gradín, *La canción de mujer en la lírica medieval*, 218; and Reckert and Macedo, "Cinquenta cantigas de amigo," 220, 227. For the link between water and sensuality, see Esther Corral, "Feminine Voices in the Galician-Portuguese *cantigas de amigo*," trans. Judith R. Cohen with Anne L. Klinck, in *Medieval Woman's Song: Cross-Cultural Approaches*, ed. Anne L. Klinck and Ann Marie Rasmussen (Philadelphia: University of Pennsylvania Press, 2002), 81–98, at 87.

32. Gradín, *La canción de mujer en la lírica medieval*, 221; Reckert and Macedo, "Cinquenta cantigas de amigo," 65, 68.

33. By comparison, it is worth noting a poem deemed by some scholars to be a *cantiga de amigo* or a *barcarola*, by the Occitan poet Raimbaut de Vaqueiras (1180–1205), "Altas undas que venez suz la mar"; for discussions of the poem's genre, see Lee, "La *chanson de femme* attribuita a Raimbaut de Vaqueiras, *Altas undas que venez suz la mar*"; Jean-Marie d'Heur, "Le motif du vent venu du pays de l'être aimé, l'invocation au vent, l'invocation aux vagues," *Zeitschrift für romanische Philologie* 88 (1972): 69–104; Giuseppe Tavani, "Raimbaut de Vaqueiras (?), *Altas undas que venez suz la mar* (BdT 392.5a)," *Lecturae Tropatorum* 1 (2008): 1–33; Saverio Guida, "Raimbaut de Vaqueiras,

[Oi] altas undas que venez suz la mar (BdT 392.5a)," *Lecturae Tropatorum* 6 (2013): 1–21. In this three-stanza, nonparallelistic text, a young woman addresses the waves that travel over the sea for news of her lover who has gone abroad. She then speaks to the "aura dulza" (sweet breeze) that originates from where her friend sleeps, asking it to carry one of his breaths to her: "[D]el dolz aleyn un beure m'aporta · y! / La bocha obre, per gran desir qu'en ai" (Bring me a mouthful of his soft breath. I open my mouth for the great desire I have; translation from *Proensa: An Anthology of Troubadour Poetry*, trans. and sel. Paul Blackburn, ed. George Economou [Berkeley: University of California Press, 1978], 138). Here, the wind clearly is phallic in the invited penetration of the woman's mouth; for the equivalence between the female mouth and vagina in Old French literature, see E. Jane Burns, *Bodytalk: When Women Speak in Old French Literature* (Philadelphia: University of Pennsylvania Press, 1993), 53.

34. On the link between the two poets, see Vicente Beltrán Pepió, "O vento lh'as levava: Don Denis y la tradición lírica peninsular," *Bulletin Hispanique* 86.1–2 (1984): 5–25, at 21, 24; Mercedes Brea, "*Levantou-s' a velida*, um exemplo de sincretismo harmónico," in *Estudos dedicados a Ricardo Carvalho Calero*, vol. 2, ed. José Luís Rodríguez (Santiago de Compostela: Universidade de Santiago de Compostela, 2000), 139–51, at 145, 147; Rip Cohen, "Girl in the Dawn: Textual Criticism and Poetics," *Portuguese Studies* 22 (2006): 173–87, at 176; Ferreira, *Águas doces, águas salgadas*, 131–32.

35. The *cervo* in Meogo's *cantigas* is a symbol of the (eroticized) male lover (Blouin, *El ciervo y la fuente*, 26). For Barletta, Meogo's mountain stags "are of course a metaphoric reference to *eros*, but they are also, and more significantly, spatio-temporal indices of remoteness and of the productive and no less erotic reverberations in force between the *there* of insult and hidden liaison and the *here* of performance" ("Songs of Stance," 90; emphasis in original).

36. It bears noting that King Dinis was invested in building the Portuguese navy. He ordered a pine forest to be planted in Leiria to provide timber for ships. Another of his nautically minded *cantigas de amigo* is "Ai flores, ai flores do verde pino," in which the young woman addresses flowering pines and asks for news of her friend. In addition to the "flores" as part of a Western, sylvan imaginary (some aspects of which Joaquim-Francisco Coelho explores in *Letras de Jornal* [Lisbon: Assírio e Alvim, 2010], 81–85), the trees possess a privileged knowledge because they will become the planks from which future ships will be built, like the one responsible for carrying away the *amigo*.

37. Helder Macedo, "Uma cantiga de Dom Dinis," in Stephen Reckert and Helder Macedo, eds., *Do cancioneiro de amigo*, 3rd ed., Lisbon: Assírio e Alvim, 1996, 59–70, at 66.

38. Lara Farina, "Wondrous Skins and Tactile Affection: The Blemmye's Touch," in *Reading Skin in Medieval Literature and Culture*, ed. Katie L. Walter (New York: Palgrave Macmillan, 2013), 11–28, at 18.

39. Farina, "Wondrous Skins and Tactile Affection," 20.

40. *Sense and Sensibilia*, trans. J.nI. Beare, in *The Complete Works of Aristotle: The Revised Oxford Translation*, vol. 1, ed. Jonathan Barnes (Princeton, NJ: Princeton University Press, 1984), 693–713, at 697.

41. Katie L. Walter, "The Form of the Formless: Medieval Taxonomies of Skin, Flesh, and the Human," in Walter, *Reading Skin in Medieval Literature and Culture*, 119–39, at 122.

42. "Songs of Stance," 80; emphasis in original.

43. The alternation between the masculine and feminine nouns *marinero/marinera* is the basis of the *moto* and Camões's gloss on it, so I have translated *marinera* as "sailoress" to reflect the gendered pairing in the original.

44. Helder Macedo, "Love as Knowledge: The Lyric Poetry of Camões," *Portuguese Studies* 14 (1998): 51–64, at 54.

45. Manuel da Costa Fontes, "The Art of 'Sailing' in *La Lozana andaluza*," *Hispanic Review* 66 (1998): 433–45.

CHAPTER TWO

1. Portuguese envoys in Kotte and Bengal in 1506 and 1521 claimed that Manuel I was King of the Sea, and "on the basis of this assertion the crown went on to pronounce the Indian Ocean a Portuguese *mare clausum*—a sea under Portugal's sole jurisdiction" (A. R. Disney, *A History of Portugal and the Portuguese Empire: From Beginnings to 1807*, vol. 2 [Cambridge: Cambridge University Press, 2009], 156). This oceanic sovereignty was part of the *Estado da Índia* (State of India), a vast geographic domain stretching from Africa to Asia that was a major component of Portugal's commercial empire. The founding of the *carreira da Índia* is the cornerstone of the *governo do mar*, but it is beset by recurrent tragedy, as Adamastor predicts in canto V with a series of "naufrágios, perdições de toda sorte" (shipwrecks [and] disasters of all kinds; V.44. vii). Steve Mentz realizes that "inside the ambivalent triumph and curse of the *Lusiads*, Portuguese expansion into the East Indies looks less like straightforward conquest or mercantile expansion than arrival into an ecologically complex world marked by catastrophe" (*Shipwreck Modernity*, xvi).

2. Homer's and Virgil's epics were brought into the Iberian vernacular in Castilian translation. The *Odyssey* was translated by Gonzalo Pérez as *La Ulixea* and published in 1550. Enrique de Villena, at the behest of Juan II, King of Navarre, produced an adaptation and translation of the *Aeneid* (*La Eneida*) in 1427.

3. Doris is the daughter of Ocean and Tethys and mother of the Nereids.

4. Scholars have debunked the legend that Gama was the first to round Good Hope or to sail the waters of the Indian Ocean: "The Javanese, Indians and Chinese had all made it across to the Cape many decades, if not centuries, before Da Gama. It has no less been forgotten that Da Gama only managed to navigate across to India because he was guided by an unnamed Gujarati Muslim pilot" (John M. Hobson, *The Eastern Origins of Western Civilisation* [Cambridge: Cambridge University Press, 2004], 21).

5. Simone Pinet, *Archipelagoes: Insular Fictions from Chivalric Romance to the Novel* (Minneapolis: University of Minnesota Press, 2011), 30.

6. The Latin text and translation are from Virgil, *Eclogues/Georgics/Aeneid 1–6*, trans. H. R. Fairclough, rev. G. P. Goold (Cambridge, MA: Harvard University Press, 1999), 262–63.

7. The Latin original is from Damião de Góis, *Elogio da cidade de Lisboa/Vrbis Olisiponis Descriptio*, ed. Aires A. Nascimento (Lisbon: Guimarães Editores, 2002), 188; the English translation is from *Lisbon in the Renaissance: A New Translation of the Urbis Olisiponis Descriptio*, trans. Jeffrey S. Ruth (New York: Italica Press, 1996), 35.

8. Ovid mentions the Hippocrene in *Metamorphoses* 5.256–59. Maria Helena da

Rocha Pereira suggests that Camões's source for the inspirational fountain could have come from the work of Portuguese humanist André de Resende ("Musas e Tágides n' *Os Lusíadas*," in *Actas da VI Reunião Internacional de Camonistas*, ed. Seabra Pereira and Manuel Ferro [Coimbra: Imprensa da Universidade de Coimbra, 2012], 51–61, at 53).

9. Glaser contends that *fúria*, along with *engenho* and *arte* mentioned at the end of the second stanza of canto I, forms a triad of characteristics referring to poetic talent and skill based on classical and contemporary theories of poetry (*Portuguese Studies* [Paris: Fundação Calouste Gulbenkian; Centro Cultural Português, 1976], 75–83).

10. Hélio J. S. Alves, "O Som e a Fúria d'*Os Lusíadas*," *Santa Barbara Portuguese Studies* 8 (2003): 49–65.

11. Alves, "O som e a fúria d'*Os Lusíadas*," 58. Alves goes on to note that "the style of epic verse is identified with the grandeur and violence of a vast fluvial current" (59).

12. The *in medias res* convention was influentially formulated by Horace in the *Ars poetica*, where the Latin poet makes this comment about Homer and the *Odyssey*: "semper ad eventum festinat et in medias res / non secus ac notas auditorem rapit" (Ever [the poet] hastens to the issue, and hurries his hearer into the story's midst, as if already known; *Satires/Epistles/Ars Poetica*, trans. H. R. Fairclough [Cambridge, MA: Harvard University Press, 1929], 462–63). The Horatian observation identifies the "artificial order" allowed a poet in narrating events in contradistinction to the "natural order" of history, which tells events in the order they actually occurred (see Bernard Weinberg, *A History of Literary Criticism in the Italian Renaissance*, vol. 1 [Chicago: University of Chicago Press, 1961], 40, 87). Hélio J. S. Alves, however, argues that in the practice of epic in the Portuguese sixteenth century the use of *in medias res* was Neo-Aristotelian, which postulated not an alternate temporal order but a beginning according to Aristotle's precept in the *Poetics* ("Teoría de la épica en el renacimiento portugués," in *La teoría de la épica en el siglo XVI [España, Francia, Italia y Portugal]*, ed. María José Vega and Lara Vilà [Pontevedra: Academia del Hispanismo, 2010], 137–73, at 156–57). The other major epic figure of the Portuguese sixteenth century alongside Camões was Jerónimo Corte-Real (1533–88). Corte-Real's poem *Sucesso do segundo cerco de Diu* (The Feat of the Second Siege of Diu, 1574) contains lines very parallel to Camões's I.19; for comparative comments, see Alves, "Poesia oceânica: Camões, da navegação ao naufrágio, ante o precedente de Corte-Real/Oceanic poetry: Camões, from Seafaring to Shipwreck, Faced with Corte-Real's Precedent," *Limite: Revista de Estudios Portugueses y de la Lusofonía* 13.1 (2019), 53–81, at 61–64.

13. The Latin text and English translation are from *Eclogues/Georgics / Aeneid 1–6*, trans. Fairclough, rev. Goold (Cambridge, MA: Harvard University Press, 1999), 264–65.

14. *Cortar* (to cleave, to rend [water]) is Camões's primordial verb of nautical movement over maritime space, and implies inscription of maritime space into the purposes and designs of empire.

15. The ship's cleaving of the water symbolically expresses a sexual component to (masculine) imperial seafaring, as I have argued elsewhere (Josiah Blackmore, *Moorings: Portuguese Expansion and the Writing of Africa* [Minneapolis: University of Minnesota Press, 2009], 145). Mary Gaylord Randel proposes an identification between navigation, conquest, and sexual aggression (especially as represented by the mast of

a ship) in Luis de Góngora's *Soledades* ("Metaphor and Fable in Góngora's *Soledad Primera*," *Revista Hispánica Moderna* 40.3/4 [1978–79], 97–112, at 103–5). Góngora, a reader of Camões, may have based his poetic rendering of the mast and ship in part on *Os Lusíadas*.

16. I follow the traditional attribution of Velho as author of the *Roteiro*. Some scholars believe the text was written by João de Sá, the secretary of the *São Rafael*; for discussions of the authorship question, see Glenn J. Ames, ed. and trans., *Em Nome de Deus: The Journal of the First Voyage of Vasco da Gama to India, 1497–99* (Leiden: Brill, 2009) 19–25, and Sanjay Subrahmanyam, *The Career and Legend of Vasco da Gama* (Cambridge: Cambridge University Press, 1997), 81-83.

17. Also see Ames, *Em Nome de Deus*, Appendix III, for translations of letters describing the voyage.

18. André Brink notes that "Da Gama's extensive journal of his first journey was lodged in the wonderful library of Coimbra, and . . . it seems to have been accessible to scholars; certainly the facts . . . were widely known by the time Camões sat down to draw on them for his epic" ("A Myth of Origin," in *T'Kama-Adamastor: Inventions of a South African Painting*, ed. Ivan Vladislavić [Johannesburg: University of the Witwatersrand, 2000], 41–47, at 41).

19. For further details, see "Roteiros," *Dicionário de história dos descobrimentos portugueses*, ed. Luís de Albuquerque and Francisco Contente Domingues, vol. 2 (Lisbon: Caminho, 1994), and C. R. Boxer, "Portuguese *Roteiros*, 1500–1700," in *From Lisbon to Goa, 1500–1750: Studies in Portuguese Maritime Enterprise* (London: Variorum, 1984), 171–86. My comments on *roteiros* here, in addition to Velho's account, are based on readings of the following: *Roteiros de D. João de Castro*, 2nd ed., 3 vols., ed. A. Fontoura da Costa (Lisbon: Agência Geral das Colónias, 1939–40); *Livro de marinharia de Bernardo Fernandes*, ed. A. Fontoura da Costa (Lisbon: Agência Geral das Colónias, 1940); *Roteiros portugueses inéditos da carreira da Índia do século XVI*, ed. A. Fontoura da Costa (Lisbon: Agência Geral das Colónias, 1940); *O livro de marinharia de Manuel Álvares*, ed. Luís Mendonça de Albuquerque (Lisbon: Junta de Investigações do Ultramar, 1969); *Le "Livro de marinharia" de Gaspar Moreira (Bibliothéque National de Paris, Cod. Port. n.º 58)*, ed. Léon Bourdon and Luís de Albuquerque (Lisbon: Junta de Investigações Científicas do Ultramar, 1977); *Livro de marinharia de André Pires*, 2nd ed., ed. Luís de Albuquerque (Lisbon: Vega, [1989?]); *Roteiro do Mar Roxo de Dom João de Castro, MS. Cott. Tib. Dix da British Library* (Lisbon: Inapa, 1991).

20. For a discussion of some of the scientific topics and methodologies addressed by Castro, see J. S. da Silva Dias, *Os descobrimentos e a problemática cultural do século XVI* (Lisbon: Presença, 1982), 83–93. A. R. Disney considers Castro's *roteiros* to be examples of an intellectual current that he calls "empirical humanism," a "tradition based on direct observation and not, like Classical Humanism, on written authorities from the Ancient past"; these *roteiros* "were arguably the most rigorous scientific writings on nautical astronomy, navigation and voyaging of the whole European Renaissance" (*A History of Portugal and the Portuguese Empire*, vol. 1 [Cambridge: Cambridge University Press, 2009], 165, 166).

21. Margaret Cohen, "The Chronotopes of the Sea," in Franco Moretti, ed., *The Novel*, vol. 2 (Princeton, NJ: Princeton University Press, 2006), 647–66.

22. Cohen, "The Chronotopes of the Sea," 647.

23. Cohen, "The Chronotopes of the Sea," 648.

24. *Diário da navegação de Pero Lopes de Sousa (1530–1532)* (Lisbon: Agência Geral do Ultramar, 1968).

25. For a list and synopsis of many of these texts from the sixteenth century, see A. Fontoura da Costa, *A marinharia dos descobrimentos*, 3rd ed. (Lisbon: Agência Geral do Ultramar, 1960), 288–330.

26. *Crónica dos feitos notáveis que se passaram na conquista da Guiné por mandado do Infante D. Henrique*, ed. Torquato de Sousa Soares, 2 vols. (Lisbon: Academia Portuguesa da História, 1978–81). José de Bragança believes that an early version of the chronicle may have been presented in Rome in 1452–53 to lobby for the concession of the bull *Romanus pontifex* (January 1455) by Nicholas V (*Crónica de Guiné*, ed. José de Bragança, [(Porto): Livraria Civilização, 1973], lxxix). This bull, the so-called charter of Portuguese imperialism (C. R. Boxer, *The Portuguese Seaborne Empire, 1415–1825* [New York: Alfred A. Knopf, 1969], 21), resolved a long-standing conflict between Portugal and Castile over trading rights in a vast West African domain by granting the Portuguese crown a monopoly over the region and exclusive rights to trade with the "Saracens." For the text of this bull with English translation, see Frances Gardner Davenport, ed., *European Treaties Bearing on the History of the United States and Its Dependencies to 1648* (Gloucester, MA: Peter Smith, 1967), 13–26.

27. Zurara, *Crónica dos feitos notáveis que se passaram na conquista da Guiné*, vol. 1, 13.

28. Cohen, "The Chronotopes of the Sea," 653.

29. Vitorino Magalhães Godinho, "A ideia de descobrimento e os descobrimentos e expansão," *Anais do Clube Militar Naval* 120 (1990): 627-42, at 633.

30. *Roteiro da África do sul e sueste desde o Cabo da Boa Esperança até ao das Correntes (1576)/"Roteiro" of the [sic] South and South-East Africa, from the Cape of Good Hope to Cape Corrientes (1576)*, ed. A. Fontoura da Costa (Lisbon: Agência Geral das Colónias, 1939).

31. Maria Fernanda Alegria, Suzanne Daveau, João Carlos Garcia, and Francesc Relaño, "Portuguese Cartography in the Renaissance," in *The History of Cartography*, vol. 3, pt. 1, ed. David Woodward (Chicago: University of Chicago Press, 2007), 975–1068, at 1021.

32. The original manuscript of the *Roteiro* is lost. Three manuscript copies survive, and the drawings in them are likely based on originals by Perestrelo.

33. Perestrelo, *Roteiro da África do sul*, 4, 6; hereafter cited as RAS with page numbers. I cite Perestrelo's Portuguese as it appears in the 1939 edition, which does not always follow modern orthographic conventions.

34. The imperial motive behind Perestrelo's journey is again explicitly evident in the description of the bay at Cape St. Bras (modern Mossel Bay): "Nesta baia . . . deixei posta uma cruz de pau. E nela amarrado, com fio de arame, um canudo tapado com cortiça e cera; e dentro um escrito que dizia: 'A louvor de nosso senhor Jesus Cristo e exalçamento da sua santa fé, e por serviço e acrescentamento dos reinos e estados de dom Sebastião, serenissimo Rei de Portugal, Manuel da misquita perestrelo, que por seu mandado veiu descobrir esta costa, poz aqui esta cruz aos sete dias de Janeiro de mil quinhentos setenta e seis anos'" (RAS 26, 28) (In this bay . . . I left a wooden cross. Tied to it with a brass wire was a tube sealed with cork and wax; inside there was a document

which reads "To the praise of Our Lord Jesus Christ and the exaltation of His faith, and for the service and enlargement of the kingdoms and states of King Sebastian, most serene King of Portugal, Manuel de Mesquita Perestrelo, who by the king's command arrived to discover this coast, placed here this cross on the seventh day of January, 1576"). Perestrelo inscribes the land with a text, a ceremonial possession in the name of King and God that is tantamount to the cartographer's own version of a *padrão* (a stone pillar surmounted by a cross), the placing of which was the habitual symbolic act of possession of foreign lands by Portuguese imperial travelers.

35. Fernão Lopes de Castanheda, *História do descobrimento e conquista da Índia pelos Portugueses*, bk. 1, 3rd ed., ed. Pedro de Azevedo (Coimbra: Imprensa da Universidade, 1924), 2; hereafter cited as HDCI with page numbers.

36. The use and/or incorporation of this *roteiro* appears to be further corroborated by the fact that descriptions of other sea voyages in the *História* do not contain the same level of nautical or other types of detail that could only have been gathered by an eyewitness. These other voyages are more summary in nature.

37. François Hartog, *The Mirror of Herodotus: The Representation of the Other in the Writing of History*, trans. Janet Lloyd (Berkeley: University of California Press, 1988), 261.

38. João de Barros, *Ásia de João de Barros: Dos feitos que os Portugueses fizeram no descobrimento e conquista dos mares e terras do Oriente. Primeira Década* ([Lisbon]: Imprensa Nacional-Casa da Moeda, 1988), 1.

39. The uncharted or un-navigated seas Camões touts in his opening stanza are a fiction. Bernhard Klein observes that "Camões plays with the fantasy that the Indian Ocean is uncharted space," and that the Portuguese arrived "in overcrowded waters" ("Camões and the Sea," 162). However, this does not prevent Camões from casting his epic narrative as "a founding moment of historic proportion" (162).

40. Álvaro Velho, *Roteiro da primeira viagem de Vasco da Gama (1497–1499)*, ed. A. Fontoura da Costa (Lisbon: Agência-Geral do Ultramar, 1969), 3.

41. For an analysis of the common mariner as the (heroic) centerpiece of Camões's seafaring epic and as the defining element of the poem's modernity, see Klein, "Camões and the Sea," 159–61, 164, 166, 177–80.

42. Shankar Raman, "Back to the Future: Forging History in Luís de Camões's *Os Lusíadas*," *Travel Knowledge: European "Discoveries" in the Early Modern Period*, ed. Ivo Kamps and Jyotsna G. Singh (New York: Palgrave, 2001), 137–47, at 142.

43. Neil Safier and Ilda Mendes dos Santos, "Mapping Maritime Triumph and the Enchantment of Empire: Portuguese Literature of the Renaissance," in *The History of Cartography*, vol. 3, pt. 1, ed. David Woodward (Chicago: University of Chicago Press, 2007), 461–68, at 462.

44. Klein, "Camões and the Sea," 167, 165.

45. Fernando Gil addresses this first-person presence in "*The Lusiads* Effect," trans. K. David Jackson, in *The Traveling Eye: Retrospection, Vision, and Prophecy in the Portuguese Renaissance*, ed. Fernando Gil and Helder Macedo (Dartmouth, MA: University of Massachusetts Dartmouth, 2009), 33–85.

46. Shankar Raman, *Framing "India": The Colonial Imaginary in Early Modern Culture* (Stanford, CA: Stanford University Press, 2001), 182; emphasis in original.

47. Gil, "*The Lusiads* Effect," 37.

48. For a list and description of many manuscript codices of this genre of maritime book, see Luís de Albuquerque, "Introdução," in *Memória das armadas que de Portugal pasaram ha Índia e esta primeira e ha com que Vasco da Gama partio ao descobrimento dela por mamdado de el Rei Dom Manvel no segvmdo anno de sev reinado e no do nacimento de XPO de 1497* (Lisbon: Academia das Ciências de Lisboa, 1979), 5–13. Also see *Relação das náos e armadas da India com os successos dellas que se puderam saber, para noticia e instrucção dos curiozos, e amantes da historia da India (British Library, Códice Add. 20902)*, ed. Maria Hermínia Maldonado (Coimbra: Biblioteca Geral da Universidade, 1985).

49. This expectation becomes explicit in canto V when Gama remarks on the first sighting of African boats on the river of "Bons Sinais" (Good Signs, now the River Kwakwa) on his approach to Mozambique: "Num rio, que ali sai ao mar aberto, / Batéis à vela entravam e saíam. / Alegria mui grande foi, por certo, / Acharmos já pessoas que sabiam / Navegar" (On a river that there empties into the open sea, vessels of sail came and left. There was of course great joy for us to encounter people who knew how to sail; V.75.iii-vii).

50. Phaëthon, son of Apollo, took the reins of the chariot of the sun for one day against his father's wishes. He was unable to control the chariot; it swooped downward and scorched the earth and caused the skin of Ethiopians to become black (thus goes Ovid's account of the racial origin of Africans in the *Metamorphoses* [2.103–236]). Interestingly, Ovid likens Apollo's chariot under Phaëthon's control to ships, which, "without their proper ballast, roll in the waves, and, unstable because too light, are borne out of their course" (labant curvae iusto sine pondere naves / perque mare instabiles nimia levitate feruntur, lines 163–64) and says of Phaëthon "he is borne along just as a ship driven before the headlong blast, whose pilot has let the useless rudder go and abandoned the ship to the gods and prayers" (ut acta / praecipiti pinus borea, cui victa remisit / frena suus rector, quam dis votisque reliquit, lines 184–85). Such comparisons might underlie Camões's scenario of seafaring encounter, since they cast the story of Phaëthon as a nautical one.

51. *Mouro* is the word Camões uses to designate non-Europeans and non-Christians from Africa to India. The word bears a heavy semantic weight as one of the lexical indicators of expansionist ideology.

52. That Gama would need the expertise of Arab navigators to traverse the Indian Ocean reflects the paltry knowledge of the Portuguese in the late fifteenth century on this geographic zone. Giancarlo Casale notes that "[the Portuguese explorers] faced repeated reminders of their comparative intellectual backwardness in the face of Islam's cosmopolitan world civilization. Vasco da Gama . . . might never even have reached India had he not been guided there from the African coast by an experienced Arab pilot" (*The Ottoman Age of Exploration* [New York: Oxford University Press, 2010], 15–16). This pilot was Ahmad ibn-Mājid, "a great Arab seaman [who] helped to bring about the undoing of Arab navigation, for the Arabs could neither drive out nor compete with the Portuguese and other European nations which followed them" (George Fadlo Hourani, *Arab Seafaring in the Indian Ocean in Ancient and Early Medieval Times*, expanded ed., rev. and exp. John Carswell [Princeton, NJ: Princeton University Press, 1995], 83–84).

53. Raman, "Back to the Future," 136–37. Raman focuses specifically on idolatry as a form of misrepresentation by non-Christian peoples, so that "the adequation of

representation to its object is the preserve of Christian truth alone. The prior legitimacy of Christian doctrine asserts the inherent superiority of Christian representations of the world over the counterfeit and inauthentic images produced by the alien peoples encountered in the course of 'discovering' the east" (139).

54. *Degredados* or exiled criminals were frequently sent on overseas voyages.

55. *Regimentos* were nautical guides that contained all manner of information for navigation as well as specific instructions regulating actions by those sailing under a monarch's orders.

56. Latin text and English translation are from Horace, *Odes and Epodes*, ed. and trans. Niall Rudd (Cambridge, MA: Harvard University Press, 2004), 30–31.

57. See Ode 6, in *Poemas Lusitanos*, 2nd ed., ed. T. F. Earle (Lisbon: Fundação Calouste Gulbenkian, 2008), 114–15.

58. Christopher D. Johnson, *Hyperboles: The Rhetoric of Excess in Baroque Literature and Thought* (Cambridge, MA: Harvard University Department of Comparative Literature, 2010), 167.

59. For example, see José Madeira, *Camões contra a expansão e o império: Os Lusíadas como antiepopeia* (Lisbon: Fenda, 2000), 37–57. Helder Macedo argues against an anti-imperialist attitude as part of the rhetoric of *Os Lusíadas*: "The existence of such an attitude is not only implausible in the spirit of the time but is belied by the spirit of the poem. Even in the most outspokenly critical passages . . . Camões only condemns the evils of imperial power in order better to defend what he regards as the proper exercise of that power" ("'The Lusiads': Epic Celebration and Pastoral Regret," *Portuguese Studies* 6 [1990]: 32–37, at 34).

60. Macedo, "'The Lusiads': Epic Celebration and Pastoral Regret," 32, 33.

61. There is an etymological dimension to this placement of seeing on board the ships. The morphemes of *desterrar* (to exile) mean to "unland," so the view that is exiled is detached from land and placed aboard the flagship.

62. Frank Pierce, ed., *Os Lusíadas* (Oxford: Clarendon Press, 1973), 175n4.

63. Marina Brownlee, "The Dark Side of Myth in Camões' 'Frail Bark,'" *Comparative Literature Studies* 32 (1995): 176–90, at 178.

64. Robert M. Durling, trans. and ed., *Petrarch's Lyric Poems: The Rime sparse and Other Lyrics* (Cambridge, MA: Harvard University Press, 1976), 270–71; hereafter cited as PLP with page numbers.

65. Ernst Robert Curtius, *European Literature and the Latin Middle Ages*, trans. Willard R. Trask (New York: Pantheon, 1953), 128.

66. Curtius, *European Literature and the Latin Middle Ages*, 128.

67. Pedro de Mariz, "Ao estudioso da lição Poetica," in *Os Lvsiadas do grande Lvis de Camoens. Principe da poesia heroica. Commentados pelo licenciado Manoel Correa . . .* (Lisbon: Pedro Crasbeeck, 1613), [v]-[x], at [viii].

68. The book was translated into English by Rebecca D. Catz as *The Travels of Mendes Pinto* (Chicago: University of Chicago Press, 1989); hereafter cited as TMP with page numbers.

69. For Michael Murrin, the *Peregrinação* "is a picaresque narrative that shows the dirty underside of the Portuguese in the East" (*Trade and Romance* [Chicago: University of Chicago Press, 2014], 124); for Murrin's study of the negative side of empire as presented in *Os Lusíadas*, see his chapter 7.

Notes to Pages 82–91   189

70. Portuguese text is from *Fernão Mendes Pinto and the* Peregrinação: *Studies, Restored Portuguese Text, Notes, and Indexes*, vol. 2, *Restored Portuguese Text*, ed. Elisa Lopes da Costa (Lisbon: Fundação Oriente, 2010), 29; English translation is from TMP 1.

71. These are chapters 53 and 54.

72. *Peregrinação, Restored Portuguese Text*, 177, 179.

73. Carmen Nocentelli, *Empires of Love: Europe, Asia, and the Making of Early Modern Identity* (Philadelphia: University of Pennsylvania Press, 2013), 46, 49.

74. Nocentelli, *Empires of Love*, 49, 50–55.

75. Nocentelli, *Empires of Love*, 59.

76. Denise Saive, "'The lover becomes the thing beloved': Queering Love in *Os Lusíadas*," in *Beyond Binaries: Sex, Sexualities, and Gender in the Lusophone World*, ed. Paulo Pepe and Ana Raquel Fernandes (Oxford: Peter Lang, 2019), 11–37, at 12, 14.

77. Saive, "'The lover becomes the thing beloved,'" 16, 18–19. Saive also finds gendered divisions in question in the brief sequence of stanzas in which Leonardo, a sailor who is unfortunate in love, pursues the nymph Efire and pleads with her repeatedly not to escape him, since the assertive behavior of the nymph loosens gender divides (27).

78. The *máquina do mundo* joins a cosmological tradition to a legacy of prophetic views of the universe influentially established by Cicero in the *Somnium Scipionis* in book 6 of *De re publica* (a Portuguese translation of the *Somnium* was published by Duarte de Resende in Coimbra in 1531). As Nicolás Wey Gómez explains, the term *machina mundi* (which dates back to the poet Lucretius [ca. 99–55 BCE]) was a cosmological concept that postulated the orderly workings of the geocentric universe into a universal harmony (*The Tropics of Empire: Why Columbus Sailed South to the Indies* [Cambridge, MA: MIT Press, 2008], 61, 93–96).

79. James Nicolopulos, *The Poetics of Empire in the Indies: Prophecy and Imitation in* La Araucana *and* Os Lusíadas (University Park: The Pennsylvania State University Press, 2000), 3–4.

80. Hélio J. S. Alves, "A máquina do mundo n'Os Lusíadas," in *Dicionário de Luís de Camões*, ed. Vítor Aguiar e Silva (Lisbon: Caminho, 2011), 555–59, at 558.

81. The Apollonian gaze that Tethys and Gama enjoy, in Denis Cosgrove's analysis, "authorized both an individualist, imperial quest for *Fama* (Fame) and a more structured metaphysics of global order and harmony" as part of "the Portuguese crown's claim to universal empire" (*Apollo's Eye: A Cartographic Genealogy of the Earth in the Western Imagination* [Baltimore: Johns Hopkins University Press, 2001], 123, 120).

82. A similar panoramic survey of the reach of Spanish empire is presented to Carlos V in the *Suma de Geographía* of Martín Fernández de Enciso; see Andrés Prieto, "Alexander and the Geographer's Eye: Allegories of Knowledge in Martín Fernández de Enciso's *Suma de Geographía* (1519)," *Hispanic Review* 78.2 (2010): 169–88.

CHAPTER THREE

1. Richard Helgerson, *A Sonnet from Carthage: Garcilaso de la Vega and the New Poetry of Sixteenth-Century Europe* (Philadelphia: University of Pennsylvania Press, 2007), 13.

2. See Helgerson, *A Sonnet from Carthage*, 68–70.

3. Leah Middlebrook, *Imperial Lyric: New Poetry and New Subjects in Early Modern Spain* (University Park: The Pennsylvania State University Press, 2009), 11.

4. Middlebrook, *Imperial Lyric*, 102.

5. Marguerite Waller advocates for nautical motifs as structuring a journey of "self-interpretive problems" (*Petrarch's Poetics and Literary History* [Amherst: University of Massachusetts Press, 1980], 80). For Waller's discussion of the ship motif, see 80–83.

6. Giuseppe Mazzotta, *The Worlds of Petrarch* (Durham, NC: Duke University Press, 1993), 4, 58.

7. See "Il sonetto CLXXXIX," *Lectura Petrarce* 9/10 (1989–90): 151–77, and "Il motivo della 'navigatio' nel Canzoniere del Petrarca," *Atti e Memorie della Accademia Petrarca di Lettere, Arti e Scienze*, new ser., 51 (1989): 291–307. M[aría] Pilar Manero Sorolla also registers the figure of the poet as a ship on the sea in *Imágenes petrarquistas en la lírica española del Renacimiento: Repertorio* (Barcelona: PPU, 1990), 210.

8. Johannes Bartuschat, "Il ritratto di Laura (*RVF* 76–80)," in *Il Canzoniere: Lettura micro e macrotestuale*, ed. Michelangelo Picone (Ravenna: Longo, 2007), 207–23, at 210–11. Also see Picone, "Il sonetto CLXXXIX," 157–58.

9. At one point in his book on solitude, Petrarch comments on the inhabitants of the Fortunate Isles (Canaries), which, for Cachey, signals the beginning of viewing Canarians as savages to be repressed by Christian European civilization ("Petrarch, Boccaccio, and the New World Encounter," *Stanford Italian Review* 10.1 [1991]: 45–59, at 54). Petrarch observes, "You might say that [the Canarians] did not so much lead the solitary life as roam about in solitudes either with wild beasts or with their flocks" (*The Life of Solitude*, trans. Jacob Zeitlin [(Urbana): University of Illinois Press, 1924], 267). The verb translated as "roam" is the Latin *errare*, and Cachey argues that "the metaphorical, moral resonance of *errare* is unmistakable here, guaranteed by the human nature of these primitives which otherwise might have been in doubt, guided as they are by their natural instinct rather than their free will" ("Petrarch, Boccaccio, and the New World Encounter," 52).

10. The lack of nautical agency is one metaphor for the passionate, passive suffering that characterizes Petrarch's relationship to love in the *Canzoniere*, according to Ross Knecht: "Petrarch is not so much an active lover as one who suffers from love.... He habitually portrays the action of love as invasion, intrusion, influence, or inspiration—as a penetrative, overwhelming force acting from without upon a passive subject" ("'Invaded by the World': Passion, Passivity, and the Object of Desire in Petrarch's *Rime sparse*," *Comparative Literature* 63.3 [2011]: 235–52, at 237–38).

11. Mary Malcolm Gaylord, "The Making of Baroque Poetry," in *The Cambridge History of Spanish Literature*, ed. David T. Gies (Cambridge: Cambridge University Press, 2004), 222–37, at 228.

12. Knecht, "'Invaded by the World,'" 235–36.

13. George Mariscal, *Contradictory Subjects: Quevedo, Cervantes, and Seventeenth-Century Spanish Culture* (Ithaca, NY: Cornell University Press, 1991), 4–5.

14. Mariscal, *Contradictory Subjects*, 32.

15. The reliable, documentary evidence of Camões's biography is scant. For a critical overview in Portuguese, see *Luís de Camões: Obra completa*, ed. Antônio Salgado Júnior (Rio de Janeiro: Aguilar, 1963), xxvii-lv; in English, see Clive Willis, *Camões, Prince of Poets* (Bristol: HiPLAM, 2010), chapters 7 and 9.

16. *Petrarch's Guide to the Holy Land: Itinerary to the Sepulcher of Our Lord Jesus Christ (Itinerarium ad sepulchrum domini nostri Yehsu Christi); Facsimile Edition of Cremona, Biblioteca Statale, Deposito Libreria Civica, manuscript BB.1.2.5*, ed. and trans. Theodore J. Cachey Jr. (Notre Dame, IN: University of Notre Dame Press, 2002), 2.

17. Cachey, *Petrarch's Guide to the Holy Land*, 17, 25.

18. As with many of Camões's sonnets, the authorship of this one is uncertain (see Leodegário A. de Azevedo Filho, *Lírica de Camões*, vol. 1, *História, metodologia, corpus* [Lisbon: Imprensa Nacional-Casa da Moeda, 1985], 255–56). Most scholars have resolved attribution in favor of Camões.

19. A poem by Álvaro de Brito equates a stormy sea voyage and emotional suffering in a Petrarchan vein ("Cuydados deyxan magora," in *Cancioneiro Geral*, ed. Andrée Crabbé Rocha, vol. 1 [Lisbon: Centro do Livro Brasileiro, 1973], 241–44), and lyrics by Afonso Valente and Diogo Brandão play on the names of their *senhoras* that contain sea-related terms ("Triste eu seguy o mar," *Cancioneiro Geral*, vol. 2, 128, and "Quem bem sabe naueguar," vol. 3, 44).

20. Similarly, the related noun *perdição* (perdition) often meant "shipwreck."

21. Virgil, *Eclogues; Georgics; Aeneid I–VI*, trans. H. Rushton Fairclough, rev. G. P. Goold (Cambridge, MA: Harvard University Press, 1999).

22. Dante Alighieri, *The Divine Comedy: Inferno*, vol. 1, pt. 1, *Text*, trans. Charles S. Singleton (Princeton, NJ: Princeton University Press, 1989), 4–5.

23. Robert Hollander, *Allegory in Dante's "Commedia"* (Princeton, NJ: Princeton University Press, 1969), 85.

24. Hollander, *Allegory in Dante's "Commedia,"* 86. For Hollander's comparative reading of the two scenes, see 83–86.

25. Charles S. Singleton, *The Divine Comedy: Inferno*, vol. 1, pt. 2, *Commentary* (Princeton, NJ: Princeton University Press, 1989), 8.

26. John Freccero, *Dante: The Poetics of Conversion*, ed. Rachel Jacoff (Cambridge, MA: Harvard University Press, 1986), 31.

27. Freccero, *Dante: The Poetics of Conversion*, 31. Peter S. Hawkins finds that this moment is the spiritual shipwreck of the pilgrim (*Dante's Testaments: Essays in Scriptural Imagination* [Stanford, CA: Stanford University Press, 1999], 277).

28. Dante does not use the words "shipwreck" or "swimmer" in his verses, although the parallel established by Hollander (*Allegory in Dante's "Commedia"*) with the *Aeneid* suggests shipwreck as the reason for the exhausted traveler.

29. According to Hollander, there is a "human immediacy [in] the exhaustion of the barely surviving swimmer" (*Allegory in Dante's "Commedia,"* 86). For C. S. Lewis, the shipwrecked man is one of Dante's "psychological similes" that establishes an emotional connection between poet and reader ("Dante's Similes," in *Studies in Medieval and Renaissance Literature*, coll. Walter Hooper [Cambridge: Cambridge University Press, 1966], 64–77, at 70). Singleton, based on passages in St. Augustine and Hugh of St. Victor, reads the water from which Dante escapes (*pelago*) as a metaphor for the "lake of the heart" of humankind into which cupidity flows; see Charles S. Singleton, "'Sulla fiumana ove'l mar non ha vanto' (*Inferno*, II, 108)," *Romanic Review* 39 (1948): 269–77, at 274–76. Freccero relates the lake of the heart (*lago del cor*) to Aristotelian physiology as the place where the body's vital spirits reside (*Dante: The Poetics of Conversion*, 36–37).

30. Cachey, *Petrarch's Guide to the Holy Land*, 20.

31. Roland Greene, *Unrequited Conquests: Love and Empire in the Colonial Americas* (Chicago: University of Chicago Press, 1999), 143. The endless voyage, Greene continues, "is a symptom of what I am calling early modern anaculturalism. This is the outlook of poets who have paced the borders between races, religions, and worldviews; have experienced the contingency of transcultural reality and the unfulfillability of desire; and imagine their personae, however abstractly or hypothetically, as voyagers among worlds of difference" (145–46). These voyagers, it should be added, often move nautically between worlds of difference, especially in sixteenth-century texts. Greene includes Camões's "Como quando do mar tempestuoso" in this anacultural outlook (144–45).

32. Theodore J. Cachey, "From Shipwreck to Port: *Rvf* 189 and the Making of the *Canzoniere*," *MLN* 120 (2005): 30–49, at 33, 35.

33. Original Catalan and English translation are from Ausiàs March, *Selected Poems*, ed. and trans. Arthur Terry (Austin: University of Texas Press, 1976), 58–59.

34. Lola Badia, *Tradició i modernitat als segles XIV i XV: Estudis de cultura literària i lectures d'Ausiàs March* (Valencia: Institut Universitari de Filologia Valenciana; Barcelona: Publicacions de l'Abadia de Montserrat, 1993), 221–29; for the comparison to Petrarch, see 213–19. March's poetry enjoyed a second life in early modern Iberia in the translations into Castilian by the Portuguese poet and novelist Jorge de Montemor (Jorge de Montemayor, author of *La Diana*) in 1560 (*Las obras del excellentíssimo poeta mossén Ausias March caballero valenciano*, in Jorge de Montemayor, *Poesía completa*, ed. Juan Bautista de Avalle-Arce [Madrid: Biblioteca Castro, 1996], 1061–1257). Camões likely was familiar with these translations.

35. Steve Mentz, *At the Bottom of Shakespeare's Ocean* (London: Continuum, 2009), 35.

36. Mentz, *Shipwreck Modernity*, 118, 176.

37. For an overview of the legend in Iberian poetry after Garcilaso de la Vega, see Antonio Alatorre, "Sobre la 'gran fortuna' de un soneto de Garcilaso," *Nueva Revista de Filología Hispánica* 24.1 (1975): 142–77, and Gutierre de Cetina, *Rimas*, ed. Jesús Ponce Cárdenas (Madrid: Cátedra, 2014), 428–29. For some classical texts, see Fernando de Herrera, *Anotaciones a la poesía de Garcilaso*, ed. Inoria Pepe and José María Reyes (Madrid: Cátedra, 2001), 452–56. A number of Iberian texts in English translation can be found in Philip Krummrich, trans., *The Hero and Leander Theme in Iberian Literature, 1500–1800: An Anthology of Translations* (Lewiston, NY: Edwin Mellen Press, 2006).

38. Jason McCloskey, "'Navegaba Leandro el Helesponto': Love and Early Modern Navigation in Juan Boscán's *Leandro*," *Revista de Estudios Hispánicos* 47 (2013): 3–27.

39. McCloskey, "'Navegaba Leandro el Helesponto,'" 4.

40. McCloskey, "'Navegaba Leandro el Helesponto,'" 5, 8, 11. Ovid's Leander expresses the metaphor in this way: "Cum patietur hiemps, remis ego corporis utar" (When the storm permits, I shall make use of the oarage of my arms; *Heroides and Amores*, vol. 1, 2nd ed., trans. Grant Showerman, rev. G. P. Goold [Cambridge, MA: Harvard University Press, 1977], 259). The Spanish poet Diego Ramírez Pagán (ca. 1524–62), in one of four sonnets on Hero and Leander, makes explicit the relationship between body and ship: "Hazia Sesto Leandro nauegaua / Al tiempo que la mar

embrauecia, / Su cuerpo de nauío le seruía, / El mismo era la barca, y el remaua" (Toward Sestos Leander sailed. As the sea became fierce, his body was his ship, he himself was the boat and the oarsman; *Floresta de varia poesía* [Valencia, 1562], fol. v [r]).

41. Hero's fire is bivalent as it is the lamp that guides Leander as well as the flame of love burning within him. The nature of Hero's light is present in classical antecedents: Musaeus opens his poem with a brief treatment of the lamp and later describes "love's firebrand" (*Hero and Leander*, lines 1–15 and 88–91, in Callimachus, *Aetia, Iambi, Lyric Poems, Hecale, Minor Epic and Elegiac Poems, and Other Fragments*, trans. and ed. C. A. Trypanis/Musaeus, *Hero and Leander*, ed. Thomas Gelzer, trans. Cedric Whitman [Cambridge, MA: Harvard University Press, 1975], 289–389). Ovid specifies both the light and the flame (*lumen, ignis*) in Leander's letter to Hero (*Heroides and Amores*, 2nd ed., trans. Grant Showerman, rev. G. P. Goold [Cambridge, MA: Harvard University Press, 1977], 250; also see Clelia Bettini, "De Cartago ao Helesponto: Dois sonetos camonianos de inspiração clássica," in *Comentário a Camões*, vol. 2, ed. Rita Marnoto [Lisbon: Centro Interuniversitário de Estudos Camonianos; Cotovia, 2012], 75–101, at 92–94, 99–101).

42. M. S. Bate also notes that Ovid's Leander "literally becomes the *naufragus*" ("Tempestuous Poetry: Storms in Ovid's *Metamorphoses, Heroides* and *Tristia*," *Mnemosyne* 57 [2004]: 295–310, at 306).

43. This single-mindedness of purpose is especially apparent in Jorge de Montemayor's Leander sonnet: "Leandro en amoroso fuego ardía / a la orilla del mar, acompañado / de un solo pensamiento enamorado" (Leander in love's fire burned at sea's edge, beset by a single, amorous thought; Jorge de Montemayor, *Poesía completa*, 593).

44. In a similar line of thought, Isabel Torres, in comments on Garcilaso de la Vega's Eclogue II, notes that water "encapsulates the fundamental ambivalence of erotic experience, embracing the polarities of pleasure and pain within the antithetical metaphor of life and death" (*Love Poetry in the Spanish Golden Age: Eros, Eris, and Empire* [Woodbridge: Tamesis, 2013], 45). The waters of the Hellespont are doubly significant: they are Leander's doom, but they are also symbolically the desire that fatally engulfs him. Death is one form of amorous surrender.

45. See Alatorre, "Sobre la 'gran fortuna,'" 172–73. Jane Whetnall further notes that "after Camões the impact of Garcilaso's sonnet on this tradition is much attenuated" ("Hipólita de Narváez and the Leander Sonnet Tradition," *Bulletin of Hispanic Studies* 86.6 [2009]: 893–909, at 894).

46. Francisco de Sá de Miranda, *Obras completas*, vol. 1, 4th ed., ed. Rodrigues Lapa (Lisbon: Sá da Costa, 1976), 298.

47. Whetnall, "Hipólita de Narváez and the Leander Sonnet Tradition," 895, 896.

48. Jonathan Culler, *Theory of the Lyric* (Cambridge, MA: Harvard University Press, 2015), 190, 212, 239.

49. Culler, *Theory of the Lyric*, 187, 213, 216.

50. Whetnall, "Hipólita de Narváez and the Leander Sonnet Tradition," 899 and n. 21.

51. Sá de Miranda's sonnet also gestures toward the possibility of a deathly, silent voice in the closing tercet: "En fin, ondas, venceis (dixo, cubierto / ya de ellas)" (Waves, you triumph in the end [he said, already covered by them]; Sá de Miranda, *Obras completas*, 298). *Cubierto* might imply that the youth was already underwater

when he spoke, but it seems more likely that the adjective denotes an action in progress, that Leander was sinking as he addressed the water.

52. Ovid categorically opposes the pilot and the swimmer in Hero's letter to Leander: "quod cupis, hoc nautae metuunt, Leandre, natare; / exitus hic fractis puppibus esse solet" (What you are eager for, Leander—to swim—is the sailor's fear; 'tis that follows ever on the wreck of ships; *Heroides* 272–73).

53. Ovid has Leander succinctly state in letter 18 "fiat modo copia nandi, / idem navigium, navita, vector ero!" (If only I may swim, I will be at once ship, seaman, passenger!; *Heroides* 254–55). One aspect of Leander's letter in the *Heroides* that clearly would have appealed to the early modern Iberian poets is that the letter was sent to Hero by ship. The youth's missive is thus a seaborne text of love and navigation. In Camões and other poets, Leander's body replaces Ovid's seagoing letter and becomes a living letter that does not reach its addressee.

54. Culler, *Theory of the Lyric*, 223.

55. The Spanish text is from Gutierre de Cetina, *Rimas*, 432.

56. Diogo Bernardes, *Obras completas*, vol. 1, ed. Marques Braga (Lisbon: Sá da Costa, 1945), 66.

57. The name Dinamene as a possible reference to Camões's lover who drowned in the Mekong River in a shipwreck is a biographical legend generated by this sonnet. In comments on "Ah! minha Dinamene!," Faria e Sousa claims to have seen the manuscripts of Camões's *Rimas* in which the poem bears the title "Ad Dinamenem aquis extinctam" (To Dinamene, drowned) (*Rimas varias de Luis de Camoens, principe de los poetas heroycos, y lyricos de España*, bk. 1 [Lisbon: Theotonio Damaso de Mello, 1685], 278).

58. Trevor Dadson argues that this sonnet is one of Camões's compositions that doubts "the immortalising powers of the spoken word" ("From Voice to Silence: Orpheus and the Epitaph in Garcilaso and Camões," *Portuguese Studies* 21 [2005]: 101–11, at 109).

59. Sannazaro's *Piscatory Eclogues* (*Piscatoriae Eclogae*) were published in 1526.

60. Jacopo Sannazaro, *Latin Poetry*, trans. Michael C. J. Putnam (Cambridge, MA: Harvard University Press, 2009), 112–13.

61. Interestingly, Sannazaro's fisherman Lycon dreams of being a world-traveling, oceanic explorer: "Externas trans pontum quaerere terras / iam pridem est animus, quo numquam navita, numquam / piscator veniat; fors illic nostra licebit / fata queri. Boreae extremo damnata sub axe / stagna petam et rigidis numquam non cana pruinis / an Libyae rapidas Austrique tepentis harenas, / et videam nigros populos Solemque propinquum?" (It has long since been my thought to seek out foreign lands across the sea, never reached by a sailor, never by a fisherman. There chance will allow me to lament my fate. Shall I go in search of sluggish waters, consigned beneath the farthest pole of Boreas, eternally white with stiffening chill, or shall I view the scorching sands of Libya and of the searing Auster, and dark-skinned races and the nearby Sun?; Sannazaro, *Latin Poetry*, 116–17). An incipient "epic" impulse in Lycon seems to harbor a sad remedy for amorous anguish, while Camões's Sereno is resigned to a solitary existence in Portugal.

62. Greene, *Unrequited Conquests*, 143.

63. Maria de Lurdes Saraiva, ed., *Luís de Camões: Lírica completa*, vol. 3 ([Lisbon]: Imprensa Nacional-Casa da Moeda, 1981), 335.

64. Vítor Manuel Pires de Aguiar e Silva, *Maneirismo e barroco na poesia lírica portuguesa* (Coimbra: Centro de Estudos Românicos, 1971), 229–35. Marimilda Rosa Vitali argues for "Como quando do mar tempestuoso" as a Camonian example of the *navigium amoris* ("As cadeias da esperança," in *Comentário a Camões*, vol. 2, ed. Rita Marnoto [Lisbon: Centro Interuniversitário de Estudos Camonianos; Cotovia, 2012], 103–27, at 104), although there is no voyage in the sonnet, only its disastrous end.

65. For an overview of some Portuguese travelers in early modernity, see Josiah Blackmore, "Travelers: Voyages to Known and Unknown Worlds," in *A Cultural History of the Sea in the Early Modern Age*, ed. Steve Mentz, vol. 3 of *A Cultural History of the Sea*, 6 vols., ed. Margaret Cohen (London: Bloomsbury Academic, 2021), 157–77.

66. The *como* . . . *así* construction appears in sonnets by Juan Boscán, whom Camões admired. These include Sonnets 107 ("Como'l patrón que, 'n golfo navegando"), 112 ("Como después del tempestoso día"), and 123 ("Si en mitad del dolor tener memoria") (*Obra completa*, ed. Carlos Clavería [Madrid: Cátedra, 1999]). Boscán's similes establish the emotional states of the lyric subject. The Catalan poet builds the *como* . . . *así* comparison around two different grammatical subjects, with the second always being the first-person *yo* as the subject of the *así* clause. This swerve to the first person presents an emotional state or experience as constitutive of the poetic subject, a state that turns on the extremes or pronounced changes of emotion. There is, consequently, a discernible tension in the *como* clause toward resolution, and this appears with *así* and the inscription of the first-person subject into the poem. What Camões evidently gleaned from Boscán in these similes was a syntactical structure of establishing contrasting and conflictual emotional experiences of the poetic subject as essential to that subject.

67. In a sonnet exploring the survival of hope as an illogical consequence of love when amorous experience has been definitively relegated to the past, Francisco de Sá de Miranda invokes the mariner who, having escaped maritime danger, yearns to return to the sea because he takes offense at life on land. The final stanza reads: "Quem do mar escapou / quanto mal conta, / que perigos sem fim! E logo brada / outra vez òs da nau: na terra afronta!" (He who has escaped from the sea, what terrors he relates, what dangers without end! And then he calls out to those on board the ship: the land offends!; Sá de Miranda, *Obras completas*, vol. 1, 294).

68. Emotion as an oceanic depth also informs Juan Boscán's Sonnet 107, "Como'l patrón que, 'n golfo navegando." Boscán compares a pilot's fearless control of a ship in good weather to the poet's calm plumbing of the depths of his affect ("yo por lo hondo travesando / de mi querer"; I, traveling the depths of my desire) in untroubled times.

69. The sonnet appears in Bernardo Cappello, *Rime* (Venice: Guerra, 1560), 6. I thank Konrad Eisenbichler of the University of Toronto for the English translation. Cappello led a life in politics marked by numerous scandals. Not much is available on him or his work; see Alberto M. Ghisalberti, ed., *Dizionario biografico degli italiani* (Rome: Istituto della Enciclopedia Italiana, 1960–[2019]), s.v. "Cappello, Bernardo." One of Camões's early editors and critics, Manuel de Faria e Sousa, partially quotes Cappello's poem in relation to Camões's sonnet in *Rimas varias*, bk. 1, 159.

70. "luctantem Icariis fluctibus Africum / mercator metuens otium et oppidi / lau-

dat rura sui; mox reficit ratis / quassas, indocilis pauperiem pati" (When a gale from Africa fights with the Icarian waves, the frightened trader recommends an easy life on a farm near his home town; a little later he repairs his shattered fleet, for he cannot learn to put up with modest means; Horace, *Odes and Epodes*, ed. and trans. Niall Rudd, [Cambridge, MA: Harvard University Press, 2004], 22–23).

71. Ovid, *Metamorphoses* 1.131, 132–33.

72. Vítor Manuel de Aguiar e Silva, *Camões: Labirintos e fascínios* (Lisbon: Cotovia, 1994), 168. For an analysis of Camões's ideas and their relation to Neoplatonism, see 170–77.

73. Garcilaso de la Vega, *Obra poética y textos en prosa*, ed. Bienvenido Morros (Barcelona: Crítica, 2007), 92.

74. Marimilda Rosa Vitali, "Amor, co a esperança já perdida," in *Comentário a Camões*, vol. 2, ed. Rita Marnoto (Lisbon: Centro Interuniversitário de Estudos Camonianos; Cotovia, 2012), 35–38, at 35. For a study of votive offerings from mariners in early modern Spanish poetry, see Elizabeth B. Davis, "La promesa del náufrago: El motivo marinero del *ex-voto*, de Garcilaso a Quevedo," in *Studies in Honor of James O. Crosby*, ed. Lía Schwartz (Newark: Juan de la Cuesta, 2004), 109–23. Davis's comments on Garcilaso's sonnet and its relation to Horace's Ode V are found on 113–15. Vitali examines the topoi of the ex-voto of the soaked garments and of shipwreck in numerous Spanish and Italian poets in "As cadeias da esperança," in *Comentário a Camões*, vol. 2, Rita Marnoto, ed. (Lisbon: Centro Interuniversitário de Estudos Camonianos; Cotovia, 2012), 103–27. Daniel L. Heiple notes that the motif of the votive offering is found in Virgil, Horace, and the *Greek Anthology* and was popular in Renaissance Neoplatonic poetry (*Garcilaso de la Vega and the Italian Renaissance* [University Park: The Pennsylvania State University Press, 1994], 251).

75. See Sílvio Castro, "Metáfora do naufrágio e viagem em Camões," in *Actas da V Reunião Internacional de Camonistas: São Paulo, 20 a 24 de julho de 1987* ([São Paulo]: A Universidade, 1987), 713–20, and "Naufrágio como metáfora e palinódia em Camões," *Revista Camoniana*, 3rd ser., 13 (2003): 135–48.

76. "Que dias há que n' alma me tem posto / um não sei quê, que nasce não sei onde, / vem não sei como, e doi não sei porquê" (For, a while ago, love placed in my soul I don't know what, from I don't know where, coming to me I don't know how, and aching I don't know why). This is one instance of the use of the *nescio quid* topos (Maria Micaela Dias Pereira Ramon Moreira, *Os sonetos amorosos de Camões: Estudo tipológico* [Braga: Universidade do Minho, Centro de Estudos Humanísticos, 1998], 143).

77. I follow Costa Pimpão's numbering of the poems.

78. Carlos Ascenso André, *Mal de ausência: O canto do exílio na lírica do humanismo português* (Coimbra: Minerva, 1992), 29, 48.

79. Maria do Céu Fraga, "O tempo e o espaço: a errância na lírica camoniana," *Floema* 7 (2010): 43–59, at 47–48.

80. Laurence E. Hooper, "Exile and Petrarch's Reinvention of Authorship," *Renaissance Quarterly* 69 (2016): 1217–56, at 1229.

81. Francesco Petrarca, *Rerum familiarum libri I–VIII*, trans. Aldo S. Bernardo (Albany: State University of New York Press, 1975), 8. Cachey remarks that "the incessantly wandering, incessantly writing Petrarchan subject conflates the planes of textual and territorial space in order to extend the range of the Petrarchan self and to

authenticate the reality of that self by fixing it against the backdrop of cartographical-geographical space" (*Petrarch's Guide to the Holy Land*, 25). The same may be said about Camões, except that the Portuguese poet wandered a vastly expanded, transoceanic geographical space, and a dimension of his lyric, maritime subjectivity is premised on a senselessness experienced in the new or emerging corners of the world.

82. Teófilo Braga first transcribed the dedication to this sonnet: "A Pero Moniz, que morreu no mar do Monte Felix, em epitaphio" (Epitaph for Pero Moniz, who died at sea near Mount Felix) (*Camões: Epoca e vida* [Porto: Chardron, 1907], 558).

83. Roland Greene, *Five Words: Critical Semantics in the Age of Shakespeare and Cervantes* (Chicago: University of Chicago Press, 2013), 146, 148.

84. Ayesha Ramachandran, *The Worldmakers: Global Imagining in Early Modern Europe* (University of Chicago Press, 2015), 125.

85. "Esta é a ditosa pátria minha amada, / À qual se o Céu me dá, que eu sem perigo / Torne, com esta empresa já acabada, / Acabe-se esta luz ali comigo" (This is my beautiful, beloved homeland, to which, if Heaven permits, I will safely return, this my undertaking having been completed; there may my light be extinguished; *Os Lusíadas*, III.21.i-iv).

86. *Rimas varias*, bk. 1, "Vida del poeta," §13. For a discussion of the legend of Camões's amorous exile, see Antônio Salgado Júnior, ed., *Luís de Camões: Obra completa*, xlvi-xlviii.

87. The poet spent three years in military service in Goa, most likely arriving there in September of 1553. In the same year, Camões participated in an expedition to the Malabar Coast against the Sultan of Chembe (the "Rei da pimenta," or Pepper King) under the command of the viceroy Afonso de Noronha (Willis, *Camões, Prince of Poets*, 210).

88. Willis, *Camões, Prince of Poets*, 176.

89. Cicero refers to Simonides and Themistocles in *De oratore*, bk. 2, trans. E. W. Sutton (Cambridge, MA: Harvard University Press, 1948), 464-67, and in *De finibus bonorum et malorum*, II, trans. H. Rackham (Cambridge, MA: Harvard University Press, 1931), 197; Quintilian tells the story in *The Orator's Education*, bks. 11-12, trans. Donald A. Russell (Cambridge, MA: Harvard University Press, 2001), 63-67. For a discussion of the classical treatises of memory, including Simonides's technique, see Frances A. Yates, *The Art of Memory* (Chicago: University of Chicago Press, 1966), chapter 1. In his life of Themistocles, Plutarch mentions Simonides but not the poet's memory arts (Plutarch, *Lives: Themistocles and Camillus; Aristides and Cato Major; Cimon and Lucullus*, trans. Bernadotte Perrin [Cambridge, MA: Harvard University Press, 1914]).

90. Translations of this elegy are from Luís de Camões, *Sonnets and Other Poems*, trans. Richard Zenith (Dartmouth: University of Massachusetts, Dartmouth, 2009), 131-45.

91. Vítor Aguiar e Silva, *A lira dourada e a tuba canora* (Lisbon: Cotovia, 2008), 176.

92. Jorge A. Osório, "Na elegia de Camões: 'O Poeta Simónides, falando,'" *Via Spiritus* 16 (2009): 189-213, at 206.

93. The addressee ("Senhor") of the elegy is unidentified.

94. Maria do Céu Fraga, *Os géneros maiores na poesia lírica de Camões* (Coimbra: Universidade de Coimbra, 2003), 218.

95. Cristóvão Falcão's eclogue *Trovas de Crisfal* (1554), for example, claims that

the poem was recorded for posterity by a nymph who inscribed the lovelorn story on a poplar tree so that, in growing, the tree would raise the sad story high so lowly thoughts could not assail it. In Camões's piscatory eclogue, the fisherman Sereno, in his anguished lament on the inaccessible Galatea, calls the nymph's attention to her name written in the sand by Love, who will protect it from obliteration. In Love's gathering of shells at the eclogue's close, Faria e Sousa finds a transposition of the material objects of writing to the maritime world: the sand becomes paper and the shells, a pen (*Rimas varias*, bk. 4, 9). The scene of arenaceous inscription is not in Sannazaro's "Galatea."

96. Vítor Aguiar e Silva, "A elegia na lírica de Camões," in *Actas da VI Reunião Internacional de Camonistas*, ed. Seabra Pereira and Manuel Ferro (Coimbra: Imprensa da Universidade de Coimbra, 2012), 19–31, at 31.

97. Helder Macedo, "O poeta Simónides e o capitão Temístocles," in *O amor das letras e das gentes: In honor of Maria de Lourdes Belchior Pontes*, ed. João Camilo dos Santos and Frederick G. Williams (Santa Barbara: Center for Portuguese Studies, University of California—Santa Barbara, 1995), 100–104, at 102, and "Love as Knowledge: The Lyric Poetry of Camões," *Portuguese Studies* 14 (1998): 51–64, at 59.

98. Camões here plays on the two meanings of *cabo* as "cape" and "end." The expression *Cabo da Esperança*, instead of *Cabo da Boa Esperança*, is a reference to the geographic locale but literally means "the end of hope."

99. Camões, *Sonnets and Other Poems*, trans. Richard Zenith, 224n11. Virgil also extols the rustic life in book 2 of the *Georgics*; Horace's commendation ("Beatus ille," mirrored in Camões's "Ditoso seja") is the subject of his Epode 2, and Tibullus's praise occurs in book 1 of his poems. (For a comparative reading of this portion of Camões's elegy and the *Georgics*, see Osório, "Na elegia de Camões," 207–11.) Faria e Sousa characteristically provides a catalogue of classical and vernacular instances of the conceit; see *Rimas*, bk. 2, pt. 2, 16–17.

100. *Culex*, lines 58, 60, in Virgil, *Aeneid 7–12; Appendix Vergiliana*, trans. H. R. Fairclough, rev. G. P. Goold (Cambridge, MA: Harvard University Press, 2000).

101. Gordon Braden, *Petrarchan Love and the Continental Renaissance* (New Haven, CT: Yale University Press, 1999), 40. In *Rime* 23, the Italian poet notes, "[L]e vive voci m'erano interditte, / ond' io gridai con carta et con incostro" (Words spoken aloud were forbidden me; so I cried out with paper and ink; PLP 64–65).

102. Interestingly, Virgil also ascribes a voice to the sea in book 3 of the *Aeneid*: as Aeneas approaches Aetna and the danger of shipwreck at Scylaceum, he says: "et gemitum ingentem pelagi pulsataque saxa / audimus longe fractasque ad litora voces" (From afar we hear the loud moaning of the main, the beating of the rocks, and recurrent crash of waves upon the shore; *Aeneid* 1.555–56). On Virgil's use of *voces* (voices), translated in this version as "crash," R. D. Williams (whose own translation reads: "and the voice of the breakers reverberating on the shore") notes that "this is a very unusual use of *voces*," and explains that Virgil is developing a personification of the sea begun with *gemitus*, and the meaning of *fractae* is probably "the pulsating or reverberating effect of a noise low in pitch. There is probably also a suggestion of the idea of 'breaking' waves" (*The Aeneid of Virgil, Books 1-6* [Basingstoke: Macmillan; St Martin's Press, 1972], 315–16). Perhaps this is one of Camões's sources for voicing the coastal sea.

103. Scholars have proposed various candidates for the identity of the *ilha* men-

tioned here. Faria e Sousa thinks that it is Goa (*Rimas varias*, bk. 2, 44), while Hernâni Cidade opts for Ternate (*Luís de Camões I: O lírico* [Lisbon: Imprensa Nacional, 1936], 228) and Landeg White adds Ambon as a possibility (*The Collected Lyric Poems of Luís de Camões* [Princeton, NJ: Princeton University Press], 12).

104. Garcilaso de la Vega, *Obra poética y textos en prosa*, 84; translation from Roland Greene, *Unrequited Conquests: Love and Empire in the Colonial Americas* (Chicago: University of Chicago Press, 1999), 161.

105. Fernando de Herrera, *Anotaciones a la poesía de Garcilaso*, ed. Inoria Pepe and José María Reyes (Madrid: Cátedra, 2001), 299.

106. Greene, *Unrequited Conquests*, 161.

107. Michael C. J. Putnam, "Vergil, Ovid, and the Poetry of Exile," in *A Companion to Vergil's Aeneid and Its Tradition*, ed. Joseph Farrell and Michael C. J. Putnam (Chichester: Wiley-Blackwell, 2010), 80–95, at 80.

108. "Assi só . . . / se via em terra estranha, / a cuja triste dor não acha igual. // Só sua doce Musa o acompanha, / nos versos saüdosos que escrevia" (Thus alone . . . he found himself in a foreign land, suffering an unequalled sadness. Only his Muse was with him in the sad and yearning verses he wrote).

109. This location on the Tagus has led some critics to postulate that Camões was exiled to nearby Santarém. See Antônio Salgado Júnior, "Biografia de Luís de Camões," in Luís de Camões, *Obra completa*, xxvii-lv, xlvi.

110. Camões locates his voice in this poem on Cape Aromata (Cape Guardafui) in the Gulf of Aden. This part of the Arabian Peninsula was called Arabia Felix by early geographers. Camões participated in an excursion to the Red Sea in 1555, and remained for some time at Guardafui.

111. Tomé Pires, in his *Suma Oriental* (written 1512–15), provides a description of Arabia Felix and the Gulf of Aden that is similar to Camões's: "[E] casy tudo he deserto he desabitado he trr̃a escaluada ssem fruto. . . . [T]em este estreito vemtos quemtes. . . ." (It is almost all entirely desert—uninhabited, sterile land that bears no fruit. . . . In the strait there are hot winds; *A suma oriental de Tomé Pires e o livro de Francisco Rodrigues*, ed. Armando Cortesão [Coimbra: Por ordem da Universidade, 1978], 137).

112. Cleonice Berardinelli, "'Junto dum seco, fero e estéril monte,'" in *Estudos Camonianos*, 2nd rev. ed. (Rio de Janeiro: Nova Fronteira; Cátedra Padre António Vieira, 2000), 235–42, at 239.

CHAPTER FOUR

1. References to the Portuguese original are cited as RSV with page numbers.

2. *Historia da muy notauel perda do Galeão grande sam João. Em q̃ se contam os innumeraveis trabalhos e grandes desauenturas q̃ aconteceram ao Capitão Manoel de Sousa de Sepulueda E o lam̃etauel fim q̃ elle e sua molher e filhos e toda a mais gente ouverão. O que se perdeo no anno de M.D.LII. a vinte e quatro de Junho, na terra do Natal em xxxj graos.* This became the most well-known and widely translated of the Portuguese shipwreck narratives. Camões's contemporary Jerónimo de Corte-Real composed an epic poem on the Sepúlveda story (*Navfragio e lastimoso sucesso da perdicam de Manoel de Sousa de Sepulueda, & dona Lianor de Sá, sua molher & filhos*, 1594).

3. English translations of selected narratives can be found in C. R. Boxer, ed. and

trans., *The Tragic History of the Sea*, ed. Josiah Blackmore (Minneapolis: University of Minnesota Press, 2001).

4. The original pamphlet (*folheto*) of the *Relação* was printed in Coimbra in 1564. It is common practice to refer to individual Portuguese shipwreck narratives by the name of the doomed vessel. The main types of Portuguese high-seas ships were the *caravela* (caravel), *galeão* (galleon), and *nau* (carrack or great ship); smaller vessels used in the fifteenth century were the *barca* (bark) and *barinel*. The *galeão* and *nau* predominated on the *carreira da Índia*. Both were awkward and unwieldy vessels, built for strength rather than sailing agility. A wealth of information on ships, nautical practices, and technology during the early modern empire is in C. R. Boxer, "Introduction," in *The Tragic History of the Sea*, 1–50; Roger C. Smith, *Vanguard of Empire: Ships of Exploration in the Age of Columbus* (New York: Oxford University Press, 1993); and Domingues, "Vasco da Gama's Voyage," 3. A partial English translation of Perestrelo's narrative is in *Records of South-Eastern Africa, Collected in Various Libraries and Archive Departments in Europe*, ed. and trans. George McCall Theal, vol. 1 (Cape Town: Government of the Cape Colony, 1898), 218–85, but translations here are mine.

5. Such positional disadvantage for Western imperial travelers is common in shipwreck texts. Shipwreck literature affords numerous examples of a dynamic of imperial power relations that "acknowledge both the multi-directional fluidity of cross-cultural contact and instances of indigenous agency" (Klein, "Camões and the Sea," 177).

6. The use of *formosa* (beautiful) to describe the wrecked ship is noteworthy. I find here an example of Steve Mentz's assertion that "[a] vision of the ocean as utopian no-place . . . opens up the underlying thalassophilia of shipwreck narratives, a frightened but powerful longing for the destructive element" (*Shipwreck Modernity*, xxiii).

7. Mentz, *Shipwreck Modernity*, xxxiii.

8. C. R. Boxer notes, "The Crown *regimentos* stressed that only experienced mariners should be entered as sailors for the India voyage, but these have never been too plentiful in Portugal. As early as the first decade of the sixteenth century, a captain found that his rustic crew could not distinguish between starboard and larboard until he tied a bunch of onions to one side of the ship and a bunch of garlic to the other. Those makeshift seamen who survived a couple of India voyages presumably became 'old salts', but complaints abounded in the years 1570–1650 that tailors, cobblers, lackeys, ploughmen and 'ignorant boys' of all kinds were freely shipped as deep-sea mariners" (*The Tragic History of the Sea*, 9–10).

9. Thomas R. Hart, ed., *Gil Vicente: Farces and Festival Plays* (Eugene: University of Oregon, 1972), 54.

10. Ricardo Padrón notes that "the distortions inherent in the way itinerary maps figure territory do not allow the reader's eye to wander in any useful or meaningful way off the network of routes" (*The Spacious Word: Cartography, Literature, and Empire in Early Modern Spain* [Chicago: University of Chicago Press, 2004], 61).

11. Wes Folkert, *The Sound of Shakespeare* (London: Routledge, 2002), 34.

12. Bruce R. Smith, *The Acoustic World of Early Modern England: Attending to the O-Factor* (Chicago: University of Chicago Press, 1999), 44.

13. Dominic Pettman, *Sonic Intimacy: Voice, Species, Technics (Or, How to Listen to the World)* (Stanford, CA: Stanford University Press, 2017), 90.

14. *On Things Heard*, trans. T. Loveday and E. S. Forster, in *The Complete Works of*

Aristotle: *The Revised Oxford Translation*, vol. 1, ed. Jonathan Barnes (Princeton, NJ: Princeton University Press, 1995), 1229–36, at 1232.

15. Susan Boynton, Sarah Kay, Alison Cornish, and Andrew Albin, "Sound Matters," *Speculum* 91.4 (2016): 998–1039, at 1001.

16. Boynton et al., "Sound Matters," 1005.

17. Boynton et al., "Sound Matters," 1006.

18. Smith, *The Acoustic World of Early Modern England*, 46; emphasis in original.

19. See Josiah Blackmore, "Portuguese Scenes of the Senses, Medieval and Early Modern," in Ryan D. Giles and Steven Wagschal, eds., *Beyond Sight: Engaging the Senses in Iberian Literatures and Cultures, 1200–1750* (Toronto: University of Toronto Press, 2018), 209–24, at 216–17.

20. "Hearing is a physiological constant; listening is a psychological variable" (Smith, *The Acoustic World of Early Modern England*, 7).

21. Haroldo de Campos, *A arte no horizonte do provável e outros ensaios* (São Paulo: Perspectiva, 1977), 148–49. The onomatopoeia of stanza 8 is also noted by Adrien Roig, "L'utilisation poétique de l'écho dans *Les Lusiades*," *Quadrant* 9 (1992): 21–33, at 21–22. Onomatopoeia is part of the tradition of epic storm-writing (M. P. O. Morford, *The Poet Lucan: Studies in Rhetorical Epic* [New York: Barnes and Noble, 1967], 24–25). Stephen Reckert identifies other instances in *Os Lusíadas* and in Camões's lyric poetry where certain sounds (*nd*, *r*, *v*, and *l*) onomatopoetically evoke the sea and being at sea ("'Micro-significantes' na semiótica de Camões," in *IV Reunião Internacional de Camonistas: Actas* [Ponta Delgada: Universidade dos Açores, 1984], 523–40, at 527–29 and 530–32). Manuel de Faria e Sousa also recognizes the sonic character of this stanza: "Antes que diga cosa alguna, sobre lo tocante a esta e. dirè, que todas las vezes que la recito, me parece voy entrando por algunas profundas cuevas: i que me perturba el oido algun son horrendo: i finalmente que me hallo navegando por el mar" (Before I make any comment on matters related to this stanza I will note that, every time I recite it, I seem to be entering deep caves and my ear is assaulted by a horrible sound. In the end I find myself sailing on the sea; *Lusíadas Commentadas*, vol. 2, col. 18).

22. Brayton, *Shakespeare's Ocean*, 68.

23. In the *Metamorphoses*, Ovid also describes Triton's shell blast as reaching the world's every part. This occurs in the description of the world flood in book 1. Triton is summoned from the deep and sounds his horn—above the surface of the water, it should be noted—which reaches "the shores that lie beneath the rising and setting sun" (litora voce replet sub utroque iacentia Phoebo; 1.338). Yet in this Ovidian scene the waters that cover the earth, in response to Triton's call, recede, uncovering shores, riverbanks, hills, land, and trees. Ovid's aquatic world becomes diminished at the sound; water and the sound of the conch do not overlap but are in opposition. Camões's seas are the sympathetic courier and amplifier of Triton's blast, and wash over the entire world. Now the world seas act as networks of communication and influence and allow a Portuguese thalassocracy, the empirical and political counterpart to Camões's poetic, globe-finding voice that is the symbolic registration of Portuguese fame.

24. Steven Feld and Keith H. Basso, *Senses of Place* (Santa Fe: School of American Research Press, 1996).

25. Sara V. Torres, "Oceanic Epic: The Translations of the *Lusiads* in the Global Renaissance," *Digital Philology: A Journal of Medieval Cultures* 8.1 (2019): 105–22, at 111.

26. Angela Leighton, *Hearing Things: The Work of Sound in Literature* (Cambridge, MA: Belknap/Harvard University Press, 2018), 30.

27. *As obras de Gil Vicente*, vol. 2, ed. José Camões ([Lisbon]: Centro de Estudos de Teatro; Imprensa Nacional-Casa da Moeda, 2002), 93.

28. For a comparative study of some of these antecedents, see Maria Helena Rocha Pereira, "A tempestade marítima de 'Os Lusíadas': estudo comparativo," in *Actas da V Reunião Internacional de Camonistas, São Paulo, 20 a 24 de julho de 1987* (São Paulo: [Universidade de São Paulo], 1987), 205–15.

29. Hélio J. S. Alves, *Camões, Corte-Real e o sistema da epopeia quinhentista* (Coimbra: Universidade de Coimbra, 2001), 407–9, and Murrin, *Trade and Romance*, 163–79.

30. Klein, "Camões and the Sea," 166.

31. David Novak, "Noise," in *Keywords in Sound*, ed. David Novak and Matt Sakakeeny (Durham, NC: Duke University Press, 2015), 125–38, at 125.

32. Ramachandran, *The Worldmakers*, 113. For comments on the storm as a battle with the elements and the allegorical feminization of the natural world that boasts Lucretian precedents, see 119–20.

33. In book 11 of *Metamorphoses*, Ovid writes: "undarum incursu gravis unda, tonitribus aether . . . et modo, cum fulvas ex imo vertit harenas, concolor est illis" (The waves run mountain-high and seem to reach the very heavens. . . . Now the water is tawny with the sands swept up from the bottom of the sea; 11.154–57).

34. Rodrigo Toromoreno, "'Ora pro nobis': The Public Expansion of the Private Portuguese Voyage in *Os Lusíadas*," *Idiom: English Undergraduate Journal* [University of Toronto] 3 (2009): 45–52.

35. Toromoreno, "'Ora pro nobis,'" 51.

36. For Luís de Oliveira e Silva, in Camões's pen the gods are paralyzed by the weight of destiny and are thus unable to effect lasting change; Camões "definitively inters Greco-Roman mythology" and "de-theologizes" it ("Consílio dos deuses marinhos," in *Dicionário de Luís de Camões*, ed. Vítor Aguiar e Silva [Lisbon: Caminho, 2011], 283–86, at 283, 286).

37. Philip Hardie, *Virgil's* Aeneid: *Cosmos and Imperium* (Oxford: Clarendon Press, 1986), 176.

38. Klein, "Mapping the Waters," 243.

39. See Katharina N. Piechocki, *Cartographic Humanism: The Making of Early Modern Europe* (Chicago: University of Chicago Press, 2019), 218–19.

WORKS CITED

[Abreu, Lisuarte de]. *Livro de Lisuarte de Abreu*, Lisbon: Comissão Nacional para as Comemorações dos Descobrimentos Portugueses, 1992.

Alatorre, Antonio. "Sobre la 'gran fortuna' de un soneto de Garcilaso," *Nueva Revista de Filología Hispánica* 24.1 (1975): 142–77.

Albuquerque, Luís de. "Introdução," in *Memória das armadas que de Portugal pasaram ha Índia e esta primeira e ha com que Vasco da Gama partio ao descobrimento dela por mamdado de el Rei Dom Manvel no segvmdo anno de sev reinado e no do nacimento de XPO de 1497*, Lisbon: Academia das Ciências de Lisboa, 1979, 5–13.

Albuquerque, Luís de, and Francisco Contente Domingues, eds. *Dicionário de história dos descobrimentos portugueses*, vol. 2, Lisbon: Caminho, 1994.

Alegria, Maria Fernanda, Suzanne Daveau, João Carlos Garcia, and Francesc Relaño. "Portuguese Cartography in the Renaissance," in *The History of Cartography*, vol. 3, part 1, David Woodward, ed., Chicago: University of Chicago Press, 2007, 975–1068.

Alighieri, Dante. *The Divine Comedy: Inferno*, vol. 1, parts 1 and 2, Charles S. Singleton, trans., Princeton, NJ: Princeton University Press, 1989.

Alves, Hélio J. S. *Camões, Corte-Real e o sistema da epopeia quinhentista*, Coimbra: Universidade de Coimbra, 2001.

———. "A máquina do mundo n'Os Lusíadas," in *Dicionário de Luís de Camões*, Vítor Aguiar e Silva, ed., Lisbon: Caminho, 2011, 555–59.

———. "Poesia oceânica: Camões, da navegação ao naufrágio, ante o precedente de Corte-Real/Oceanic Poetry: Camões, from Seafaring to Shipwreck, Faced with Corte-Real's Precedent," *Limite: Revista de Estudios Portugueses y de la Lusofonía* 13.1 (2019): 53–81.

———. "O som e a fúria d'*Os Lusíadas*," *Santa Barbara Portuguese Studies* 8 (2003): 49–65.

———. "Teoría de la épica en el renacimiento portugués," in *La teoría de la épica en el siglo XVI (España, Francia, Italia y Portugal)*, María José Vega and Lara Vilà, eds., Pontevedra: Academia del Hispanismo, 2010, 137–73.

Ames, Glenn J., ed. and trans. *Em Nome de Deus: The Journal of the First Voyage of Vasco da Gama to India, 1497–99*, Leiden: Brill, 2009.

André, Carlos Ascenso. *Mal de ausência: O canto do exílio na lírica do humanismo português*, Coimbra: Minerva, 1992.

Aristotle. *Metaphysics*, W. D. Ross, trans., in *The Complete Works of Aristotle: The Revised Oxford Translation*, vol. 2, Jonathan Barnes, ed., Princeton, NJ: Princeton University Press, 1984, 1552–1728.

———. *On Things Heard*, T. Loveday and E. S. Forster, trans., in *The Complete Works of Aristotle: The Revised Oxford Translation*, vol. 1, Jonathan Barnes, ed., Princeton, NJ: Princeton University Press, 1995, 1229–36.

———. *Sense and Sensibilia*, J. I. Beare, trans., in *The Complete Works of Aristotle: The Revised Oxford Translation*, vol. 1, Jonathan Barnes, ed., Princeton, NJ: Princeton University Press, 1984, 693–713.

Arte de Trovar do Cancioneiro da Biblioteca Nacional de Lisboa, Giuseppe Tavani, ed., Lisbon: Colibri, 1999.

Asensio, Eugenio. *Poética y realidad en el cancionero peninsular de la Edad Media*, 2nd rev. ed., Madrid: Gredos, 1970.

Badia, Lola. *Tradició i modernitat als segles XIV i XV: Estudis de cultura literària i lectures d'Ausiàs March*, Valencia: Institut Universitari de Filologia Valenciana; Barcelona: Publicacions de l'Abadia de Montserrat, 1993.

Baïf, Lazare de. *De re vestiaria, vascularia, & nauali*, Lutetiae: Apud Carolum Stephanum, Typographum Regium, 1553.

Barletta, Vincent. "The *Lusiads* Affect: Standing in the Middle of the Sea," in *A Companion to World Literature*, vol. 3, Christopher Lupke and Evan Nicoll-Johnson, eds., Hoboken: John Wiley and Sons, 2020, 1469–79.

———. "Songs of Stance," in *Portuguese Literature and the Environment*, Victor K. Mendes and Patrícia Vieira, eds., Lanham, MD: Lexington Books, 2019, 79–92.

Barros, João de. *Ásia de João de Barros: Dos feitos que os Portugueses fizeram no descobrimento e conquista dos mares e terras do Oriente. Primeira Década*, [Lisbon]: Imprensa Nacional-Casa da Moeda, 1988.

Bartuschat, Johannes. "Il ritratto di Laura (*RVF* 76-80)," in *Il Canzoniere: Lettura micro e macrotestuale*, Michelangelo Picone, ed., Ravenna: Longo, 2007, 207–23.

Bate, M. S. "Tempestuous Poetry: Storms in Ovid's *Metamorphoses*, *Heroides*, and *Tristia*," *Mnemosyne* 57 (2004): 295–310.

Beltran, Vicenç. *La poesía tradicional medieval y renacentista: Poética antropológica de la lírica oral*, Kassel: Edition Reichenberger, 2009.

Berardinelli, Cleonice. "'Junto dum seco, fero e estéril monte,'" in *Estudos Camonianos*, 2nd rev. ed., Rio de Janeiro: Nova Fronteira; Cátedra Padre António Vieira, 2000, 235–42.

Bernardes, Diogo. *Obras completas*, 3 vols., Marques Braga, ed., Lisbon: Sá da Costa, 1945–46.

Bettini, Clelia. "De Cartago ao Helesponto: Dois sonetos camonianos de inspiração clássica," in *Comentário a Camões*, vol. 2, Rita Marnoto, ed., Lisbon: Centro Interuniversitário de Estudos Camonianos; Cotovia, 2012, 75–101.

Biedermann, Zoltán. "(Dis)connected History and the Multiple Narratives of Global Early Modernity," *Modern Philology* 119.1 (2021): 13–32.

Works Cited

Blackmore, Josiah. *Moorings: Portuguese Expansion and the Writing of Africa*, Minneapolis: University of Minnesota Press, 2009.

———. "Portuguese Scenes of the Senses, Medieval and Early Modern," in *Beyond Sight: Engaging the Senses in Iberian Literatures and Cultures, 1200–1750*, Ryan D. Giles and Steven Wagschal, eds., Toronto: University of Toronto Press, 2018, 209–24.

———. "Travelers: Voyages to Known and Unknown Worlds," in *A Cultural History of the Sea in the Early Modern Age*, Steve Mentz, ed., vol. 3 of *A Cultural History of the Sea*, 6 vols., Margaret Cohen, ed., London: Bloomsbury Academic, 2021, 157–77.

Blouin, Egla Morales. *El ciervo y la fuente: Mito y folklore del agua en la lírica tradicional*, Madrid: José Porrúa Turanzas; Potomac: Studia Humanitatis, 1981.

Blum, Hester. *The View from the Masthead: Maritime Imagination and Antebellum American Sea Narratives*, Chapel Hill: University of North Carolina Press, 2008.

Boscán, Juan. *Obra completa*, Carlos Clavería, ed., Madrid: Cátedra, 1999.

Boxer, C. R. "Portuguese *Roteiros*, 1500–1700," in *From Lisbon to Goa, 1500–1750: Studies in Portuguese Maritime Enterprise*, London: Variorum, 1984, 171–86.

———. *The Portuguese Seaborne Empire, 1415–1825*, New York: Alfred A. Knopf, 1969.

———, trans. *The Tragic History of the Sea*, Josiah Blackmore, ed., Minneapolis: University of Minnesota Press, 2001.

Boynton, Susan, Sarah Kay, Alison Cornish, and Andrew Albin. "Sound Matters," *Speculum* 91.4 (2016): 998–1039.

Braden, Gordon. *Petrarchan Love and the Continental Renaissance*, New Haven, CT: Yale University Press, 1999.

Braga, Teófilo. *Camões: Epoca e vida*, Porto: Chardron, 1907.

Brayton, Dan. *Shakespeare's Ocean: An Ecocritical Exploration*, Charlottesville: University of Virginia Press, 2012.

Brea, Mercedes. "*Levantou-s' a velida*, um exemplo de sincretismo harmónico," in *Estudos dedicados a Ricardo Carvalho Calero*, vol. 2, José Luís Rodríguez, ed., Santiago de Compostela: Universidade de Santiago de Compostela, 2000, 139–51.

Brink, André. "A Myth of Origin," in *T'Kama-Adamastor: Inventions of a South African Painting*, Ivan Vladislavić, ed., Johannesburg: University of the Witwatersrand, 2000, 41–47.

Brito, Bernardo Gomes de, comp. *Historia tragico-maritima em que se escrevem chronologicamente os naufragios que tiveraõ as naos de Portugal, depois que se poz em exercicio a navegaçaõ da India*, Lisbon: Congregaçaõ do Oratorio, 1735–36.

Brownlee, Marina. "The Dark Side of Myth in Camões' 'Frail Bark,'" *Comparative Literature Studies* 32 (1995): 176–90.

Burns, E. Jane. *Bodytalk: When Women Speak in Old French Literature*, Philadelphia: University of Pennsylvania Press, 1993.

Cachey, Theodore J., Jr. "From Shipwreck to Port: *Rvf* 189 and the Making of the *Canzoniere*," *MLN* 120 (2005): 30–49.

———. "Petrarch, Boccaccio, and the New World Encounter," *Stanford Italian Review* 10.1 (1991): 45–59.

Camões, Luís de. *The Collected Lyric Poems of Luís de Camões*, Landeg White trans., Princeton, NJ: Princeton University Press, 2008.

———. *Lírica completa*, vol. 3, Maria de Lurdes Saraiva, ed., [Lisbon]: Imprensa Nacional-Casa da Moeda, 1981.

———. *Lírica de Camões*, vol. 3, bk. 1, Leodegário A. de Azevedo Filho, ed., [Lisbon]: Imprensa Nacional-Casa da Moeda, 1995.

———. *Obra completa*, Antônio Salgado Júnior, ed., Rio de Janeiro: Aguilar, 1963.

———. *Os Lusíadas*, Frank Pierce, ed., Oxford: Clarendon Press, 1973.

———. *Rhythmas de Lvis de Camoes. Diuididas em cinco partes. Dirigidas ao muito Illustre Senhor D. Gonçalo Coutinho*, Lisbon: Manoel de Lyra, 1595.

———. *Rimas de Lvis de Camões. Accrescentadas nesta segunda impressaõ. Dirigidas a D. Gonçalo Coutinho*, Lisbon: Pedro Crasbeeck, 1598.

———. *Sonnets and Other Poems*, Richard Zenith, trans., Dartmouth: University of Massachusetts, Dartmouth, 2009.

Campos, Haroldo de. *A arte no horizonte do provável e outros ensaios*, São Paulo: Perspectiva, 1977.

"Cantigas Medievais Galego-Portuguesas," accessed March 17, 2021, https://cantigas.fcsh.unl.pt.

Cappello, Bernardo. *Rime*, Venice: Guerra, 1560.

Casale, Giancarlo. *The Ottoman Age of Expansion*, New York: Oxford University Press, 2010.

Castanheda, Fernão Lopes de. *História do descobrimento e conquista da Índia pelos Portugueses*, bks. 1 and 2, 3rd ed., Pedro de Azevedo, ed., Coimbra: Imprensa da Universidade, 1924.

Castro, João de. *Roteiro do Mar Roxo de Dom João de Castro, MS. Cott. Tib. Dix da British Library*, Lisbon: Inapa, 1991.

———. *Roteiros de D. João de Castro*, 3 vols., 2nd ed., A. Fontoura da Costa, ed., Lisbon: Agência Geral das Colónias, 1939–40.

———. *Tratado da Sphœra; Da Geografia; Notação Famosa; Informação sobre Maluco*, A. Fontoura da Costa, ed., Lisbon: Agência Geral das Colónias, 1940.

Castro, Sílvio. "Metáfora do naufrágio e viagem em Camões," in *Actas da V Reunião Internacional de Camonistas: São Paulo, 20 a 24 de julho de 1987*, [São Paulo]: A Universidade, 1987, 713–20.

———. "Naufrágio como metáfora e palinódia em Camões," *Revista Camoniana*, 3rd ser., 13 (2003): 135–48.

Cetina, Gutierre de. *Rimas*, Jesús Ponce Cárdenas, ed., Madrid: Cátedra, 2014.

Chaplin, Joyce E. *Round about the Earth: Circumnavigation from Magellan to Orbit*, New York: Simon and Schuster, 2012.

Cicero. *De finibus bonorum et malorum*, H. Rackham, trans., Cambridge, MA: Harvard University Press, 1931.

———. *De oratore*, bks. 1–2, E. W. Sutton, trans., Cambridge, MA: Harvard University Press, 1948.

———. *De re publica/De legibus*, Clinton Walker Keyes, trans., Cambridge, MA: Harvard University Press, 1928.

Cidade, Hernâni. *Luís de Camões I: O lírico*, Lisbon: Imprensa Nacional, 1936.

Classen, Albrecht. *Water in Medieval Literature: An Ecocritical Reading*, Lanham, MD: Lexington Books, 2018.

Coelho, Joaquim-Francisco. *Letras de jornal*, Lisbon: Assírio e Alvim, 2010.

Cohen, Margaret. "The Chronotopes of the Sea," in Franco Moretti, ed., *The Novel*, vol. 2, Princeton, NJ: Princeton University Press, 2006, 647–66.

———. *The Novel and the Sea*, Princeton, NJ: Princeton University Press, 2010.

Cohen, Rip. *Erotic Angles on the* Cantigas d'Amigo, London: Department of Iberian and Latin American Studies, Queen Mary, University of London, 2012.

———. "Girl in the Dawn: Textual Criticism and Poetics," *Portuguese Studies* 22 (2006): 173–87.

Corral, Esther. "Feminine Voices in the Galician-Portuguese *cantigas de amigo*," Judith R. Cohen, trans., with Anne L. Klinck, in *Medieval Woman's Song: Cross-Cultural Approaches*, Anne L. Klinck and Ann Marie Rasmussen, eds., Philadelphia: University of Pennsylvania Press, 2002, 81–98.

Corte-Real, Jerónimo. *Navfragio e lastimoso sucesso da perdicam de Manoel de Sousa de Sepulueda, & dona Lianor de Sá, sua molher & filhos*, [Lisbon]: s. Lopez, 1594.

———. *Sucesso do segūdo cerco de Diu: Estando dō Ioham Mazcarenhas por capitam da fortaleza, 1546*, Lisbon: A. Gonçaluez, 1574.

Cosgrove, Denis. *Apollo's Eye: A Cartographic Genealogy of the Earth in the Western Imagination*, Baltimore: Johns Hopkins University Press, 2001.

Costa, A. Fontoura da. *A marinharia dos descobrimentos*, 3rd ed., Lisbon: Agência Geral do Ultramar, 1960.

———, ed. *Roteiros portugueses inéditos da carreira da Índia do século XVI*, Lisbon: Agência Geral das Colónias, 1940.

Culler, Jonathan. *Theory of the Lyric*, Cambridge, MA: Harvard University Press, 2015.

Cunha, Celso Ferreira da. *O cancioneiro de Martin Codax*, Rio de Janeiro: Departamento de Imprensa, 1956.

Curtius, Ernst Robert. *European Literature and the Latin Middle Ages*, Willard Trask, trans., New York: Pantheon, 1953.

Dadson, Trevor. "From Voice to Silence: Orpheus and the Epitaph in Garcilaso and Camões," *Portuguese Studies* 21 (2005): 101–11.

Davenport, Frances Gardner, ed. *European Treaties Bearing on the History of the United States and Its Dependencies to 1648*, Gloucester: Peter Smith, 1967.

Davis, Elizabeth B. "La promesa del náufrago: El motivo marinero del *ex-voto*, de Garcilaso a Quevedo," in *Studies in Honor of James O. Crosby*, Lía Schwartz, ed., Newark: Juan de la Cuesta, 2004, 109–23.

d'Heur, Jean-Marie. "Le motif du vent venu du pays de l'être aimé, l'invocation au vent, l'invocation aux vagues," *Zeitschrift für romanische Philologie* 88 (1972): 69–104.

Dias, J. S. da Silva. *Os descobrimentos e a problemática cultural do século XVI*, Lisbon: Presença, 1982.

Disney, A. R. *A History of Portugal and the Portuguese Empire: From Beginnings to 1807*, 2 vols., Cambridge: Cambridge University Press, 2009.

Dobrin, Sidney I. *Blue Ecocriticism and the Oceanic Imperative*, London: Routledge, 2021.

Domingues, Francisco Contente. "Vasco da Gama's Voyage: Myths and Realities in Maritime History," *Portuguese Studies* 19 (2003): 1–8.

Falcão, Cristóvão. *Trovas de Crisfal: Reprodução fac-simile da primeira edição*, Guilherme G. de Oliveira Santos, ed., Lisbon: Livraria Portugal, 1965.

Farina, Lara. "Wondrous Skins and Tactile Affection: The Blemmye's Touch," in *Read-*

ing Skin in Medieval Literature and Culture, Katie L. Walter, ed., New York: Palgrave Macmillan, 2013, 11–28.

Feld, Steven, and Keith H. Basso, *Senses of Place*, Santa Fe: School of American Research Press, 1996.

Ferreira, António. *Poemas Lusitanos*, 2nd ed., T. F. Earle, ed., Lisbon: Fundação Calouste Gulbenkian, 2008.

Ferreira, Maria do Rosário. *Águas doces, águas salgadas: Da funcionalidade dos motivos aquáticos na Cantiga de Amigo*, Porto: Granito, 1999.

Filho, Leodegário A. de Azevedo. *Lírica de Camões*, vol. 1, *História, metodologia, corpus*, Lisbon: Imprensa Nacional-Casa da Moeda, 1985.

Flint, Valerie I. J. *The Imaginative Landscape of Christopher Columbus*. Princeton, NJ: Princeton University Press, 1992.

Folkerth, Wes. *The Sound of Shakespeare*, London: Routledge, 2002.

Fontes, Manuel da Costa. "The Art of 'Sailing' in *La Lozana andaluza*," *Hispanic Review* 66 (1998): 433–45.

Foulke, Robert. *The Sea Voyage Narrative*, New York: Routledge, 2002.

Fraga, Maria do Céu. *Os géneros maiores na poesia lírica de Camões*, Coimbra: Universidade de Coimbra, 2003.

———. "O tempo e o espaço: A errância na lírica camoniana," *Floema* 7 (2010): 43–59.

Freccero, John. *Dante: The Poetics of Conversion*, Rachel Jacoff, ed., Cambridge, MA: Harvard University Press, 1986.

Garza, Luz Pozo. *Ondas do mar de Vigo: Erotismo e conciencia mítica nas cantigas de amigo*, A Coruña: Espiral Maior, 1996.

Gaylord, Mary Malcolm. "The Making of Baroque Poetry," in *The Cambridge History of Spanish Literature*, David T. Gies, ed., Cambridge: Cambridge University Press, 2004, 222–37.

Ghisalberti, Alberto M., ed. *Dizionario biografico degli italiani*, Rome: Istituto della Enciclopedia Italiana, 1960–[2019].

Gil, Fernando. "*The Lusiads* Effect," K. David Jackson, trans., in *The Traveling Eye: Retrospection, Vision, and Prophecy in the Portuguese Renaissance*, Fernando Gil and Helder Macedo, eds., Dartmouth: University of Massachusetts at Dartmouth, 2009, 33–85.

Glaser, Edward. *Portuguese Studies*, Paris: Fundação Calouste Gulbenkian; Centro Cultural Português, 1976.

Godinho, Vitorino Magalhães. "A ideia de descobrimento e os descobrimentos e expansão," *Anais do Clube Militar Naval* 120 (1990): 627–42.

Góis, Damião de. *Elogio da cidade de Lisboa/Vrbis Olisiponis Descriptio*, Aires A. Nascimento, ed. and trans., Lisbon: Guimarães Editores, 2002.

———. *Lisbon in the Renaissance: A New Translation of the Urbis Olisiponis Descriptio*, Jeffrey S. Ruth, trans., New York: Italica Press, 1996.

Gradín, Pilar Lorenzo. *La canción de mujer en la lírica medieval*, Santiago de Compostela: Universidade de Santiago de Compostela, 1990.

Greene, Roland. *Five Words: Critical Semantics in the Age of Shakespeare and Cervantes*, Chicago: University of Chicago Press, 2013.

———. *Unrequited Conquests: Love and Empire in the Colonial Americas*, Chicago: University of Chicago Press, 1999.

Works Cited

Gschwend, Annemarie Jordan, and Kate Lowe. "Princess of the Seas, Queen of Empire: Configuring the City and Port of Renaissance Lisbon," in *The Global City: On the Streets of Renaissance Lisbon*, Annemarie Jordan Gschwend and K. J. P. Lowe, eds., London: Paul Holberton, 2015, 12–35.

Guida, Saverio. "Raimbaut de Vaqueiras, *[Oi] altas undas que venez suz la mar (BdT 392.5a)*," *Lecturae Tropatorum* 6 (2013): 1–21.

Hardie, Philip. *Virgil's Aeneid: Cosmos and Imperium*, Oxford: Clarendon Press, 1986.

Hart, Thomas R., ed. *Gil Vicente: Farces and Festival Plays*, Eugene: University of Oregon, 1972.

Hartog, François. *The Mirror of Herodotus: The Representation of the Other in the Writing of History*, Janet Lloyd, trans., Berkeley: University of California Press, 1988.

Hawkins, Peter S. *Dante's Testaments: Essays in Scriptural Imagination*, Stanford, CA: Stanford University Press, 1999.

Heiple, Daniel L. *Garcilaso de la Vega and the Italian Renaissance*, University Park: The Pennsylvania State University Press, 1994.

Helgerson, Richard. *A Sonnet from Carthage: Garcilaso de la Vega and the New Poetry of Sixteenth-Century Europe*, Philadelphia: University of Pennsylvania Press, 2007.

Herrera, Fernando de. *Anotaciones a la poesía de Garcilaso*, Inoria Pepe and José María Reyes, eds., Madrid: Cátedra, 2001.

Historia da muy notauel perda do Galeão grande sam João. Em q̃ se contam os innumeraveis trabalhos e grandes desauenturas q̃ aconteceram ao Capitão Manoel de Sousa de Sepulueda E o lamẽtauel fim q̃ elle e sua molher e filhos e toda a mais gente ouverão. O que se perdeo no anno de M.D.LII. a vinte e quatro de Junho, na terra do Natal em xxxj graos, Lisbon: 15(??).

Hobson, John M. *The Eastern Origins of Western Civilization*, Cambridge: Cambridge University Press, 2004.

Hollander, Robert. *Allegory in Dante's "Commedia,"* Princeton, NJ: Princeton University Press, 1969.

[Homer]. *La Ulixea de Homero, traducida de griego en lengua castellana por el secretario Gonzalo Pérez*, 2 vols., J. R. Muñoz Sánchez, ed., Málaga: Universidad de Málaga, 2015.

Hooper, Laurence E. "Exile and Petrarch's Reinvention of Authorship," *Renaissance Quarterly* 69 (2016): 1217–56.

Horace. *Odes and Epodes*, Niall Rudd, ed. and trans., Cambridge, MA: Harvard University Press, 2004.

———. *Satires/Epistles/Ars Poetica*, H. R. Fairclough, trans., Cambridge, MA: Harvard University Press, 1929.

Hourani, George Fadlo. *Arab Seafaring in the Indian Ocean in Ancient and Early Medieval Times*, expanded ed., John Carswell, rev. and exp., Princeton, NJ: Princeton University Press, 1995.

Jensen, Frede. *The Earliest Portuguese Lyrics*, [Odense]: Odense University Press, 1978.

———, ed. and trans. *Medieval Galician-Portuguese Poetry: An Anthology*, New York: Garland, 1992.

Johnson, Christopher D. *Hyperboles: The Rhetoric of Excess in Baroque Literature and Thought*, Cambridge, MA: Harvard University Department of Comparative Literature, 2010.

Jowitt, Claire, Craig Lambert, and Steve Mentz. "Introduction: Oceans in Global History and Culture 1400–1800; Expanding Horizons," in *The Routledge Companion to Marine and Maritime Worlds, 1400–1800*, Claire Jowitt, Craig Lambert, and Steve Mentz, eds., London: Routledge, 2020, 1–29.

Jue, Melody. *Wild Blue Media: Thinking through Seawater*, Durham, NC: Duke University Press, 2020.

Kado, Martina. "The Ship as Assemblage: Melville's Literary Shipboard Geographies," *Atlantic Studies* 15.1 (2018): 40–61.

Klein, Bernhard. "Camões and the Sea: Maritime Modernity in *The Lusiads*," *Modern Philology* 111.2 (2013): 158–80.

———. "Mapping the Waters: Sea Charts, Navigation, and Camões's *Os Lusíadas*," *Renaissance Studies* 25.2 (2011): 228–47.

Knecht, Ross. "'Invaded by the World': Passion, Passivity, and the Object of Desire in Petrarch's *Rime sparse*," *Comparative Literature* 63.3 (2011): 235–52.

Krummrich, Philip, trans. *The Hero and Leander Theme in Iberian Literature, 1500–1800: An Anthology of Translations*, Lewiston, NY: Edwin Mellen Press, 2006.

Lee, Charmaine. "La *chanson de femme* attribuita a Raimbaut de Vaqueiras, *Altas undas que venez suz la mar*," in *Studi di filologia romanza offerti a Valeria Bertolucci Pizzorusso*, vol. 2, Pietro G. Beltrami, Maria Grazia Capusso, Fabrizio Cigni, and Sergio Vatteroni, eds., Ospedaletto (Pisa): Pacini, 2006, 868–81.

Leighton, Angela. *Hearing Things: The Work of Sound in Literature*, Cambridge, MA: Belknap/Harvard University Press, 2018.

Lewis, C. S. "Dante's Similes," in *Studies in Medieval and Renaissance Literature*, Walter Hooper, coll., Cambridge: Cambridge University Press, 1966, 64–77.

Livro de marinharia de André Pires, 2nd ed., Luís de Albuquerque, ed., Lisbon: Vega, [1989?].

Livro de marinharia de Bernardo Fernandes, A. Fontoura da Costa, ed., Lisbon: Agência Geral das Colónias, 1940.

Le "Livro de marinharia" de Gaspar Moreira (Bibliothéque National de Paris, Cod. Port. n.° 58), Léon Bourdon and Luís de Albuquerque, eds., Lisbon: Junta de Investigações Científicas do Ultramar, 1977.

Lopes, Graça Videira. "Galician-Portuguese as a Literary Language in the Middle Ages," in *A Comparative History of Literatures in the Iberian Peninsula*, vol. 1, Fernando Cabo Aseguinolaza, Anxo Abuín Gonzalez, and César Domínguez, eds., Amsterdam: John Benjamins, 2010, 396–412.

Macedo, Helder. "Uma cantiga de Dom Dinis," in *Do cancioneiro de amigo*, 3rd ed., Stephen Reckert and Helder Macedo, eds., Lisbon: Assírio e Alvim, 1996, 59–70.

———. "Love as Knowledge: The Lyric Poetry of Camões," *Portuguese Studies* 14 (1998): 51–64.

———. "'The Lusiads': Epic Celebration and Pastoral Regret," *Portuguese Studies* 6 (1990): 32–37.

———. "O poeta Simónides e o capitão Temístocles," in *O amor das letras e das gentes: In honor of Maria de Lourdes Belchior Pontes*, João Camilo dos Santos and Frederick G. Williams, eds., Santa Barbara: Center for Portuguese Studies, University of California—Santa Barbara, 1995, 100–104.

Works Cited

Madeira, José. *Camões contra a expansão e o império: Os Lusíadas como antiepopeia*, Lisbon: Fenda, 2000.

Manero Sorolla, M[aría] Pilar. *Imágenes petrarquistas en la lírica española del Renacimiento: Repertorio*, Barcelona: PPU, 1990.

March, Ausiàs. *Selected Poems*, Arthur Terry, ed. and trans., Austin: University of Texas Press, 1976.

Mariscal, George. *Contradictory Subjects: Quevedo, Cervantes, and Seventeenth-Century Spanish Culture*, Ithaca, NY: Cornell University Press, 1991.

Mariz, Pedro de. "Ao estudioso da lição Poetica," in *Os Lvsiadas do grande Lvis de Camoens. Principe da poesia heroica. Commentados pelo licenciado Manoel Correa . . .* , Lisbon: Pedro Crasbeeck, 1613, [v]-[x].

Matos, Maria Vitalina Leal de. "O mar em Camões," *Oceanos* 23 (1995): 54–65.

Mazzotta, Giuseppe. *The Worlds of Petrarch*, Durham, NC: Duke University Press, 1993.

McCloskey, Jason. "'Navegaba Leandro el Helesponto': Love and Early Modern Navigation in Juan Boscán's *Leandro*," *Revista de Estudios Hispánicos* 47 (2013): 3–27.

Mentz, Steve. *At the Bottom of Shakespeare's Ocean*, London: Continuum, 2009.

———. "Introduction: Wet Globalization; The Early Modern Ocean as World-System," in *A Cultural History of the Sea in the Early Modern Age*, Steve Mentz, ed., vol. 3 of *A Cultural History of the Sea*, 6 vols., Margaret Cohen, ed., London: Bloomsbury Academic, 2021, 1–23.

———. *Shipwreck Modernity: Ecologies of Globalization, 1550–1719*, Minneapolis: University of Minnesota Press, 2015.

Middlebrook, Leah. *Imperial Lyric: New Poetry and New Subjects in Early Modern Spain*, University Park: The Pennsylvania State University Press, 2009.

Miranda, Francisco de Sá de. *Obras completas*, 2 vols., Rodrigues Lapa, ed., Lisbon: Sá da Costa, 1976.

Monteiro, Luis Nuno Sardinha. "Fernando Oliveira's Art of War at Sea (1555): A Pioneering Treatise on Naval Strategy," *Naval War College Review* 68.4 (2015): 94–107.

Montemayor, Jorge de. *Poesía completa*, Juan Bautista de Avalle-Arce, ed., Madrid: Biblioteca Castro, 1996.

Morais, Carlos Alexandre de. *Cronologia geral da Índia portuguesa, 1498–1962*, 2nd rev. ed., Lisbon: Estampa, 1997.

Morford, M. P. O. *The Poet Lucan: Studies in Rhetorical Epic*, New York: Barnes and Noble, 1967.

Morison, Samuel Eliot. *Portuguese Voyages to America in the Fifteenth Century*, Cambridge, MA: Harvard University Press, 1940.

Murrin, Michael. *Trade and Romance*, Chicago: University of Chicago Press, 2014.

Musaeus. *Hero and Leander*, in Callimachus, *Aetia, Iambi, lyric poems, Hecale, minor epic and elegiac poems, and other fragments*, C. A. Trypanis, trans. and ed./Musaeus, *Hero and Leander*, Thomas Gelzer, ed., Cedric Whitman, trans., Cambridge, MA: Harvard University Press, 1975, 289–389.

Navegação de S. Brandão nas fontes portuguesas medievais, Aires A. Nascimento, ed. and trans., Lisbon: Colibri, 1998.

Nicolopulos, James. *The Poetics of Empire in the Indies: Prophecy and Imitation in* La Araucana *and* Os Lusíadas, University Park: The Pennsylvania State University Press, 2000.

Nocentelli, Carmen. *Empires of Love: Europe, Asia, and the Making of Early Modern Identity*, Philadelphia: University of Pennsylvania Press, 2013.

Novak, David. "Noise," in *Keywords in Sound*, David Novak and Matt Sakakeeny, eds., Durham, NC: Duke University Press, 2015, 125-38.

Oliveira, Fernando. *Liuro da fabrica das naos*, Lisbon: Academia de Marinha, 1991.

Oliveira, Fernando de. *Arte da guerra do mar: Estratégia e guerra naval no tempo dos descobrimentos*, Lisbon: Edições 70, 2008.

Oliveira, Fernão de. *Gramática da linguagem portuguesa (1536)*, Amadeu Torres and Carlos Assunção, eds., Lisbon: Academia das Ciências de Lisboa, 2000.

O livro de marinharia de Manuel Álvares, Luís Mendonça de Albuquerque, ed., Lisbon: Junta de Investigações do Ultramar, 1969.

Osório, Jorge A. "Na elegia de Camões: 'O Poeta Simónides, falando,'" *Via Spiritus* 16 (2009): 189-213.

Ovid. *Heroides and Amores*, vol. 1, 2nd ed., Grant Showerman, trans., G. P. Goold, rev., Cambridge, MA: Harvard University Press, 1977.

———. *Metamorphoses*, 2 vols., Frank Justus Miller, trans., G. P. Goold, rev., Cambridge, MA: Harvard University Press, 1977-84.

Oxford Latin Dictionary, 2 vols., 2nd ed., P. G. W. Glare, ed., Oxford: Oxford University Press, 2012.

Padrón, Ricardo. *The Spacious Word: Cartography, Literature, and Empire in Early Modern Spain*, Chicago: University of Chicago Press, 2004.

Pagán, Diego Ramírez. *Floresta de varia poesía*, Valencia, 1562.

Pastore, Christopher L. "Knowledges: Constructing the Early Modern Ocean, 1450-1700," in *A Cultural History of the Sea in the Early Modern Age*, Steve Mentz, ed., vol. 3 of *A Cultural History of the Sea*, 6 vols., Margaret Cohen, ed., London: Bloomsbury Academic, 2021, 25-51.

Paviot, Jacques. "L'imaginaire géographique des decouvertes au XVe siècle," in *La Découverte, le Portugal et l'Europe: Actes du Colloque, Paris, les 26, 27 et 28 mai 1988*, Jean Aubin, ed., Paris: Fondation Calouste Gulbenkian; Centre Culturel Portugais, 1990, 141-58.

Pepió, Vicente Beltrán. "O vento lh'as levava: Don Denis y la tradición lírica peninsular," *Bulletin Hispanique* 86.1-2 (1984): 5-25.

Pereira, Maria Helena da Rocha. "Musas e Tágides n'*Os Lusíadas*," in *Actas da VI Reunião Internacional de Camonistas*, Seabra Pereira and Manuel Ferro, eds., Coimbra: Imprensa da Universidade de Coimbra, 2012, 51-61.

———. "A tempestade marítima de 'Os Lusíadas': Estudo comparativo," in *Actas da V Reunião Internacional de Camonistas, São Paulo, 20 a 24 de julho de 1987*, São Paulo: [Universidade de São Paulo], 1987, 205-15.

Perestrelo, Manuel de Mesquita. *Relação sumária da viagem que fez Fernão d'Álvares Cabral, desde que partiu deste Reino por capitão-mor da Armada que foi no ano de 1553 às partes da Índia até que se perdeu no cabo de Boa Esperança no ano de 1554*, in Giulia Lanciani, ed., *Sucessos e naufrágios das naus portuguesas*, Lisbon: Caminho, 1997, 215-313.

———. *Roteiro da África do sul e sueste desde o Cabo da Boa Esperança até ao das Correntes (1576)/"Roteiro" of the [sic] South and South-East Africa, from the Cape of

Good Hope to Cape Corrientes (1576), A. Fontoura da Costa, ed., Lisbon: Agência Geral das Colónias, 1939.

Petrarch. *The Life of Solitude*, Jacob Zeitlin, trans., [Urbana]: University of Illinois Press, 1924.

———. *Petrarch's Guide to the Holy Land: Itinerary to the Sepulcher of Our Lord Jesus Christ (Itinerarium ad sepulchrum domini nostri Yehsu Christi); Facsimile Edition of Cremona, Biblioteca Statale, Deposito Libreria Civica, Manuscript BB.1.2.5*, Theodore J. Cachey, ed. and trans., Notre Dame, IN: University of Notre Dame Press, 2002.

———. *Petrarch's Lyric Poems: The Rime sparse and Other Lyrics*, Robert M. Durling, trans. and ed., Cambridge, MA: Harvard University Press, 1976.

———. *Rerum familiarum libri I–VIII*, Aldo S. Bernardo, trans., Albany: State University of New York Press, 1975.

Pettman, Dominic. *Sonic Intimacy: Voice, Species, Technics (Or, How to Listen to the World)*, Stanford, CA: Stanford University Press, 2017.

Picone, Michelangelo. "Il motivo della 'navigatio' nel Canzoniere del Petrarca," *Atti e Memorie della Accademia Petrarca di Lettere, Arti e Scienze*, new ser., 51 (1989): 291–307.

———. "Il sonetto CLXXXIX," *Lectura Petrarce* 9/10 (1989–90): 151–77.

Piechocki, Katharina N. *Cartographic Humanism: The Making of Early Modern Europe*, Chicago: University of Chicago Press, 2019.

Pinet, Simone. *Archipelagoes: Insular Fictions from Chivalric Romance to the Novel*, Minneapolis: University of Minnesota Press, 2011.

Pinto, Fernão Mendes. *Fernão Mendes Pinto and the* Peregrinação: *Studies, Restored Portuguese Text, Notes, and Indexes*, vol. 2, *Restored Portuguese Text*, Elisa Lopes da Costa, ed., Lisbon: Fundação Oriente, 2010.

———. *The Travels of Mendes Pinto*, Rebecca D. Catz, ed. and trans., Chicago: University of Chicago Press, 1989.

Pires, Tomé. *A suma oriental de Tomé Pires e o livro de Francisco Rodrigues*, Armando Cortesão, ed., [Coimbra]: Por Ordem da Universidade, 1978.

Plutarch. *Lives: Themistocles and Camillus; Aristides and Cato Major; Cimon and Lucullus*, Bernadotte Perrin, trans., Cambridge, MA: Harvard University Press, 1914.

Prieto, Andrés. "Alexander and the Geographer's Eye: Allegories of Knowledge in Martín Fernández de Enciso's *Suma de Geographía* (1519)," *Hispanic Review* 78.2 (2010): 169–88.

Proensa: An Anthology of Troubadour Poetry, Paul Blackburn, trans. and sel., George Economou, ed., Berkeley: University of California Press, 1978.

Putnam, Michael C. J. "Vergil, Ovid, and the Poetry of Exile," in *A Companion to Vergil's Aeneid and Its Tradition*, Joseph Farrell and Michael C. J. Putnam, eds., Chichester: Wiley-Blackwell, 2010, 80–95.

Quint, Anne-Marie. "O mar na lírica medieval galego-portuguesa," in *Actas do quinto congresso da Associação Internacional de Lusitanistas, Universidade de Oxford, 1 a 8 de Setembro de 1996*, vol. 3, T. F. Earle, ed., Oxford-Coimbra: Associação Internacional de Lusitanistas, 1998, 1321–29.

Quint, David. *Epic and Empire: Politics and Generic Form from Virgil to Milton*, Princeton, NJ: Princeton University Press, 1993.

———. *Virgil's Double Cross: Design and Meaning in the* Aeneid, Princeton, NJ: Princeton University Press, 2018.

Quintilian. *The Orator's Education*, bks. 11–12, Donald A. Russell, trans., Cambridge, MA: Harvard University Press, 2001.

Ramachandran, Ayesha. *The Worldmakers: Global Imagining in Early Modern Europe*, Chicago: University of Chicago Press, 2015.

Raman, Shankar. "Back to the Future: Forging History in Luís de Camões's *Os Lusíadas*," in *Travel Knowledge: European "Discoveries" in the Early Modern Period*, Ivo Kamps and Jyotsna G. Singh, eds., New York: Palgrave, 2001, 137–47.

———. *Framing "India": The Colonial Imaginary in Early Modern Culture*, Stanford, CA: Stanford University Press, 2001.

Ramon Moreira, Maria Micaela Dias Pereira. *Os sonetos amorosos de Camões: Estudo tipológico*, Braga: Universidade do Minho, Centro de Estudos Humanísticos, 1998.

Randel, Mary Gaylord. "Metaphor and Fable in Góngora's *Soledad Primera*," *Revista Hispánica Moderna* 40.3/4 (1978–79): 97–112.

Reckert, Stephen. "'Micro-significantes' na semiótica de Camões," in *IV Reunião Internacional de Camonistas: Actas*, Ponta Delgada: Universidade dos Açores, 1984, 523–40.

Reckert, Stephen, and Helder Macedo, "Cinquenta cantigas de amigo," in *Do cancioneiro de amigo*, 3rd ed., Stephen Reckert and Helder Macedo, eds., Lisbon: Assírio e Alvim, 1996, 71–247.

Records of South-Eastern Africa, Collected in Various Libraries and Archive Departments in Europe, 9 vols., George McCall Theal, ed. and trans., Cape Town: Government of the Cape Colony, 1898–1903.

Relação das náos e armadas da India com os successos dellas que se puderam saber, para noticia e instrucção dos curiozos, e amantes de historia da India (British Library, Códice Add. 20902), Maria Hermínia Maldonado, ed., Coimbra: Biblioteca Geral da Universidade, 1985.

Resende, Garcia de, comp. *Cancioneiro Geral*, 5 vols., Andrée Crabbé Rocha, ed., Lisbon: Centro do Livro Brasileiro, 1973.

Roig, Adrien. "L'utilisation poétique de l'écho dans *Les Lusiades*," *Quadrant* 9 (1992): 21–33.

Safier, Neil, and Ilda Mendes dos Santos. "Mapping Maritime Triumph and the Enchantment of Empire: Portuguese Literature of the Renaissance," in *The History of Cartography*, vol. 3, part 1, David Woodward, ed., Chicago: University of Chicago Press, 2007, 461–68.

Saive, Denise. "'The lover becomes the thing beloved': Queering Love in *Os Lusíadas*," in *Beyond Binaries: Sex, Sexualities, and Gender in the Lusophone World*, Paulo Pepe and Ana Raquel Fernandes, eds., Oxford: Peter Lang, 2019, 11–37.

Sannazaro, Jacopo. *Latin Poetry*, Michael C. J. Putnam trans., Cambridge, MA: Harvard University Press, 2009.

Sayers, William. "The Maritime Vocabulary of *Le Voyage de saint Brendan*," *Neophilologus* 97 (2013): 9–19.

Schwartz, Stuart B. "The Economy of the Portuguese Empire," in *Portuguese Oceanic Expansion, 1400–1800*, Francisco Bethencourt and Diogo Ramada Curto, eds., Cambridge: Cambridge University Press, 2007, 19–48.

Works Cited

Silva, Luís de Oliveira e. "Consílio dos deuses marinhos," in *Dicionário de Luís de Camões*, Vítor Aguiar e Silva, ed., Lisbon: Caminho, 2011, 283–86.

Silva, Maria Branco da, ed. "Conto de Amaro," in *Navegação de S. Brandão nas fontes portuguesas medievais*, Aires A. Nascimento, ed., Lisbon: Colibri, 1998, 243–81.

Silva, Vítor Manuel Pires de Aguiar e. *Camões: Labirintos e fascínios*, Lisbon: Cotovia, 1994.

―――. "A elegia na lírica de Camões," in *Actas da VI Reunião Internacional de Camonistas*, Seabra Pereira and Manuel Ferro, eds., Coimbra: Imprensa da Universidade de Coimbra, 2012, 19–31.

―――. *A lira dourada e a tuba canora*, Lisbon: Cotovia, 2008.

―――. *Maneirismo e barroco na poesia lírica portuguesa*, Coimbra: Centro de Estudos Românicos, 1971.

Singleton, Charles S. "'Sulla fiumana ove'l mar non ha vanto' (*Inferno*, II, 108)," *Romanic Review* 39 (1948): 269–77.

Smith, Bruce R. *The Acoustic World of Early Modern England: Attending to the O-Factor*, Chicago: University of Chicago Press, 1999.

Smith, Roger C. *Vanguard of Empire: Ships of Exploration in the Age of Columbus*, New York: Oxford University Press, 1993.

Soucek, Svat. "Islamic Charting in the Mediterranean," in *The History of Cartography*, vol. 2, bk. 1, J. B. Harley and David Woodward, eds., Chicago: University of Chicago Press, 1992, 263–92.

Sousa, Manuel de Faria e. *Lusíadas de Luis de Camoens, principe de los poetas de España... comentadas por Manuel de Faria...* 2 vols., Madrid: Juan Sánchez, 1639.

―――. *Rimas varias de Luis de Camoens, principe de los poetas heroycos, y lyricos de España*, 4 bks., Lisbon: Theotonio Damaso de Mello, 1685.

[Sousa, Pero Lopes de]. *Diário da navegação de Pero Lopes de Sousa (1530–1532)*, Lisbon: Agência Geral do Ultramar, 1968.

Subrahmanyam, Sanjay. *The Career and Legend of Vasco da Gama*, Cambridge: Cambridge University Press, 1997.

Tavani, Giuseppe. *Ensaios portugueses: Filologia e linguística*, Lisbon: Imprensa Nacional-Casa da Moeda, 1988.

―――. "Raimbaut de Vaqueiras (?), *Altas undas que venez suz la mar* (*BdT* 392.5a)," *Lecturae Tropatorum* 1 (2008): 1–33.

Toromoreno, Rodrigo. "'Ora pro nobis': The Public Expansion of the Private Portuguese Voyage in *Os Lusíadas*," *Idiom: English Undergraduate Journal* (University of Toronto) 3 (2009): 45–52.

Torres, Isabel. *Love Poetry in the Spanish Golden Age: Eros, Eris, and Empire*, Woodbridge: Tamesis, 2013.

Torres, Sara V. "Oceanic Epic: The Translations of the *Lusiads* in the Global Renaissance," *Digital Philology: A Journal of Medieval Cultures* 8.1 (2019): 105–22.

Vasconcelos, Carolina Michaëlis de, ed. *Cancioneiro da Ajuda*, 2 vols., Halle a.S.: Max Niemeyer, 1904.

Vega, Garcilaso de la. *Obra poética y textos en prosa*, Bienvenido Morros, ed., Barcelona: Crítica, 2007.

Velho, Álvaro. *Roteiro da primeira viagem de Vasco da Gama (1497–1499)*, A. Fontoura da Costa, ed., Lisbon: Agência-Geral do Ultramar, 1969.

Vicente, Gil. *As obras de Gil Vicente*, 5 vols., José Camões, ed., [Lisbon]: Centro de Estudos de Teatro; Imprensa Nacional-Casa da Moeda, 2002.

Villena, Enrique de. *Obras completas II and III: Traducción y glosas de la Eneida*, Madrid: Biblioteca Castro, 1994, 2000.

Villiers, John. "Ships, Seafaring, and the Iconography of Voyages in the Age of Vasco da Gama," in *Vasco da Gama and the Linking of Europe and Asia*, Anthony Disney and Emily Booth, eds., Oxford: Oxford University Press, 2000, 72–83.

Virgil. *The Aeneid of Virgil, Books 1–6*, R. D. Williams, ed., Basingstoke: Macmillan; St Martin's Press, 1972.

———. *Eclogues/Georgics/Aeneid 1–6*, H. Rushton Fairclough, trans., G. P. Goold rev., Cambridge, MA: Harvard University Press, 1999.

Vitali, Marimilda Rosa. "Amor, co a esperança já perdida," in *Comentário a Camões*, vol. 2, Rita Marnoto, ed., Lisbon: Centro Interuniversitário de Estudos Camonianos; Cotovia, 2012, 35–38.

———. "As cadeias da esperança," in *Comentário a Camões*, vol. 2, Rita Marnoto, ed., Lisbon: Centro Interuniversitário de Estudos Camonianos; Cotovia, 2012, 103–27.

Waller, Marguerite. *Petrarch's Poetics and Literary History*, Amherst: University of Massachusetts Press, 1980.

Walter, Katie L. "The Form of the Formless: Medieval Taxonomies of Skin, Flesh, and the Human," in *Reading Skin in Medieval Literature and Culture*, Katie L. Walter, ed., New York: Palgrave Macmillan, 2013, 119–39.

Weinberg, Bernard. *A History of Literary Criticism in the Italian Renaissance*, vol. 1, Chicago: University of Chicago Press, 1961.

Wey Gómez, Nicolás. *The Tropics of Empire: Why Columbus Sailed South to the Indies*, Cambridge, MA: MIT Press, 2008.

Whetnall, Jane. "Hipólita de Narváez and the Leander Sonnet Tradition," *Bulletin of Hispanic Studies* 86.6 (2009): 893–909.

Willis, Clive. *Camões, Prince of Poets*, Bristol: HiPLAM, 2010.

Yates, Frances A. *The Art of Memory*, Chicago: University of Chicago Press, 1966.

Zenith, Richard, trans. "Song of Clean Shirts," "Cantigas Medievais Galego-Portuguesas," accessed March 17, 2021, https://cantigas.fcsh.unl.pt.

Zurara, Gomes Eanes de. *Crónica da tomada de Ceuta por El Rei D. João I*, Francisco Maria Esteves Pereira, ed., Lisbon: Academia das Ciências de Lisboa, 1915.

———. *Crónica de Guiné*, José de Bragança, ed., Porto: Livraria Civilização, 1973.

———. *Crónica dos feitos notáveis que se passaram na conquista da Guiné por mandado do Infante D. Henrique*, 2 vols., Torquato de Sousa Soares, ed., Lisbon: Academia Portuguesa da História, 1978–81.

INDEX

Page numbers in italics refer to figures.

acoustics, 60, 135–36, 139, 155, 159–60, 163, 169; maritime, 160–69. *See also* ocean; sea; sound

Adamastor, 14, 51, 147, 182n1; voice of, 163–64

Aeneas, 4, 48, 53, 97–99, 127, *129*. *See also* Virgil

Aeneid. *See under* Virgil

Africa, 3, 5, 11, 13, 22, 48–50, 52, 54, 62, 65, 81, 85, 135, 147, 150–51, 153–55, 157–58, 187n51; and Aeneas, 98; and Camões, 94; coastline of, 60, *61*; East, 71–72, 74; Horn of, 142; in *Os Lusíadas*, 66; Portuguese and Spanish voyages to, 22; and *roteiro*, 59–61; and slaving, 57. *See also Os Lusíadas*; Perestrelo, Manuel de Mesquita; *Rimas*; Zurara, Gomes Eanes de

Africans, 5, 55, 59, 147–48; as signmakers, 73

alba (dawn song), 40

Alenquer, Pero de, 4

Alfonso X of Castile and León, 175n1; *Cantigas de Santa Maria*, 24, 179n18

Alves, Hélio J. S., 51, 89, 167, 183n12

Americas, 11

Arabic, 55, 71

Aristotle, 5, 9, 159, 191n29; *De anima*, 41; *Parva naturalia*, 41

Arte de trovar, 42; gendered voice in, 42, 178n12. *See also cantigas de amigo*

Asia, 3, 11, 48–50, 75, 85–86, 105; in *Os Lusíadas*, 65; South, 81

Atlantic Ocean, 4, 22, 54, 94–95, 168

Azores, 22

Bacchus, 68, 72–73, 161–64, 169. *See also Os Lusíadas*

Baïf, Lazare de, 9

Bantu, 55

Barletta, Vincent, 42, 175n5, 178n12

Barros, João de, 61, 63–65; and eyewitness, 65; oceanic nature of history in, 63–64. *See also* historiography

Behaim, Martin, 178n11

Belém (Portugal), 54, 75–77. *See also* Gama, Vasco da; *Os Lusíadas*; Portugal

Bernardes, Diogo, 1–2, 107–8

boat, 7, 11, 20, 25, 44–45, 79, 83, 110, 122, 130; African, 71–72; *barcarolas*, 25; in *Os Lusíadas*, 47. *See also cantigas de amigo*; *Os Lusíadas*; ships; *Voyage of St. Brendan*

body, 9–10, 144, 151, 154–55, 159; in *cantigas de amigo*, 28, 30, 35, 37, 42; as subject intensifying, 149. *See also* Perestrelo, Manuel de Mesquita; subjectivity
Bojador, Cape, 5
Bolseiro, Juião, 25
Boscán, Juan, 91, 104–5, 195n66, 195n68
Brazil, 56, 160
Brito, Álvaro de, sea voyage and emotional suffering in poem of, 191n19
Brito, Bernardo Gomes de, 111, 147

Calicut, 47, 54, 84, 160. *See also* Gama, Vasco da; India
Caminha, Pero Vaz de, 160
Camões, Luís Vaz de, 2, 4, 9, 16, 42, 47–54, 63, 65–68, 72–73, 75–80, 84, 98, 101, 118, 123, 126, 130–31, 133, 135–36, 138, 140–41, 144, 161–63, 183n12; and Aónio, 108–9; and *cantigas de amigo* tradition, 43–46; and epic frenzy, 51, 163; epic poetry of, 3, 80; epic poiesis of, 54; first-person voice of, 78–79; and *fraco batel*, 78–80; lyric poetry of, 3, 16, 43, 81, 96, 102, 111, 119, 122; lyric subject of, 95, 117; and maritime subject, 94–97; and "new poetry," 91–92; and oceanic travels, 95; and Petrarch, 79, 92–95; poetic voice of, 50, 163; as preeminent maritime poet, 12; and shipwreck, 80–81; and women's agency in lyric, 44. *See also* Asia; boat; Gama, Vasco da; India; Lisbon; *Os Lusíadas*; nautical voyage; *navegação*; navigation; ocean; Perestrelo, Manuel de Mesquita; Petrarch; Portugal; *Rimas*; sailor; sea; Sebastião, King; seafaring; sex; ships; shipwreck; subjectivity; water; waves; wind
Canaries, 5, 22, 95
cantigas, 1, 16, 19, 23, 40–42; *cantigas de amor*, 24, 30, 35, 42; *cantigas de amor*, gendered sea voyaging in, 31; *cantigas de amor*, on-deck perspective in, 31; *cantigas de escarnho e mal-dizer*, 24 *cantigas de amigo*, 24–42; *barcarolas*, 24–25, 31, 33, 37, 179n16; and Camões, 43–46; *coita* in, 26, 28, 36–37, 41; dancing in, 38; and early modern lyric subject, 30, 43–46; erotics in, 26, 34–35, 37–39, 42, 179n16, 181n33; female corporality in, 24, 30, 34–35, 38, 42; ire in, 39; love as maritime travel in, 28, 30; lovestruck woman as ship in, 37; male authors of, 16, 24, 42; male principle of fertility in, 39; *marinhas*, 24, 31, 33; nautical movement in, 27; nautical voyage in, 25, 40; nostalgia and yearning in, 24, 33, 35–37, 179n15; riverbank in, 26–27; sea, ships, and sea voyages in, 24–26, 29, 32–33, 35–37; sight in, 26, 33–34, 38, 179n20; stag in, 40, 181n35; swimming in, 34–36, 38, 41; touch in, 41; washing clothes in, 38–39; wind in, 39–41, 181n33; women's voice in, 24, 42. *See also Arte de trovar*; body; Dinis, King of Portugal; navigation; sea; seafaring; sex; subjectivity; water; waves
capitão-mor, 10, 13, 54, 66–67, 71–72. *See also* Gama, Vasco da
Cappello, Bernardo, 113–14
carreira da Índia, 3–4, 17, 54, 67–68, 96, 151, 182n11
Castanheda, Fernão Lopes de, 61–65; and nautical eyewitnessing, 64; oceanic nature of history in, 63–64; and *roteiros*, 64–65. *See also* historiography
Castro, João de, 6–7, 58; *Roteiro do Mar Roxo*, 61, 62; *roteiros* of, 55; *Tratado da Sphæra*, 6
Cetina, Gutierre de, 107, 192n37
Ceuta, 74, 133
Charinho, Paio Gomes, 1, 29–30, 179n18. *See also cantigas de amigo*
China, 81, 83, 94
Christianity, 5, 7, 20, 58, 72–73, 163; and

Index

imperialism, 59–60, 84; and Petrarch, 92
Cicero, 51, 124; and *Somnium Scipionis*, 189n78
Codax, Martim, 31–32; Bay of Vigo in, 24, 32, 37–38. See also *cantigas de amigo*
Cohen, Margaret, 4, 15, 56, 58
compass, 10, 79, 146
Corte-Real, Jerónimo, 183n12, 199n2
craft (nautical knowledge), 4, 9, 20–21, 81, 84
Cupid, 15, 85, 87

Dante, 98–100, 111; and survival of metaphorical shipwreck, 99
degredados, 73
de la Vega, Garcilaso, 91, 105–6, 115–16, 137–38, 193n44
depths, 17–18, 53, 146–69; Camonian meanings of oceanic, 12–15, 49, 66, 162, 165; of emotion, 11, 110, 112–13, 144, 148–49; forms of, 148; and self, 112. See also *Os Lusíadas*; Perestrelo, Manuel de Mesquita
Diário da navegação (Pero Lopes de Sousa), 56
Dias, Bartolomeu, 54–55
Dinis, King of Portugal, 38–41; and pine forest, 181n36; and Portuguese navy, 181n36

ecocriticism, 15–16
emotion: and depth, 112, 115, 195n68; inner voyages of, 114; and seafaring in Petrarch, 93; and water, 16. See also *cantigas de amigo*; *Os Lusíadas*; sex
empire, 7–8, 60, 95, 110, 114, 137, 147, 160, 163. See also *Os Lusíadas*; Perestrelo, Manuel de Mesquita
epic poetry, 3, 5, 11–12, 16–17, 47, 73, 76, 79–80, 98, 114, 183n12. See also *Os Lusíadas*
epistemology, 8, 162, 169–70; seafaring, 5–6, 8; ships and, 7

equivocatio, 45
Estado da Índia, 182n1
Europe, 3, 105, 160
exile, 17, 118–45; as oceanic errancy, 118, 120; and temporality, 122, 130–33, 141–42, 144. See also *Rimas*; sea; seafaring; subjectivity
expansion, imperial, 8, 52, 54, 86, 111, 114, 137–38, 169

Falcão, Cristóvão, 197n95
female lyric consciousness, 16. See also *cantigas de amigo*
Ferreira, António, 75

Galicia, 25, 32
Galician-Portuguese poetry, medieval. See *cantigas*; *cantigas de amigo*
Gama, Vasco da, 2–5, 8, 12–14, 16, 47, 51, 54, 64–66, 80, 87, 89–90, 125, 131, 147, 165; as *capitão-mor*, 4, 66, 74, 76; and false pilot, 73; flagship of (*São Gabriel*), 4, 11, 55, 67, 71–72; fleet of, 47, 52–54, 65, 68, 71, 73, 75, 78, 90, 123–24, 126–27, *128*, 161–64, 170; and historical narrative, 74; as historical protagonist and epic narrator, 76; and Muslim pilot, 73, 182n4, 187n52; as navigator, 4; portrait of, *70*; prayer of, 168–69; and rounding of Cape of Good Hope, 182n4; as viewer-narrator, 67, 71, 89; and voyage as enactment of history, 67. See also Belém (Portugal); Camões, Luís Vaz de; *capitão-mor*; *carreira da Índia*; Castanheda, Fernão Lopes de; India; Indian Ocean; *Livro de Lisuarte de Abreu*; *Os Lusíadas*; nautical voyage; navigation; ocean; pilot; Portugal; *Rimas*; *roteiro*; sailor; sea; seafaring; ships; storms; Velho, Álvaro
Ganges River, 66–67. *See also* India
Goa, 62–63, 123, 197n87, 199n103. *See also* India
Góis, Damião de, 49–50

Good Hope, Cape of, 54, 59–60, 125, 131–32, 147. *See also* Africa; Gama, Vasco da; *Os Lusíadas*
governo do mar, 3, 12, 17, 47, 163, 176n11, 182n1. *See also Os Lusíadas*
Guardafui, Cape, 123, 142, 144; as *locus horridus*, 143
Guiné, 5, 57, 65. *See also* Zurara, Gomes Eanes de

hagiography, 11, 16, 19, 21, 23. *See also Voyage of St. Brendan*
Hellespont, 104–5, 107, 193n44
Hero and Leander, 103–8; and Iberian writers, 104. *See also* Boscán, Juan; de la Vega, Garcilaso; Ovid; *Rimas*
Herrera, Fernando de, 138, 192n37
Hippocrene, 51, 182n8
historiography, 5–6, 11, 57–58, 61–62. *See also* Barros, João de; Castanheda, Fernão Lopes de; Zurara, Gomes Eanes de
Holy Land, 95
Homer, 76, 182n2; *The Odyssey*, Castilian translation of, 182n2
Horace, 75, 114, 198n99; *Ars poetica*, 183n12
human-ocean encounter, 15, 41–42, 167

Iberia, 2, 7, 11, 15, 19, 22, 24, 95, 105, 192n34; "new poetry" of, 91; seafaring and literary culture of, 12, 43, 101. *See also* Portugal; Spain
identity, 3, 11, 106, 126–27, 163; Camões's vision of, 49; sea and national, 66
ideology, imperial, 3, 82, 187n51
India, 1, 3–4, 6, 10, 13, 16, 47, 52, 54, 59, 73, 78, 85, 87, 96, 125–26, 132, 147, 163, 165, 187n51; as aquatic figure, 67; Camões in, 94; Cochin and, 147; and encounter with Portuguese, 55; expansionist presence in, 64; Malabar Coast of, 81, 84, 197n87; Portuguese, 67–68; and Portuguese conquest of, 63; sound of, 169. *See also* Calicut; Ganges River

Indian Ocean, 12, 67, 73, 75, 84, 95, 147, 160, 168, 170, 187n52
Indonesia, 59
ipseity, 8, 115

Japan, 81
João I, 74
João III, 62–63, 65, 151

Klein, Bernhard, 3, 67, 168–69, 186n39, 186n41, 200n5

Lisbon, 3, 17, 24, 52, 55–56, 65, 141; as maritime metropole, 49–50; as new Rome, 161; worldwide reach of, 13. *See also Os Lusíadas*; Portugal
Livro de Lisuarte de Abreu, 11, 67–68, 69, 70. *See also* Gama, Vasco da; *Os Lusíadas*; seafaring; ships
Lopo, 28
La Lozana andaluza (Francisco Delicado), 46
Os Lusíadas, 2–4, 7–8, 13–14, 47–54, 61, 65–81, 84–90, 118, 122, 124, 127, 128, 131–32, 146–47, 161, 169, 182n1, 197n95; anti-epic discourse in, 75; aquatic feminine in, 85–86; canto VI of, 160–70; and deck-bound view, 67–68, 71–72; divine approval of seafaring in, 21; and epic ideology, 73; epic idiom of, 53; female power in, 86–87; gender in, 85–86; *gente marítima de Luso* in, 66; *in medias res* in, 52–54, 76; Isle of Love in, 84–90, 88, 165; love and desire in, 85–86; *máquina do mundo* in, 87, 89–90; nautical movement in, 53–54, 77, 122, 183–84nn14–15; oceanic *conquista* in, 66; piloted ship in, 47; prophecy in, 13–14, 47, 65–66, 87, 89–90, 164–65; rivers in, 47; *Roteiro da primeira viagem de Vasco da Gama* and, 55; Sabine women in, 86; sea in, 12, 47–49, 51; sea as organizing principle in, 47, 84; seafaring frame of, 65; seafaring as masculine venture in, 85; storm in,

Index

161, 165–69; triumphalist reading of, 17, 175n5; Twelve of England episode in, 165; *Velho do Restelo* (Old Man of Restelo) in, 75–76. *See also* acoustics; Adamastor; Aeneas; Asia; boat; *carreira da Índia*; depths; empire; epic poetry; expansion, imperial; Gama, Vasco da; Good Hope, Cape of; *governo do mar*; India; Indian Ocean; Lisbon; Melinde (Malindi); nautical voyage; *navegação*; navigation; ocean; pilot; Portugal; sailor; sea; seafaring; ships; subjectivity; Tagus River; Triton; Velho, Álvaro; Venus; Virgil; voyaging, imperial *Lusiads, The*. See *Os Lusíadas*
lyric poetry, 2–3, 8, 11, 17, 96, 98, 103–4, 110, 118–19, 123; and empire, 91. *See also* Camões, Luís Vaz de; de la Vega, Garcilaso; Petrarch; *Rimas*

Madeira, 22
Magnus, Albertus, 41
Manuel I, 13, 47, 53–54, 66–67; orders of, 74
March, Ausiàs, 101–2
mariner. *See* sailor
maritime humanities, 15
maritime imaginary, 16, 19, 81, 104, 118, 146, 162
Mariz, Pedro de, 80, 123
Mediterranean Sea, 9, 55
Melinde (Malindi), 13, 66, 161; king of, 14, 74–75, 161. *See also* Gama, Vasco da; *Os Lusíadas*
memória das armadas. See *Livro de Lisuarte de Abreu*
Mendinho, 36–37; Bay of Vigo in, 36
Mentz, Steve, 4, 15, 103, 151, 182n1, 200n6
Meogo, Pero, 39–41
metis, 4, 10. *See also* craft (nautical knowledge)
Middle East, 3, 6, 55, 81
mirabilia, 19–20, 158
Miranda, Francisco de Sá de, 105, 193n51, 195n67

Mombassa, 73, 161
Monçaide (Muslim ally of the Portuguese), 84
Montemayor, Jorge de, 105, 192n34, 193n43
Mozambique, 52, 59, 68, 72
mundo, 121–22, 138
Musaeus, 104, 193n41
Muses, 50, 52, 140, 163

Narváez, Hipólita de, 106
nausea, 168
nautical allusions, 40, 45, 102, 125; and women's sexual agency, 45. *See also cantigas de amigo*
nautical science, 6, 8, 56–57, 65, 160
nautical voyage, 2, 5–6, 8, 11, 16, 18, 53–54, 57, 61, 64–65, 81, 118, 122, 125–26, 131–33, 153; in *cantigas de amigo*, 24–33, 35–36; and composition of poetry, 80; and history, 67; metaphor of, 7; in Petrarch, 92, 101; and *roteiros*, 58–59; telos of, 21, 23, 84, 118. *See also* Camões, Luís Vaz de; Gama, Vasco da; *Os Lusíadas*; navigation; *Rimas*; sea; ships; *Voyage of St. Brendan*
navegação, 3, 13, 90
navigation, 5, 8–9, 46, 54, 65, 146; African, 73; greed and, 114; love and, 104–6, 194n53; in lyric, 97; and narrative, 73–81. *See also* Boscán, Juan; Gama, Vasco da; *Os Lusíadas*; Petrarch; *Rimas*; sea; ships
Neptune, 2, 5, 51, 53, 126, 161–63, 168. See also *Os Lusíadas*
Nereids, 126–27, 129, 130, 162, 182n3
New World, 22, 48
Nunes, Airas, 35

ocean, 3, 11, 37–38, 42, 50–51, 125, 163–64; as form of thought, 16; inner, 97, 125; and medieval T-O maps, 164; new vision of, 161; as pathway of sound, 163; as poetic principle, 17; polysemy of, 47; as Portuguese domain, 4; transformation of, 162–63;

222   Index

ocean (*continued*)
world, 12. *See also* acoustics; Camões, Luís Vaz de; Gama, Vasco da; *governo do mar*; *Os Lusíadas*; navigation; *Rimas*; sailor; sea; ships; sound; voice; waves
Oliveira, Fernando, 8–10
onomatopoeia, 40–41; and the sea, 162
Ovid, 106, 120, 140–42, 168; *Epistulae ex Ponto*, 139–40; *Heroides*, 104, 192n40, 193nn41–42, 194n52; *Metamorphoses*, 114, 182n8, 187n50, 201n23; *Tristia*, 130, 140. See also *Os Lusíadas*; *Rimas*

Pagán, Diego Ramírez, 192n40
Palinurus, 4–5. *See also* Virgil
Peregrinação. *See* Pinto, Fernão Mendes
peregrinatio, 20, 119
peregrino, 119–20
Perestrelo, Manuel de Mesquita, 17, 59, 64; and on-deck viewing, 60–61; *Relação sumária da viagem que fez Fernão d'Álvares Cabral*, 146–50, 152–60; *Roteiro da África do sul*, 59–61. *See also* acoustics; Africa; body; shipwreck; sound; voice
Petrarch, 17, 80, 111, 119–20, 135, 138, 143–44, 191n19, 192n34; and emotional interiority as sea, 93, 102; frail bark of, 79, 81; and metaphor of *navigatio*, 92; and ship of the self, 92, 101; and ships and seafaring, 92–95; and shipwreck, 100–101. *See also* Camões, Luís Vaz de; *Rimas*; ships; subjectivity
Phaëthon, 72, 75
pilot, 4–5, 58, 73, 93, 105–6, 113, 151, 194n52, 195n68; Muslim, 73, 182n4, 187n52; women as, 46. *See also* Gama, Vasco da; ships
Pinto, Fernão Mendes, 81–84; and seafaring, 83; as shipwreck narrative, 84; and subject categories, 82
Pires, Tomé, 199n111
Pliny, 9
Plutarch, 197n89

Polo, Marco, 81
Porco, Nuno, 27
Portugal, 2–4, 6–7, 9, 11, 16, 25, 47, 54, 59, 66, 72, 96, 123, 125, 131, 147; and Castile, 185n26; as coastal nation, 49–50; history of, 74; imperial ambitions of, 89; Porto, 19; Santa Cruz de Coimbra, 19; seafaring identity of, 3, 8; seafaring in literary culture of, 12; and slave markets, 5, 57; transoceanic feats of, 87; and world's seas, 147. *See also* Belém (Portugal); Camões, Luís Vaz de; Gama, Vasco da; India; Lisbon; *Os Lusíadas*; *Rimas*; shipwreck
Prince Henry, the Navigator, 5, 21, 57, 65; and knowledge gathering, 22. *See also* Guiné; Zurara, Gomes Eanes de
profundo. *See* depths
Promised Land, 19–20
Proteus, 52–53, 87, 89, 164–65. See also *Os Lusíadas*
Psalm 130 ("De profundis"), 168

Quintilian, 51, 124

Reconquest, 28
Red Sea, 56, 61, 123, 199n110
Resende, André de, 183n8
Resende, Garcia de, 97
Rimas (lyric poetry of Camões), 2, 91, 94–99, 109, 111–45, 192n31; body/ship metaphor in, 104–5; Dinamene in, 108; and Echo, 134–36, 139; and exile, 118–45; Hero and Leander in, 103–8; "new maritime" style of, 110; and "new poetry," 91–92; and Petrarchan interiority, 94; and piscatory eclogue, 109–11, 198n95; and poetic ipseity, 115; and shipwreck swimmer, 96–99; and wind and voice, 108, 145. *See also* acoustics; Africa; boat; body; Boscán, Juan; Camões, Luís Vaz de; Dante; de la Vega, Garcilaso; emotion; India; lyric poetry; navigation; ocean; Petrarch; Portugal; Sannazaro,

Jacopo; sea; ships; sound; subjectivity; Themistocles; Virgil; voice; water; waves; wind
river, 125, 130, 138–39, 152–53; idyll of, 142; in *Os Lusíadas*, 47, 50, 66, 80. *See also* Ganges River; *Os Lusíadas*; sea; Tagus River; water
roteiro, 6, 55–61, 64–65; and chronotopes of the sea, 56; deck-bound gaze in, 59–61; definition of, 55; and first-person perspective, 58, 67; and João de Castro, 55. *See also* Castanheda, Fernão Lopes de; *Os Lusíadas*; Perestrelo, Manuel de Mesquita; Velho, Álvaro
rutter. See *roteiro*

Sá, João de, secretary of *São Rafael*, 184n16. *See also* Gama, Vasco da
sailing, 46, 126; as metaphor for sex, 46. *See also* navigation; ships
sailor, 3–4, 43, 48, 66, 72, 84, 97, 102, 114, 116, 125, 151, 161, 165; body of, 151; as epic achiever, 75; and gender, 43; and love, 43–44; as lover, 117; Muslim, 71; and nymphs, 86; shipbound, 77. *See also cantigas de amigo*; Gama, Vasco da; *Os Lusíadas*; Perestrelo, Manuel de Mesquita; ships; shipwreck
Sannazaro, Jacopo, 109–10, 194n61, 198n95
Santiago, Rui Fernandes de, 30–31
São Bento (ship). *See* Perestrelo, Manuel de Mesquita: *Relação sumária da viagem que fez Fernão d'Álvares Cabral*
saudade, 125–26, 130–32, 135, 140–41, 145
Scylla and Charybdis, 101
sea, 3, 4, 8, 13, 43, 73, 97, 99, 110–11, 117, 125, 132, 143–46; as allegory, 20; apostrophe to, 37, 44, 105–8; as body, 130; Camonian, 15; in *cantigas*, 24–26, 29, 32–33, 35–38, 43; eroticization of, 85, 87; erotic movement of, 130; and exile, 118–45; horizontal surveillance of, 89; as idea and principle, 1, 11; and literary culture, 12; as locus of temporality, 57; and lyric consciousness, 131; as medium of history, 74; metaphoric realms of, 3, 8, 11; and national identity, 66; nature of, 1; as new historical and epistemological regime, 162; as place, 1, 20; sound of, 109; and supernatural will and human agency, 53; as text, 130; as undomesticated, 48, 90, 163, 169; unity of, 89–90; and voice, 198n102. *See also* Camões, Luís Vaz de; *cantigas de amigo*; Gama, Vasco da; Iberia; *Os Lusíadas*; maritime imaginary; nautical allusions; nautical voyage; navigation; ocean; Portugal; sailing; sailor; seafaring; ships; subjectivity; *Voyage of St. Brendan*; water; waves
seafarer. *See* sailor
seafaring, 2–5, 7–11, 44, 49, 57, 118–20, 123, 126, 147, 162; African, 72–73; in *cantigas de amigo*, 40; Christian, 73; as constitutive of history, 58; and historical narrative, 74; and historical order, 78; and horizontality, 146; and human and divine will, 48; as imperative, 76; imperial, 13, 16; as masculine, 85–87; polysemy of, 47; as principle, 11. *See also* Camões, Luís Vaz de; *cantigas de amigo*; Gama, Vasco da; historiography; *Livro de Lisuarte de Abreu*; *Os Lusíadas*; nautical voyage; navigation; Petrarch; *Rimas*; sea; ships; shipwreck; subjectivity; *Voyage of St. Brendan*
seamanship, 4, 10, 21, 61, 151, 165; Portuguese books of, 57. See also *roteiro*
sea nymphs, 87, 127–30, *128*, 169, 198n95. *See also Os Lusíadas*; Nereids; *Rimas*
Sebastião, King, 52–53, 59–60; and sexuality, 86. *See also Os Lusíadas*
sex, 16, 26, 33–35, 37–39; in *Os Lusíadas*, 85; and ships, 46; and the stag, 40; and women as ship's pilot, 46. *See also* body; *cantigas de amigo*; ships

Shakespeare, 155, 162
ships, 4–11, 44–46, 67–68, 72, 75, 83, 112, 124, 126, 132, 146, 149–51, 161, 168, 177n6; African, 71, 187n49; architecture of, 8–10, 45–46, 72, 101–2, 151; and body, 104–5, 151; and cleaving water, 53; as clock, 57; daily time on, 56–57, 59; and deck-bound view, 54, 58; as expression of maritime might, 52–54; as eyewitness, 61, 64; and gender, 103; and history, 74; lover as, 100; and male anatomy, 46; and men as passive sexual objects, 45; metaphoric dimension of, 21; Moorish, 9; piloted, 47; and poem, 77; and poetic psyche, 113; and *roteiros*, 56; route of, 153; and seafaring in Petrarch, 92–95, 100–101; and sexual potency, 45–46; as sign of divine will, 21; steerage of, 55; and subjectivity, 11; symbolism of, 20–21; types of Portuguese, 200n4; and women's sexual choice, 45–46. *See also* Camões, Luís Vaz de; *cantigas de amigo*; Gama, Vasco da; *Livro de Lisuarte de Abreu*; *Os Lusíadas*; navigation; sea; seafaring; *Voyage of St. Brendan*
shipwreck, 17, 59, 80–84, 102–3, 105, 111, 113–14, 116–18, 146–47, 150–51, 153–54, 160, 168, 182n1, 194n57; aftereffects of, 148, 158; corporeality of, 154–55, 159; and Echo, 157; as icon of Portuguese culture, 111; inward turn of, 150; and love, 97; and lyric poetry of Camões, 96–98; of Manuel de Sousa de Sepúlveda, 147; and maritime labor, 149, 151–52, 156; and poetic interiority, 115; Portuguese narratives of, 84, 111, 146–48, 151, 167; and soundscape, 155–56, 158–60; and space, 150, 153, 155; survivor of, 97–99, 114, 147, 149–50, 152–54, 157–58; and time, 149–50, 160. *See also* body; Camões, Luís Vaz de; *Os Lusíadas*; Perestrelo, Manuel de Mesquita; *Rimas*; sea; ships; subjectivity; swimmer

Simonides of Ceos, 123–24, 131. *See also* Themistocles
sound, 18, 42, 109, 110–11, 135, 139, 163, 166, 168–69; and depth, 146; and empire, 60; and shipwreck, 155–60; of water, 52, 135. *See also* acoustics; *Os Lusíadas*; Perestrelo, Manuel de Mesquita; *Rimas*; shipwreck
Sousa, Manuel de Faria e, 123, 194n57, 195n69, 198n95, 198n99, 199n103, 201n21
Spain, 9, 91, 92, 104, 189n82; and subjectivity, 94. *See also* Boscán, Juan; de la Vega, Garcilaso; Iberia; Portugal
storms, 95–99, 112–13, 125, 132, 152, 169; in *Os Lusíadas*, 161–69. See also *Os Lusíadas*; shipwreck
subjectivity, 79, 81, 96, 104, 106, 114, 116–17, 121, 195n66; in *cantigas de amigo*, 37, 42; maritime, 7–8, 11, 17, 92, 94–95, 102–3, 115, 118, 197n81; masculine and lyric, 103; and "new poetry," 92; oceanic, 176n19; and shipwreck, 149; and subject boat, 11, 78, 92, 102, 132. *See also* Camões, Luís Vaz de; Gama, Vasco da; *Livro de Lisuarte de Abreu*; *Os Lusíadas*; Perestrelo, Manuel de Mesquita; Petrarch; *Rimas*; sea; ships; swimmer
swimmer, 17, 80, 87, 103–4, 115, 117, 156, 194n52; and shipwreck, 96–99, 102–3, 105–6, 111–12, 115–18. *See also* Hero and Leander; *Rimas*; subjectivity

Tagus River, 24, 49–50, 127, 130, 141–42, 163; as gateway to worldwide oceans, 51. See also *Os Lusíadas*; *Rimas*; river
Ternate, 123, 199n103
Tethys, 80–81, 84, 87, 89–90, 182n3. See also *Os Lusíadas*
Themistocles, 96, 123–27, 129–33; ship of, 124. *See also* Camões, Luís Vaz de; exile; *Rimas*; sea
Tibullus, 132
time, 6, 10–11, 122, 130–33, 141–42, 144, 165; liturgical, 20; and mariner's

clock, 149; ships and daily, 56–57, 59; and shipwreck, 149. *See also* Perestrelo, Manuel de Mesquita; *Rimas*; *roteiro*; ships

Torneol, Nuno Fernandes, 25

Toromoreno, Rodrigo, 168

Triton, 51; conch blast of, 163–64; in *Metamorphoses*, 201n23. *See also Os Lusíadas*; sound; voice

Tupi, 160

Ulysses, 48, 76, 120, 138

University of Coimbra, 64

Valdés, Juan de, 106

Vaqueiras, Raimbaut de, 180n33

Velho, Álvaro, 58; *Roteiro da primeira viagem de Vasco da Gama*, 5–7, 55, 61, 64–66; as source of *Os Lusíadas*, 55. *See also* Gama, Vasco da; *Os Lusíadas*; *roteiro*; ships

Venus, 15, 68, 73, 169; and Isle of Love, 84–90. *See also* Camões, Luís Vaz de; *Os Lusíadas*; sex

Vicente, Gil, 45–46; *Triunfo do Inverno*, 151–52, 166–67. *See also* shipwreck; sound

Virgil, 5, 17, 52–53, 98–99, 127, 129, 169, 191n28; *Aeneid*, 5, 49, 51–52, 97–98, 198n102; Castilian translation of *Aeneid*, 182n2; *Culex*, 132–33; *Georgics*, 198n99. *See also* Aeneas; *Os Lusíadas*; Palinurus

Vitruvius, 10

voice, 17–18, 106, 109, 130, 134, 144, 156–58, 160, 164, 167–68, 198n102; Aristotle and, 159; boat and, 110; and depth, 146–60; as traveler, 169; and Triton's conch blast, 163; water and, 48–54, 105, 135–36, 139, 193n51; wind and, 108–9, 145. *See also Os Lusíadas*; Perestrelo, Manuel de Mesquita; *Rimas*; sea; shipwreck; subjectivity

Voyage of St. Brendan, 16, 19–23, 23; in African waters, 22; Anglo-French version of, 177n5; horizontality of, 23; as marker of geographic and cartographic knowledge, 22; meaning of ship in, 20–21; St. Brendan's Isles, 19–22, 178n8, 178n11; sea in, 20–21; telos of, 23; whale in, 19–20, 22, 23. *See also* hagiography

voyaging, imperial, 10, 13–14, 48, 89, 95–96

water, 16, 24, 47, 131, 169; in *cantigas de amigo*, 43, 180n29; fluvial, 51; touch and, 41; and voice, 48–54, 105, 135–36, 139. *See also cantigas de amigo*; *Os Lusíadas*; *Rimas*; subjectivity

waves, 10, 20, 105, 110, 135, 162, 168; in *cantigas de amigo*, 31–32, 35–37, 179n22, 181n33. *See also Os Lusíadas*; sea; water

wind, 6, 12, 21, 55, 68, 101, 107–10, 145, 164, 167; in *cantigas de amigo*, 31, 39–41; as carrier of desire, 110; in *Os Lusíadas*, 52–53. *See also Livro de Lisuarte de Abreu*; *Os Lusíadas*; *Rimas*; ships

Zorro, João, 24, 26–27, 179n14. *See also cantigas de amigo*

Zurara, Gomes Eanes de, 5–7, 21–22, 57–58, 176n19; and naturalizing view of historical action, 58; and nautical expeditions, 57; and oceanic turn of history, 58; and St. Brendan's Isles, 21–22. *See also* Africa; epistemology; Guiné; historiography; Prince Henry, the Navigator